IN THE BLOOD OF OUR BROTHERS

Abolitionism and the End of the Slave Trade
in Spain's Atlantic Empire, 1800–1870

JESÚS SANJURJO

The University of Alabama Press   Tuscaloosa

The University of Alabama Press
Tuscaloosa, Alabama 35487-0380
uapress.ua.edu

Inquiries about reproducing material from this work
should be addressed to the University of Alabama Press.

Typeface: Adobe Caslon

Cover image: section of *Seascape 6, with Alizarin
Crimson* by Jake Wood-Evans, 120 x 104 cm, oil
on linen, 2018; courtesy of Jake Wood-Evans

Cover design: Michele Myatt Quinn

Cataloging-in-Publication data is available
from the Library of Congress.
ISBN: 978-0-8173-2105-5
E-ISBN: 978-0-8173-9374-8

To my nephews, Mateo and Diego

Contents

Acknowledgments

Writing a book can sometimes feel isolating, and there have been moments of frustration and fatigue. But this monograph has a much more powerful meaning to me. Thanks to this book I have met some fascinating people, traveled to beautiful and breathtaking places, and discovered the struggle of those who risked it all to live in a more decent society.

I am very grateful to Manuel Barcia and Gregorio Alonso for their guidance, kindness, and encouragement. Without their unwavering support this book would not have been completed. For financial support, I was helped enormously by the White Rose College of Arts and Humanities, the Arts and Humanities Research Council, the universities of Leeds, York, and Cardiff, the Association of Hispanists of Great Britain and Ireland, the Spanish embassies in London and Havana, and the Leeds Humanities Research Institute. I am also grateful to the University of Alabama Press for passionately believing in this project when it was only an early draft.

In the course of writing this study, I have met many academics with whom I have had fascinating conversations and who offered their advice and insightful comments. I owe special thanks to María del Carmen Barcia, Catherine Davis, Fernando Durán, Marcela Echeverri, Mercedes García, Richard Huzzey, Jean-François Manicom, David Murray, Gabriel Paquette, José Antonio Piqueras, Eduardo Posada-Carbó, Karen Racine, Martín Rodrigo, Romy Sánchez, Ismael Sarmiento, Adrian Shubert, Natalia Sobrevilla, Randy Sparks, Lisa Surwillo, and William Van Norman for their help. I am also very thankful to the two anonymous peer reviewers for their very constructive feedback.

I am grateful to the support of my friends and colleagues in Leeds, York, and Cardiff. I am profoundly indebted to Michael Abbey, RJ Arkhipov, Diana Battaglia, Lawrence Black, Graham Carson, Jack Chadwick, Richard Cleminson, Sam Critchell, Hanna Diamond, Daniel Evans, Conor Di Fante, Julio García, María García-Florenciano, Charlotte Hammond, David Huyssen, Tom Johnson, Joel Kirk, Conor J. Lewis, Lucía López, Daniel Mourenza, Juan Muñoz, Jennifer Nelson, Lourdes Parra, Kristina Pla, Stewart Rusell-Moya,

Angel Smith, Montse Venrell, Sam Wetherell, and Joey Whitfield. I am also thankful to Jake Wood-Evans, who kindly authorized the use of his painting *Seascape 6, with Alizarin Crimson* for the cover of this book.

I would also like to thank the Centre for the Study of International Slavery at the University of Liverpool, the Latin American Centre at the University of Oxford, the Research Group Historia Constitucional de España, the Centre de recherche d'histoire de l'Amérique Latine et du monde ibérique at the University of Paris 1 Panthéon-Sorbonne, the Casa de Altos Estudios Don Fernando Ortiz at the University of Havana, and the universities of Cadiz, La Laguna, and Pompeu Fabra for inviting me to present some of my work and offering invaluable discussion and feedback.

I want to express my gratitude to the staff at the Archivo Nacional de la República de Cuba and the Biblioteca Nacional de Cuba José Martí in Havana, the Archivo del Congreso de los Diputados and Archivo Histórico Nacional in Madrid, the Archivo de Indias in Seville, the Bodleian Library in Oxford, and the National Archives in London for their efficiency and assistance with my research.

Sections of the Introduction and chapters 1, 2, and 3 are derived in part from articles published by Wiley in the *Bulletin of Latin American Studies* in 2017, available online: https://onlinelibrary.wiley.com/doi/abs/10.1111/blar .12746, and by Taylor & Francis in the *Journal of Iberian and Latin American Studies* in 2020, copyright Taylor & Francis, available online: https://www .tandfonline.com/doi/10.1080/14701847.2020.1789377.

Finally, I am also thankful for my loving family!

In the Blood of Our Brothers

Introduction

It was a momentous night. The British Prime Minister William Wyndham Grenville rose from the red benches in the House of Lords to move a second reading of the Bill for the Abolition of the Slave Trade. "What right do we derive from any human institution, or any divine ordinance," he asked, "to tear the natives of Africa, to deprive them by force of the means of laboring for their own advantage, and to compel them to labor for our profit?"[1] The legislation was passed. Watching from the chamber's public gallery, a young Spaniard, Agustín de Argüelles (1876–1844), felt that he had witnessed an event of monumental significance. Little did he know that three years later he would attempt to put an end to the "infamous traffic" across the dominions of the Spanish crown.

Argüelles had arrived in London in 1806 and was working for the Spanish government as a secret agent. He would become one of the most important statesmen of his generation and a central figure in Spanish politics for more than forty years. The abolition of the slave trade and slavery would be a recurrent concern during his life, and in many ways his inconsistent convictions and thoughts, his changing attitudes and political action, mirror the complex ways in which Spaniards from both sides of the Atlantic thought about the slave trade and slavery.

Spain officially abolished the slave trade in 1820, but its effective eradication took place only around fifty years later. An intricate system of slave traders, planters, financial backers, and public institutions introduced more than 700,000 African men, women, and children into Cuba, the most important remaining colony of a shrinking empire, between 1800 and 1870. The slave trade in the Spanish imperial territories was profitable until its very last day, and its abolition and much later eradication can be comprehensibly explained only as the consequence of a complex and fragmented process. Since the early abolitionist discourses advanced by Isidoro de Antillón, José María Blanco White, Miguel Guridi, and Argüelles in the 1800s and 1810s, to the antislavery poetry of Concepción Arenal in the second half of the 1860s, discourses against the slave trade and slavery adopted multiple forms and were advocated by Liberal and Absolutist, progressive and conservative, egalitarian and racist actors.[2]

This book examines the processes of production, circulation, and reception of abolitionist ideas in Spain's Atlantic empire at the beginning of the nineteenth century and their development through to the decade of the 1860s. It charts British ideological, political, and diplomatic influence on the construction of anti–slave trade discourses and policies in Spain and stresses the multiplicity of abolitionist and antiabolitionist ideas between 1802 and 1867. It appraises the emergence and development of public and political expressions of abolitionism and antiabolitionism, studying the ideological backgrounds, political pressures, and motivations that operated during this process.

This book tells the story of people who campaigned for and against the slave trade and slavery but who knew that they would never be enslaved themselves. This is only part of the story: enslaved and free men and women around the world argued, agitated, and fought for freedom, and their contribution is essential to understand the success of the abolitionist cause across the Atlantic. Without the revolts, the activism, and the struggle of Black men and women, the end of the slave trade and slavery would have never happened.

This book resituates Spanish abolitionism in the light of international scholarship on the slave trade, slavery, and abolitionism in the Atlantic World and, in so doing, contributes to filling a significant gap in the Spanish and English-speaking historiographies. The results of this work provide a more consistent and comprehensive theory of the history of the abolition and eradication of the slave trade in Spain's Atlantic empire.[3]

∽

This book shows that the ultimate eradication of the slave trade responded to international political negotiations that excluded the Spanish authorities and ignored Spanish political actors. However, the contribution of Spanish anti–slave trade activists was crucial to debilitating the public legitimacy of the traffic and challenged the dominant rhetoric affirming the necessity of its continuation. Their writings, speeches, campaigns and political initiatives eventually succeeded in consolidating the idea that the slave trade was "horrendous, atrocious and inhumane," as Argüelles described it in 1810.[4] In the long term, they contributed to building the public consensus that the slave trade was unsuitable and condemned to disappear. This shift was informed by its relationship with liberalism, which has a particular meaning in the Spanish metropolitan and colonial contexts, and wider political and ideological debates in the Atlantic World.[5] Both dimensions—the domestic and the transatlantic—co-existed and informed each other.

As Emily Berquist has pointed out, abolitionist ideas in Spain in the early nineteenth century have received little attention from historians.[6] The foundational works in the field, such as those by Arthur Corwin and David Murray, focused on British influence on the development of anti–slave trade legislation.[7] More recently, however, works by Josep Fradera, Christopher Schmidt-Nowara, José Antonio Piqueras, Manuel Barcia, Kate Ferris, Albert García Balañà, and Berquist herself, among others, have provided more innovative approaches to the construction and circulation of abolitionist ideas in the Spanish Empire during the nineteenth century.[8] In order to put together an innovative and compelling narrative of the history of Spanish anti–slave trade and anti-slavery discourses, we must embrace a transnational analysis and decisively engage with the international scholarship.[9]

The rise of political liberalism and the founding of representative institutions were key to the reception and construction of anti–slave trade ideas in Spain. However, abolitionist demands became an essential part of the Liberal program only in the context of the political radicalization of the 1860s. It was only in 1868 when the leaders of the *Revolución Gloriosa* proclaimed that "without liberty there is no honor" and demanded the abolition of slavery in the Spanish colonies of Cuba and Puerto Rico that the movement penetrated the mainstream.[10] The ties between liberalism and abolitionism, which can be clearly seen in the French and British contexts, cannot be directly transposed into the Spanish case. This position distances us from attempts to define an "ideological canon" for liberalism in Spain. As Javier Fernández Sebastián has argued, liberalism in the first decades of the nineteenth century, "far from being a stable and well-defined notion, was a variable bunch of vague and faltering concepts."[11] To assume a teleological projection, in which the English and French cases constitute a yardstick for measuring liberalism in Spain, would therefore be ineffective and would force us to think about the Spanish and Portuguese political histories as imperfect or anomalous. As Gabriel Paquette and Fernández Sebastián have concluded, "to study Iberian liberalism from the viewpoint of this 'presumed canonical liberalism' leads inexorably to a focus on the errors, imperfections, and [flawed] departures from that model."[12]

Josep Fradera argued rightly that the particular social and political conditions in Spain's empire meant that abolitionism "was never likely to unfold along similar lines" to the British process and only by adopting a transnational approach, and placing the study in dialogue with international historiography, will we be able to build a comprehensive understanding of Spanish abolitionism.[13] Fradera has also stressed that one of the questions that future researchers in the field should deal with is "why, in a country dealing with major internal upheaval but with liberal institutions in place since the 1830s, the abolitionist movement failed to make headway until reformers on all sides realized, following the US Civil War, that slavery was in its death throes."[14] A tentative answer would be that to equate liberalism and abolitionism is to misinterpret the relation of the two phenomena. So even if Spain had "liberal institutions" or a liberal parliamentary system, there is no reason to assume that it was "a contradiction" that Spanish political actors protected and even promoted the slave trade. In this regard, the ideological and political tension between Spanish liberalism and imperialism is crucial to formulating a more comprehensive examination of the reasons for the failure of anti–slave trade initiatives from 1811 to the 1860s. Spanish liberalism and the metropolitan elites prioritized the preservation of territorial integrity, the enormous wealth and revenue that Cuba produced, and the maintenance of the status quo in the colonies in the context of the imperial crisis. There was a tacit agreement between the metropolitan and the Cuban colonial elite, broken only by the rise of pro-autonomy or pro-independence movements on the island in 1868.

We need, therefore, as Duncan Bell has suggested, to revisit the concept of "liberalism" in a critical way.[15] He defined two major methodological strategies to approaching the phenomenon: (1) "stipulative": the creation of normative political philosophies and the construction of ideal types; and (2) a "canonical" methodology, based on refining "liberal" theoretical structures from exemplary writings. Bell concludes that both methodological strategies are "valuable, even essential" but "neither [is] capable of underwriting plausible comprehensive or explanatory accounts."[16] He problematized the idea of a liberal canon given the internal diversity of liberalism and its national and regional variation. His proposal to break this methodological deadlock is to develop "a comprehensive contextualized analysis of liberalism . . . in which liberal languages emerge, evolve, and come into conflict with one another, rather than trying to distil an ahistorical set of liberal commitments from conceptual or canonical investigation."[17]

In this regard, by avoiding a national(ist) approach, it is possible to obtain more comprehensive and dynamic answers to some old questions; or as, Jorge Cañizares-Esguerra put it, abandoning these approaches "has proven genuinely liberating, and it has allowed historians to escape the traditional teleological narratives of the nation."[18] If slavery and the slave trade were indeed "the most intense and lasting cohesive activities in the Atlantic World . . . for demographic, cultural, military, social and political reasons," studying the production and circulation of abolitionist ideas in Spain within the wider context of intellectual debates in the Atlantic World not only makes sense but is the only reasonable approach.[19] This book does just that.

1

Early Spanish Anti–Slave Trade Discourses, 1802–1814

Trading in the blood of our brothers is horrendous,
atrocious and inhumane and the National Congress
must not hesitate for a single moment between its high
principles and the interest of certain individuals.
—Agustín de Argüelles, 1810

Agustín de Argüelles and British politician and abolitionist William Wilberforce never met in person. Most likely, Wilberforce did not encounter his name until 1811, when Argüelles, member of parliament for the northern region of Asturias, become a central figure in Spanish politics. But Argüelles knew well who Wilberforce was. Wilberforce's fight represented, in Argüelles's mind, the very best of the British political system, capable of conducting a radical transformation from the benches of a freely elected parliament, respecting the tradition while embodying the passion of a true Jacobin. Argüelles admired Wilberforce, and if he had the chance, he wanted to become him.

The 1811 parliamentary proposal of Argüelles to abolish the slave trade, which adopted and adapted the moral condemnation elaborated by the British abolitionist movement, was crucial in expressing a new ideological stance within Spanish political discourse. His initiative was the result of a coordinated strategy with the British authorities and was key to the construction of early abolitionist discourses in Spain. This chapter explores the political, ideological, and diplomatic influence of Britain in the development of early anti-slavery and anti–slave trade discourses in Spain, between 1802 and 1814, and demonstrates the centrality of Argüelles's proposal.

The economic reforms applied by the Bourbon monarchs in the previous four decades of the eighteenth century laid the foundations for a new political, social, and economic order that brought crucial changes to Cuba.[1] The freedom to import enslaved Africans, established by the Reales Cédulas (royal decrees) of 1789 and 1791, started an agrarian revolution in Cuba, which radically transitioned the conditions of production on the island from a small-holding and livestock model to a plantation system (Figure 1.1).[2]

These developments altered the power balance between different social groups in the colony and led to the social rise of sugar producers and exporters, who became the most powerful colonial stakeholders and a counterweight to the metropolitan authorities. This economic group, labeled by Manuel Moreno Fraginals as the "sacarocracy," was characterized by a strong defense of the introduction of a freer domestic market and, at the same time, the preservation and development of slavery and the slave trade as key factors for the prosperity of the colony.[3] Moreno Fraginals has argued that the powerful owners of the sugar mills in Cuba operated as "one family in the feudal sense of the word," planning and arranging each marriage "so that accumulated fortunes would not be dispersed."[4] This phenomenon was not limited to local individuals, as these networks included Spanish military and civil officials who had arrived in the island "to gain rapid promotion, personal wealth, and political power."[5] Numerous peninsular military leaders, from across the political spectrum, served as military officials and captain generals in Cuba. In the words of Alfonso Quiroz, during the nineteenth century the Spanish colony "became a strategic hub for corrupt networks of nepotism and favoritism plaguing the Spanish state bureaucracy and delaying much needed colonial reform in Cuba."[6]

The relationship between liberalism and slave ownership was, according to Moreno Fraginals, "a constant flight from reality" as "the contradictions of the sugar regime . . . formed a nucleus of negative ideas based not on what should be but on what [the sacarocrats] did not want to be."[7] This group had to deal with the "tremendous contradiction of selling merchandise on the world market and at the same time having slaves," and concluded that this "vacillating position" was "painfully reflected in their ideological world."[8] Similarly, Candelaria Saiz Pastor has also emphasized that these "slavery-related contradictions" represented the cornerstone of the relations between the Spanish colonies and the metropolis during the nineteenth century. The terms "liberalism" and "pro-slavery," operated as a "palpable conjunction," Saiz concluded.[9] Within this ideological framework "the private ownership of the means of production, sanctioned by the liberal doctrine, applied to people," and this idea was embraced and implemented by slave owners, officials, and lawmakers alike.[10] Moreno Fraginals concluded that this attitude explains the ideological world of the sacarocrat, which made him "a champion of inviolable property in the means of production [. . . adapting] a bourgeois judicial concept to a situation which corresponded to the most primitive form of labor."[11]

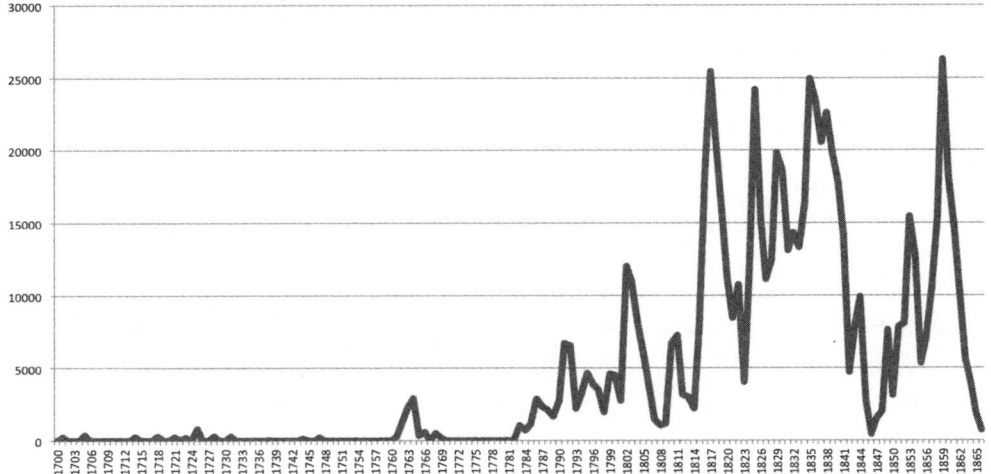

Figure 1.1. Number of enslaved Africans brought to Cuba, 1700–1866. (Data from Trans-Atlantic Slave Trade Database, http://www.slavevoyages.org/, accessed September 1, 2017)

However, as Domenico Losurdo has problematized, sheltered by the notion of "property rights," slavery also became a synonym of prosperity, stability, and progress.[12] "The rise of liberalism and the spread of racial chattel slavery are the product of a twin birth," and "slavery is not something that persisted despite the success of the three liberal revolutions. On the contrary, it experienced its maximum development following that success."[13] For slave owners, planters, and investors, slavery and the slave trade, far from representing a contradiction of their ideas and economic principles, were rooted in the fundamental belief that property rights were inviolable and compatible with a "liberal system of policy."[14]

From the second half of the eighteenth century, key representatives of this Cuban sacarocracy, such as Ignacio Pedro Montalvo, Nicolas Calvo, Antonio del Valle Hernández, Tomás Romay, José de Ilincheta, Francisco Arango y Parreño, and Captain General Luis de las Casas, defined a political strategy for the development and protection of a new colonial economy based on the plantation system. The establishment of this new economic model demanded the importation of large numbers of enslaved Africans and thus led to the consolidation of pro–slave trade discourses within the new Cuban colonial elite, which drew its wealth from the production of sugar, coffee, and tobacco.[15] During the nineteenth century, the slave trade into Cuba became a very profitable economic activity, which gradually became crucial to the material viability of the Spanish Empire.[16] The abolition of the slave trade in the

British Empire in 1807, far from stopping the trade to Cuba and Puerto Rico, "consolidated dynamic slave economies and a political order that protected and encouraged these economies."[17]

Condemning the slave trade meant having to confront not only the Cuban colonial elite but also very powerful metropolitan interests. Several aspects of the Cuban slave economy, such as the slave trade, commodity production, investment in infrastructures, and shipping, represented enormous earnings for some of the biggest fortunes in Spain and were "based on the vertical integration of all activities related to the colonial sugar economy."[18] The ideological and political reaction against slavery and the slave trade in Spain, confronting both domestic and colonial interests, was a complex and fragmented historical process. However, during the first quarter of the nineteenth century, some voices started to publicly condemn those practices and to develop a Spanish abolitionist discourse.

Antillón and Blanco White: Translating "Abolitionism"

Abolitionist ideas in Spain started to circulate at the beginning of the nineteenth century, strongly influenced by French and British forerunners. The decision of the British parliament to abolish the slave trade in 1807 signaled the beginning of a diplomatic campaign that would eventually constitute the strongest stimulus for the emergence of anti–slave trade discourses in Spain.[19]

British and French thinkers strongly influenced early antislavery and anti–slave trade discourses in Spain, as is clear from the work of the doctor of law and geography expert Isidoro de Antillón.[20] The first public speech that can be considered part of an abolitionist tradition in Spain was delivered by Antillón at the Real Academia Matritense de Derecho Español y Público, in 1802. However, as Josep Fradera has convincingly argued, "Antillon's text . . . should not be considered as merely a distillation of British or French arguments," as he inscribed his abolitionist position within a wider discourse of Spanish imperial reform.[21] His speech was entitled "Disertación sobre el origen de la esclavitud de los negros, motivos que la han perpetuado, ventajas que se le atribuyen y medios que podrían adoptarse para hacer prosperar sin ella nuestras colonias." In it Antillón argued in favor of "ameliorating" the life conditions of the enslaved Africans in the Spanish dominions and contended that gradually "European governments must, in all justice, free the African slaves in America."[22] He clarified, however, that "the time and circumstances in which freedom ought to be given to them and the preliminaries that must take place before granting them this just benefit, must be arranged wisely by governments."[23]

Antillón "focused on the politics, economics, and demography of colonial labor" to build his abolitionist position, in which humanitarian and religious arguments were secondary.[24] Antillón believed, as Schmidt-Nowara has pointed out, that Spain should not depend on "dangerous and unreliable enslaved African labour," as the British and French had done.[25] He suggested encouraging traders to introduce a balanced gender ratio, and to allow enslaved Africans to have more leisure time, and proposed the gradual replacement of slaves by free indigenous workers. Antillón argued in favor of Spain's colonial expansion in Africa as the best way to increase Spanish agricultural production and mitigate the metropolitan dependency on the American territories. He proposed establishing new settlements on African soil, where the habitants were "industrious, quiet, sweet, and too cowardly to oppose the founding of a colony."[26] He believed that the Spaniards would be welcome as "good gods" by the Africans "if those who came to occupy the land, taught them how to cultivate it instead of expatriating them forever."[27] Antillón argued that those "in favor of this infamous system, would only deserve . . . the disregard of the philosopher and the dagger of the Negro."[28] However, far from being grounded on appeals to humanitarian sentiment, his analysis aimed to prove that the slave trade was "not only anomalous but also unnecessary."[29]

Fradera has pointed out that Antillón's "abolitionist stance [was] likely to have had a wide impact" during the Peninsular War; however, his speech was not published until 1811.[30] The author himself admitted, "[I] didn't believe or expect that, in 1802, when I read my speech on the slavery of the Negroes . . . it would become in some time more than just an outburst in front of friends."[31] As he explained, his decision to publish his speech was encouraged by the recent abolition of the slave trade by Britain (which Antillón wrongly described as "the abolition of Negro slavery") and the British diplomatic campaign to extend "abolition to the whole of Europe."[32] He optimistically predicted, "Spain is going to take part in this glorious revolution of principles which is an honor to the enlightenment and the humaneness of modern peoples."[33] British political and diplomatic pressure would be, from this point forward, the primary driver of abolitionism in Spain.

In his political campaign against the slave trade, however, Antillón was not alone. José María Blanco y Crespo, better known as José María Blanco White, was a multifaceted thinker and writer in the history of early Spanish liberalism.[34] From April 1810 to June 1814, he published the Spanish-language newspaper *El Español* in London. The publication was sponsored by the Foreign Office from the outset, and by Henry Richard Vassall Fox, Lord Holland (1773–1840), a great expert in Spanish politics and a major Whig figure.[35] Before 1812 *El Español* featured translations of Jeremy Bentham, Francis Horner, John Allen, Samuel Romilly, and Lord Holland.[36] He was keen to propagate the benefits of a political alliance with Britain, and the British authorities saw his newspaper as a useful tool in their diplomatic strategy in Spain. The British Embassy in Cadiz subscribed to one hundred copies, Lord Holland was also a major subscriber, and the company Gordon and Murphy (with interests in Spain and Spanish America) transported the newspaper into the Spanish colonies for free, at the request of the British government.[37] Blanco's fascination with British society led him to believe, as Fernando Durán has pointed out, that "[learning from Britain] was the dreamed salvation for a country that seemed to have no solution."[38]

After the abolition of the slave trade was first debated at the Cortes of Cadiz, Blanco elaborated his anti–slave trade position, which was strongly influenced by that of William Wilberforce.[39] He adopted "some aspects of the evangelical religion that animated the leading British abolitionist" and "shared the . . . enthusiasm of Wilberforce."[40] In the issue of May 1811 (no. 14), only one month after Agustín de Argüelles had presented his proposal at the Cortes of Cadiz, Blanco White published the article "Abolición de la esclavitud" ("Abolition of Slavery"), in which he commented upon and supported Argüelles's ideas.[41] He described them as "extremely glorious for the Spanish nation" but criticized Guridi y Alcocer's speech on March 26, 1811, in which he proposed the abolition of slavery.[42] Blanco White mistakenly believed, at this point, that Guridi y Alcocer's initiative had succeeded and that the Spanish assembly had "emancipated black slaves all at once; . . . and this step [was] directly contrary to the good that is being attempted."[43] To support his point, he raised the specter of the Haitian Revolution and asked the Spanish deputies to follow the example of the British parliament, and to consider this issue more carefully.[44]

In September 1811 Blanco White published the translation of some excerpts of Wilberforce's *Letter on the Abolition of the Slave Trade*, originally written in 1808, including some notes on the life of the African American antislavery activist Paul Cuffee. The translation was divided into three chapters, which were published between September and November 1811.[45] Blanco White thought that this translation would help to spread the anti–slave trade message in Spain and achieve the "happy abolition of the barbaric traffic in slaves."[46] For Blanco White, Britain and Wilberforce represented a moral and political example of moderation.

In March 1814 Blanco White published the book *Bosquexo del comercio de esclavos* in London, in which he advocated the abolition of the slave trade. He presented his work as a translation of Wilberforce's *A Letter on the Abolition of the Slave Trade*, but Blanco White made a great effort to adapt the core ideas of the British abolitionist movement to the Spanish cultural and political context. Schmidt-Nowara convincingly suggested that Blanco White "used the language of slavery" to compare the violence suffered by the Spanish

people under the French occupation to that undergone by the African victims
of the slave trade. In this way Blanco White aimed to translate "Wilberforce's
evangelical outlook into an idiom more immediately comprehensible to Spanish readers struggling against the French."[47] In December 1813, while Blanco
White was working on his *Bosquexo*, he sent a letter to Wilberforce that has
hitherto remained unpublished. The Spanish author thanked Wilberforce for
his comments on his work and for inspiring him to write it in the first place:
"It was your work, Sir, that first gave me a full insight of the abominable traffic: it was your work that brought my vague compassion for the slaves into
action: it is your work that has led my pen throughout the sketch which the
[African] Institution have been pleased to look upon . . . and grant me the
blessing of being instrumental in doing away the stain which the continuation
of the slave trade casts to this day, upon the character of my native country."[48]

The *Bosquexo* had the financial support of the African Institution, one of
the most important British abolitionist lobbies, which was involved in the
translation and publication of British abolitionist propaganda into other European languages.[49] According to Wayne Ackerson, the African Institution
sponsored "the translation of one of Wilberforce's commentaries into Spanish"
and planned to distribute the book "among the Spanish clergy and throughout the Spanish government."[50] Following the moderate position and strategic
gradualism that Blanco White defended in *El Español*, he used Christian rhetoric very similar to Wilberforce's. Blanco White, unlike Antillón, referred exclusively to the slave trade and tacitly accepted the preservation of slavery. He
believed that the end of the slave trade would improve the living conditions of
the enslaved Africans, but, unlike Antillón, Blanco White appealed to Christian values to support abolition.[51] Blanco White's book was published only two
months before the end of the Cortes of Cadiz and the restoration of Fernando
VII as absolute king of Spain in May 1814. This fact made the immediate distribution of the book in Spain impossible and diminished its impact.[52]

Berquist has suggested that Antillón and Blanco White belonged to a
"broader network" of abolitionist thinkers, which fostered an "early anti-
slavery movement" in Spain.[53] Although she is right in suggesting that their
contributions should not be seen as a "sidelined anomaly" and must be understood in the wider context of abolitionism in the Atlantic World, there is no
evidence to suggest that Blanco White's and Antillón's works were part of a
coordinated effort until 1811.[54] Their works have traditionally been analyzed
as the historical background to the debates on slavery and the slave trade at
the Cortes of Cadiz, but they became politically relevant only in the context
of the Cadiz debate.[55] The *Bosquexo* was an articulate and passionate response
to the pro–slave trade arguments advanced by the slaveholders at the Cortes,
and it was "congruent with other contemporary Spanish attacks on the Cuban

slave trade."[56] Both the *Disertación* and the *Bosquexo* came about in an attempt to support Argüelles's proposal to abolish the slave trade in a gradual, nonradical way. Blanco White's publications were used by British diplomats and the abolitionist lobby to reinforce their position in Spain and proves the political determination of the British government to put the issue of the slave trade on the Spanish political agenda.

THE ABOLITION OF THE SLAVE TRADE IN SPAIN AS A BRITISH POLITICAL INITIATIVE

The British Parliament's decision to abolish the slave trade in 1807 marked the beginning of a new political stance that had an almost immediate impact in Spain. In the wake of the Peninsular War (1807–1814), Britain would become the main promoter of abolitionist ideas and an ally to many liberal Spanish politicians. The British government, in concert with the British abolitionist lobby headed by Wilberforce, Thomas Clarkson, and Zachary Macaulay, was committed to achieving the global abolition of the slave trade. British abolitionists campaigned to stop the slave trade all across the Atlantic, not only on humanitarian grounds but also to respond to the antiabolitionist position, which warned "that other nations would continue to trade in slaves regardless of Britain abolishing her role in the international trade."[57] On this point, the importance of Spain as a main antagonist was key. After the British abolition of the slave trade, Cuba became the largest slave colony in the Caribbean, with 86 percent of the enslaved Africans introduced in the island arriving after 1807. By the end of the 1820s, Cuba had also become the world's largest sugar producer.[58]

Spanish and Portuguese American territories had become the main destinations of the transatlantic slave trade, and the British government saw slavery in Cuba as a "competitive disadvantage" for British planters in Jamaica and Barbados. Therefore, lobbying the governments in Madrid and Lisbon became a priority for both the abolitionist movement and British government. As early as May 1806, the British parliament passed legislation to prevent British traders from supplying foreign colonies with enslaved Africans. Shortly after, in June, Parliament passed an address asking the king to establish diplomatic negotiations with foreign countries to achieve the international abolition of the slave trade. As David Murray has pointed out, "Cuba had been completely dependent on the foreign slave trade, and the British slave trade had been responsible for supplying a large percentage of slaves to Cuba."[59] In this context, many British slave traders began sailing under the Spanish flag to avoid British jurisdiction.[60]

British activists were anxious to expand their anti–slave trade campaign to the rest of Europe, and also in 1806 the abolitionist activist Henry Brougham

(1778–1868) wrote to Wilberforce to stress the importance of raising the issue of the Spanish slave trade and mustering support from key political figures in Britain: "I had written to Lord H. Petty very fully upon the subject of the Spanish slave trade, and I am happy to find, . . . that he is perfectly master of the subject which I had attempted to press upon his attention. He and I talked over a good part of it in presence of Mr. Fox, which I thought the best way of letting him take a share in the discussion or not, as he might choose. . . . On the slave trade, in general, we talked a great deal—and you may believe all agreed. Lord H. Petty mentions that you had a wish to begin the campaign; . . . I should add that the company present were Mr. Fox, Lord Holland, Lord H. Petty, and myself."[61]

The coordination between the British government and British anti–slave trade activists oriented to Spain was readily apparent in this period, demonstrative of how intertwined the strategies of the British anti–slave trade lobby and the British government were. In July 1808 then–prime minister Spencer Perceval (1762–1812) wrote a letter to Wilberforce to assure his cabinet's commitment to the "very interesting" question of the abolition of the slave trade in Spain.[62] He promised Wilberforce that he would do "anything in power that I think likely to be practicable and availing to forward the views you have upon it" and let him know that the Secretary of Foreign Affairs, George Canning (1770–1827), was "equally desirous to do the same."[63]

In 1808 Canning sent instructions to the British ambassador in Madrid "to expound the British reasons for abolishing the slave trade without proposing any specific measure."[64] British abolitionists saw the outbreak of the Peninsular War in 1808, the emergence of the Spanish *guerrilla* (armed actions carried out by regular troops), and the British military intervention as propitious factors to stir debate about the abolition of the slave trade. Following the popular rejection of the French occupation of Spain, and only three years after the Battle of Trafalgar in the context of the Anglo-Spanish War (1796–1808), Spain became an ally of Britain. Wilberforce praised the "extraordinary spectacle" of the Spanish people fighting against Napoleon's troops and believed that the British military intervention in the peninsula put them in a good position to influence Spanish politics.[65]

In June 1808 a group of Spanish deputies from the northern region of Asturias, headed by Andrés de la Vega (1768–1813) and José María Queipo de Llano, Count of Toreno (1786–1843), traveled to London to meet Canning and to ask the British government to support their fight against Napoleon in Spain. They were joined by Argüelles, who was already in London acting as a secret agent of the Spanish government.[66] Wilberforce did not want to lose the opportunity to communicate his abolitionist ideas to these Spanish politicians, so he sent letters to Canning, Brougham, and Lord Holland (at least) on the topic. "Just at present the Spanish must necessarily be wholly engrossed by the exigencies of their own situation, but doubtless they are precisely in the circumstances in which, if it please God they succeed, . . . that generous temper of mind be produced, which will abhor oppression and cruelty, consequently will abolish the slave trade. And surely, we ought to be immediately taking all proper preparatory measures for diffusing information on the subject. . . . I will immediately write to Canning, desiring him to mention the subject to the Spanish deputies. Do you desire Perceval to do the same I have an idea also of writing to Lord Holland, as well as to Brougham, who we ought here to carry along with us, for his knowledge of Portugal people, &c. render him capable of being a useful ally."[67]

Wilberforce believed that "to get pretty well acquainted with the Spanish and Portuguese deputies" was essential, as "advantage should be taken of their being here, to make them acquainted with the real nature of the slave trade." He invited "Canning, and Perceval, and Brougham, and Lord Holland to attend to the deputies" and requested that anti–slave trade propaganda be translated into Spanish.[68] In July 1809 Canning sent a letter to Richard Colley Wellesley, Marquis of Wellesley (1760–1842), British ambassador in Madrid, in which he stressed the importance of persuading the Spanish government of the desirability of a gradual abolition of the slave trade, "urging the adoption of a similar policy [as Brazil's] by Spain, whenever a fit opportunity shall recur for bringing that discussion forward."[69]

The war in Spain, however, blocked any immediate opportunity to debate it. As Canning explained in Parliament in March 1810, "there was hardly time to enter into any stipulation with that government with respect to its colonial policy."[70] The British authorities saw the Peninsular War as both an opportunity and a hurdle in establishing negotiations to abolish the Spanish slave trade. The French invasion made a rapprochement between Spain and Britain possible, but before the opening of the Cortes of Cadiz, in September 1810, this group of liberal Spanish politicians had no legislative power and were more concerned with winning the war against France than anything else.

The political rise of liberal figures such as Argüelles and the opening of the Cortes created a new political atmosphere conducive to reform. José María Portillo has stressed the importance of the new assembly's "political audacity" to include in the definition of the Spanish nation all the territories under the Spanish monarchy, and to allow the political representation of the American territories. "The idea of a general reform of the empire" characterized the main ambition of the Cortes.[71] But imperial reform did not necessarily include the abolition of the slave trade. It was certainly the "perseverance and insistence" of the British authorities and activists in the context of the Peninsular War that put the issue of the slave trade into the Spanish political debate.[72]

Abolitionism at the Cortes of Cadiz: An Anti–Slave Trade Morality

The opening of the Spanish Cortes in the city of Cadiz in September 1810 initiated the establishment of a new political system in Spain. For the first time, a national assembly had the right to rule the country, and a group of liberal politicians had the chance to challenge the power of traditional ruling elites. The British government and the abolitionist lobby saw the Cortes as a great platform to influence the future of Spain. However, the weight of French ideas in the construction of Spanish liberalism had been greater than that of Britain's. That said, after Napoleon's invasion the notion of "rejecting" French ideas operated as a very powerful driving force in engendering an important rise of Anglophile sentiment that may contribute to explaining the susceptibility to English ideas and discourses in Spain at the time.[73] Many Spanish deputies at the Cortes of Cadiz started to see Britain as not only an ally but a political example to be followed.[74]

The abolition of the slave trade was first debated at the Cortes of Cadiz on January 9, 1811. Domingo García Quintana, Liberal deputy for the province of Lugo, argued that the Assembly should "ban forever even the memory of slavery."[75] He also proposed that while abolition was being ratified, enslaved Africans should have "a representative in Congress that would speak for them in those matters concerning slaves, and that this representation power should go to one of the European representatives."[76] On March 26, 1811, a second resolution against slavery was introduced by the deputy from Tlaxcala (New Spain), Miguel Guridi y Alcocer (1763–1828). His proposal was the first formal project to abolish slavery in Spain. He defended the immediate abolition of the slave trade, the freedom of all children born to slave mothers, remunerations for the enslaved people, their right to purchase their freedom, and better working conditions to establish parity with free workers. He defended a gradual abolition of slavery that protected the property rights of slaveholders alongside the prohibition of the slave trade.[77] Neither proposal generated a formal debate, although Guridi y Alcocer's was brought before the Constitutional Commission for further consideration and later to a "special commission."[78]

Both antislavery proposals lacked enough support in the assembly and went beyond the political expectations of the British authorities. While the abolition of the slave trade had become a symbol of national pride in Britain and a top priority for the Foreign Office, the majority of deputies publicly opposed the abolition of slavery.[79] Following Fradera's contention that "the ubiquitous and unequal distribution of *castas* prevented the idea of slavery from being the central issue to tackle in any hypothetical reform of the empire," it was unlikely to be undertaken in a similar way to the British debate.[80] Discussions on the slave trade followed a different track. As opposed to slavery, "the backbone of Spain's largest American colonies," the transatlantic slave trade into Spanish territories was geographically very limited, chronologically recent compared to other American colonies, and economically central only after the collapse of slavery in Saint-Domingue (1791–1804).[81] Abolishing the slave trade was seen, therefore, as a realistic possibility.

On April 2, 1811, Argüelles presented his proposal to put an end to the slave trade. Argüelles was the political leader of the Liberal faction in the Spanish assembly and would go on to become the most influential abolitionist in the Cortes of Cadiz. In 1807 he had witnessed in Westminster the session of the House of Lords in which the slave trade was abolished, and, during his stay in London, he had been in contact with Lord Holland. Relying on these initial contacts, he arguably became the main link between the Cortes, the British abolitionist movement, and the British diplomatic mission in Cadiz, led by the Marquis of Wellesley, British ambassador, and Charles Vaughan (1774–1849), secretary of the embassy. Argüelles's proposal advocated the immediate abolition of the slave trade.

While García Quintana and Guridi y Alcocer had asked the Cortes for the immediate abolition of slavery, Argüelles's proposal was more limited, defending *only* the abolition of the trade in slaves: "That without HM [His Majesty] stopping over the claims of those who may be interested in continuing with the introduction in America of slaves from Africa, Congress should abolish such infamous traffic forever, and from the very day that this Decree be issued, by no means slaves from Africa must be bought or introduced in any of the possessions of the Crown on both hemispheres, not even if bought from any of the European or American powers."[82]

He concluded his short speech inviting the Cortes to inform "His Britannic Majesty" of this "philanthropic" decision in order to collaborate with Britain in its implementation, "so that the great objective the English nation has put forward in the famous Bill of Abolition of the slave trade, may be fully achieved."[83] Argüelles's anti–slave trade discourse was strongly influenced by the rhetoric of both Wilberforce and the British abolitionist movement. In his speech, the Spanish deputy referred to Wilberforce as the "dignified and indefatigable . . . author of the Bill of Abolition" and recalled his presence in the British Parliament when the abolition bill was passed: "The memorable night of 5 February 1807 in which I had the sweet joy of witnessing the triumph of Enlightenment and Philosophy in the House of Lords."[84] In his speech, Argüelles introduced the notion of "slaves as brothers" and the slave trade as both politically and religiously unacceptable, following the same strategy that

Wilberforce had successfully adopted in the British Parliament: "Trafficking . . . in slaves is not only contrary to the purity and liberality of feelings of the Spanish nation, but also to the spirit of its religion. Trading in the blood of our brothers is horrendous, atrocious and inhumane and the National Congress must not hesitate for a single moment between its high principles and the interest of certain individuals."[85]

According to nineteenth-century Cuban politician José Antonio Saco (1797–1879), Argüelles informed him, decades later, about the actual negotiation with the British government concerning the proposal to abolish the slave trade.[86] Saco argued that the British ambassador in Cadiz intended to hand a note to the Regencia (the then Spanish government) requesting the abolition of the slave trade in the Spanish colonies. Argüelles dissuaded the British ambassador, "promising to propose the same in the Cortes so that it would seem to have a national and spontaneous character free of foreign pressure."[87] Two days after Argüelles's initiative was discussed at the Cortes, Henry Wellesley, British ambassador in Spain, sent a note to the British foreign secretary, his brother Richard Wellesley, in which he informed him about the discreet conversations that he had held with different members of the Spanish parliament about the abolition of the slave trade:

> After fully considering what would be the best mode of carrying into effect the instruction . . . relative to impressing upon the Spanish Government the justice and policy of abolishing the slave trade within the Dominions of the Monarchy of Spain, I thought it might be advisable, previous to making any representation to the Council of Regency to ascertain what would be likely to be the feeling of the Cortes. . . .
>
> I therefore had a communication with some of the Deputies to Cortes soon after the receipt of your Lordships dispatches; and there seemed to be but one opinion among them of the propriety of the abolition as soon as it might be practicable. They however suggested the necessity of deferring its decision until the arrival of the deputies from Cuba and Porto Rico, whose Constituents had a greater personal interest in the question, than any other class of the subjects of His Catholic Majesty.
>
> The Deputies from these Islands arrived a short time ago, and no time has since been lost in bringing forward the subject for the consideration of the Cortes. A motion . . . was made by Mr. Argüelles on the 2nd of April, and was referred to a Committee. . . .
>
> Your Lordship will, I hope, approve my having deferred any representation to the Government upon this subject, perceiving, as I did, every disposition on the part of the Cortes to bring it forward of themselves.[88]

The report of the British ambassador in Madrid perfectly corresponds with the description made by Saco. Henry Wellesley had been in consultation with Argüelles since December 1810, and ultimately Argüelles agreed to present a proposal under two conditions. First, he would need to wait until the arrival of the Cuban and Puerto Rican deputies to Madrid; and second, the British ambassador would not put pressure on the Regencia until the proposal had been presented to the Cortes. This would also explain why Argüelles did not support, or even intervene in, the debates on the proposals made by García Quintana, and Guridi y Alcocer.

The antiabolitionist reaction to Guridi y Alcocer's and Argüelles's proposals was immediate, overwhelming, and very effective. The Catalan deputy Felip Aner d'Esteve and the Cuban representative Andrés de Jáuregui pointed out that even while "humanity contemplates" the abolition of the slave trade, the Spanish nation was not ready for this decision, as "even when fair and humane; it would be serious and dangerous." Jauregui concluded that Cuba's "public opinion is not ready to take a decision of this significance."[89] On July 20, 1811, the *ayuntamiento* (city council), the Sociedad Patriótica (a learned society initially organized to promote agriculture, commerce, education and industry), and the Consulado of Havana (an institution dedicated to promote commerce and economic development in the port) submitted a joint statement to the Cortes explaining the ruinous and dangerous effects that the abolition of the slave trade would have on Cuba's economy and political stability. The document was written by the Cuban aristocrat Francisco Arango y Parreño, who confronted Argüelles's proposal on the basis of two main ideas: Cuban slaveholders and traders had to be listened to by the Cortes, and Argüelles's proposal was a radical attack on property rights.[90]

Arango accused Argüelles of aiming to "condemn" the Cuban planters "without hearing us!"—ignoring what slaveholders, merchants, and investors had to say, and without considering normal parliamentary procedures.[91] In criticizing Argüelles, Arango referred to the British Bill of Abolition, highlighting that this man "so much praises Anglican legislation . . . but has proposed to adopt a conduct so diametrically opposed." He rhetorically asked the chamber "how has he [Argüelles] forgotten that the British Parliament never legislated precipitously about the interests of their provinces" and that while "Mr. Argüelles did not want to allow a day for the law to be published," the British parliament allowed ten months for the abolition law to come into effect.[92] Arango argued that the slave trade was so deeply rooted in Cuba's society and economy that it could not "be removed easily and, even less, suddenly."[93]

By characterizing Argüelles's proposal as unplanned and radical, Arango aimed to avoid a debate on moral grounds, to move the discussion to when and how the abolition should take place, and to consider the complex network of interests at stake. The Cuban aristocrat defined the slave trade as "infamous" and described abolition as "the cause of humanity" but argued that a sudden abolition of the traffic would "violate the rule of law, and the acquired rights according to the current laws."[94] If property rights were ignored by the Spanish authorities, some important members of Cuban society would feel marginalized by the metropolis in the context of a growing threat from the United States:[95] "We see growing in the northern part of this world a colossus that threatens to swallow, if not our entire America, at least the northern part; and instead of trying to give [to the landowners] the moral and physical force, and the will that is necessary to resist such combat; we continue idolizing the wrong principles that cause our indolence."[96]

Arango tacitly accepted the humanitarian case but countered that banning the slave trade was as unjust as slavery itself. He argued for a longer discussion about the issue and for the right of the Cuban planters to be heard. He maintained that the end of the slave trade would cause a collapse of the sugar economy and would lead to economic difficulties for the whole empire. He also affirmed that a sudden abolition of the slave trade, even its public debate at the Cortes, could spark a massive slave revolt that would destroy the colony.[97] On July 7, 1811, a letter from the captain general of Cuba, the Marquis of Someruelos, was read at the Cortes, asking the deputies to deal with this issue with extreme care, "so this important Island is not lost," and demanded that Cuban "loyal habitants" should be listened to and reassured that a repetition of the "catastrophic events [that] occurred in the neighboring Saint-Domingue, now controlled by former slaves," would never happen.[98] These ideas would become a very powerful and repeated antiabolitionist notion in the years to come. As Manuel Barcia has argued, one of "the most frequently mentioned threats up to 1820 [was] a possible revolution of the slaves and/or the free coloured men living on the Island."[99]

In March 1812 a rebellion "with ramifications in different parts of the Island, organized by free men of color and slaves, was discovered in Havana."[100] Cuban slave owners and colonial authorities blamed the Cortes for "inciting slaves to disorder," and the letter from the captain general to the Cortes was now seen as a premonition of the disastrous consequences that merely discussing the issue of slavery in Cadiz could produce in the Spanish colonies.[101] This episode, the "Aponte Conspiracy," contributed to reinforcing antiabolitionist positions at the Cortes and forced the British authorities and the Spanish abolitionist leaders to wait for a better moment to make their case.[102]

The proposals of both Argüelles and Guridi y Alcocer were relegated to a secret "special commission" chaired by the deputy Muñoz Torrero, who appointed five more members, including the Cuban representative Andrés de

Jáuregui.[103] The antiabolitionist pressure was effective, and the commission never submitted a report.[104] After 1811 British diplomatic pressure to abolish the slave trade declined as a result of the several failed attempts at the Cortes and the prevalence of the position of Cuban planters. The last time the Cortes of Cadiz discussed an abolitionist proposal was on November 23, 1813. During a debate on a motion concerning the *alcabala* (a sales tax), the deputy Antillón advocated the abolition of slavery.[105] This proposal did not have any support, and the Cuban deputy Arango intervened to reject any debate on the matter.

In March 1814 British forces commanded by William Clinton forced the French army to yield the posts of Lleida and Mequinenza and to cross the Pyrenees into France. The Peninsular War was over, and in May 1814 Fernando VII ordered the abolition of the Cadiz Constitution and the liberal leaders to be arrested. The king justified his actions by stressing that the Constitution of 1812 had been made by a Cortes illegally assembled in his absence, without his consent and without the conventional form. When Fernando VII returned to Spain, the vast dominion of the Spanish monarchy in the Americas began to collapse. In New Spain two main guerrilla groups led by Guadalupe Victoria and Vicente Guerrero controlled Puebla and Oaxaca. In northern South America, New Granadan and Venezuelan armies, under the command of Simón Bolívar, Francisco de Paula Santander, Santiago Mariño, Manuel Piar, and José Antonio Páez, carried out campaigns along the Orinoco valleys and the Caribbean coast. Also, in Upper Peru guerrilla bands controlled rural parts of the country. Gradually, during the following two decades, all the Spanish territories in the Americas became independent states, with the exception of Cuba and Puerto Rico.[106]

As Dumas has suggested for the British case, the distinction between pro–slave trade and antiabolitionist arguments is key to comprehensively understanding the complexity of the arguments advanced by both sides.[107] Argüelles's proposal had the immediate effect of moving the debate from the alleged "benefits" of the slave trade, to the "negative" consequences that abolition might have. The wickedness of the traffic was not a question. Arango briefly referred to the positive effect that the slave trade had had on the Africans, because of the "unhappy destiny" they faced in their homeland; but as Schimidt-Nowara argued, the Cuban author primarily "emphasized the centrality of Cuba's booming plantation economy to the imperial regime's well-being."[108] Jáuregui, Arango, and Someruelos adopted a clear and consistent antiabolitionist discourse as the most effective way of stopping Argüelles's proposal.

Following this line of argument, it is important to stress that Agustín de Argüelles never advocated the abolition of slavery, and it is therefore inaccurate to label him an "antislavery advocate."[109] The slave trade could have been stopped without the abolition of slavery even being considered. Berquist has questioned how "Argüelles . . . turned from impassioned speeches against the slave trade . . . to deciding to exclude slaves from citizenship altogether," and the answer lies in the fundamental differences between both: the slave trade was a relatively new and deregulated commercial activity, while slavery was a central social institution in the Spanish Americas.[110] Argüelles forced the pro–slave trade lobby to tacitly accept some moral condemnation, and this was recognized and praised by the British abolitionist leaders, who identified Argüelles as an ally.

Conclusions

From the beginning of the nineteenth century, the slave trade in Cuba was a cornerstone of the colony's economy—the production of which in turn was crucial to the material viability of the Spanish Empire. With this in mind, it is suggested here that exploration of the abolitionist ideas that surfaced in Spain prior to 1811 need consider two main currents: on the one hand, the influence of the British government and antislavery movement, and on the other, the profound ideological effect of Agustín de Argüelles's 1811 proposal to end the empire's role in the slave trade.

With respect to British ideological influence, this factor, paired with overt political intervention, constituted the main driving force in early Spanish abolitionist ideation. The beginning of the debates and the permanence of the issue of the slave trade in Spanish politics during the first quarter of the nineteenth century can be accounted for as a direct consequence of the pressure exercised by the British government and antislavery movement.

Argüelles, in spite of British political support, failed to attain his goal of putting to an immediate end the traffic in enslaved Africans, but his attempt succeeded in affixing to the Spanish political psyche the moral capacity for categorizing the slave trade as "horrendous, atrocious and inhumane."[111] The conciliatory defensive strategy resorted to by pro–slave trade representatives in their rhetoric at Cadiz is testament to the success of Argüelles's ethical arguments.

In the aftermath of the Cortes of Cadiz, the absolutist regime would be forced by the British authorities to adopt and define an anti–slave trade position, in which Argüelles's contribution was key. Although unsuccessful, the anti–slave trade and antislavery proposals prior to 1814 are fundamental to understanding the construction and development of subsequent abolitionist discourse and legislation. They set up an ideological framing of the issue, strongly influenced by the British model, which would remain intact for decades to come.

2

Defining a New Discourse on the Slave Trade

Absolutist Nuances, Toreno's Commitment, and Varela's Utopia

The longer that the People have lost their liberty, the stronger becomes in them their anxiety to recover it.
—Council of the Indies, 1816

The Spanish king Fernando VII was no abolitionist. Contrary to what he occasionally expressed, his political actions demonstrated, as this chapter shows, a general disregard for the lives of those enslaved and transported across the ocean to labor for others for free in his dominions. However, the Spanish state was heterogeneous and exposed to the new ideas circulating in the Atlantic World. Abolitionism was so persuasive as to pervade the court of the absolutist king, with important consequences for the political counsel he was given at certain junctures.

In the aftermath of the restoration, Fernando VII's government was forced by the British authorities to define a new official stance on the slave trade and to accommodate some aspects of an anti–slave trade rhetoric. This new policy was built upon a conservative tradition but also on the ideological influence of British and early Spanish abolitionism. In practice the Absolutist regime continued to protect and even promote the continuity of the slave trade in the Spanish colonies. This chapter explores the characteristics of the new official discourse on the trade and the ideological inconsistencies reared within the Spanish imperial administration as part of this process.

During the short constitutional period of 1820–1823, both abolitionist and proslavery discourses found in the reestablished Cortes a prominent platform. Some important Liberal figures, such as José María Queipo de Llano

(Count of Toreno), José María Calatrava, and Francisco Martínez de la Rosa, argued against the slave trade and, in collaboration with the British authorities, proposed different strategies to implement anti–slave trade legislation. The Cuban planters in the parliament advanced a consistently pro–slave trade discourse, urging the abrogation of all agreements reached by Spain that resolved toward abolition. This chapter suggests that both sides failed to meet their conditions of victory. The anti–slave trade discourse cemented during the previous constitutional period (1810–1814) could not be eroded, but a combination of factors interfered decisively with the passage of effective anti–slave trade legislation. By 1823 slavery and the illicit slave trade were "indispensable" engines of the new colonial economic system.[1]

A New Absolutist Discourse on the Slave Trade: From the Declaration of 1814 to the Treaty of 1817

The Treaty of Madrid of 1814

In May 1814 Fernando VII abolished the Constitution of 1812 and closed down the Cortes. Since 1811 British diplomatic pressure to abolish the slave trade had been foiled by failed attempts at the Cortes and the prevalence of the position of Cuban representatives.[2] Merchant and planter elites successfully projected the idea that the risk of losing the island to "the black slaves, the British, the Haitians, or whomever they considered the most credible threat at the time" was certain and imminent.[3] Securing the permanence of Cuba as part of the Spanish Empire, in the context of the Spanish American Wars for Independence, was seen by the metropolitan elites as a priority, and British abolitionist pressure was described as a threat to the stability of Cuba's society and economy.

In the aftermath of the Napoleonic Wars, an unprecedented popular antislavery mobilization resumed in Britain. A petition to the prince regent, George IV (1762–1830), requesting the complete abolition of the slave trade in France, Spain, and Portugal garnered nearly one million signatures, putting the issue at the top of the agenda of the British government.[4] As Seymour Drescher has pointed out, this social mobilization was "the most numerous petition in British history" and marked a point of no return for the British commitment to fighting against the slave trade in the Atlantic.[5] No future negotiation with the governments of these three nations would take place without discussing the abolition of the slave trade.[6]

Negotiations between the Foreign Office and the Spanish government started in June 1814 and concluded on August 28 of the same year, with the signing in Madrid of a Treaty of Alliance between the two countries.[7] The Spanish authorities were worried about the logistical assistance that the pro-independence armies were receiving from British merchants and about the possibility of the British Empire offering full support and international recognition to the independence of the Spanish colonies in the Americas. As Guadalupe Jiménez Codinach has argued with regard to the War of Independence in Mexico, the role that the British government played was always covert, and after 1814 the main interest was the—always officially undeclared—will of the British economic elites and merchants to control the Spanish American markets.[8] The Spanish government had no better option than to negotiate with Britain a "noninterventionist" policy in the Americas, in return for a relaxation of the Spanish position with respect to the slave trade.

By the terms of this agreement, Britain pledged not to provide arms, ammunition, or any other support to the "dissidents of the Americas," and in return Spain prohibited any Spaniard from taking part in the slave trade, except to supply Spanish dominions.[9] The treaty also included a declaration of the Spanish king, in which he condemned the slave trade. Fernando VII declared that "concurring in the fullest manner in the sentiment of His Britannic Majesty, with respect to the injustice and inhumanity of the Traffic in Slaves, [the King] will take into consideration, . . . the means of acting in conformity with those sentiments."[10] For the first time, a Spanish monarch publicly affirmed that the slave trade was unfair, cruel, and wrong.

The importance of this statement has been diminished or overlooked by most historians in the field, following the British characterization of this declaration as "unsatisfactory."[11] As David Murray has pointed out, the king's statement had no immediate legal consequences, but it should be stressed that it constitutes a milestone in the construction of a new official discourse on the slave trade in Spain, and the first official anti–slave trade statement by a Spanish head of state.[12] This declaration was seemingly the best deal that the British ambassador in Madrid, Henry Wellesley, could obtain from the Spanish authorities, but contrary to Murray's belief, this was not a small concession from the Absolutist regime.[13] In spite of its origins as a contrivance of diplomatic trade-offs, and legal impotence, the declaration signed by Fernando VII is significant for drawing the contours of a new state discourse on the slave trade that would persist until its final displacement from the Spanish colonies in the 1860s.

For the first time, the Spanish government abandoned its long-held assumption that the slave trade had a positive impact on the enslaved Africans who were "rescued" from their barbaric homeland, and who became Catholics "from the moment [they] set foot in any of the Spanish Possessions."[14] This declaration represented the most significant alteration of the Spanish official position on the slave trade since its establishment.

However, in practical terms, the treaty's additional article did not imply any actual commitment on the Spanish side to abolishing the slave trade. Neither did it stipulate or even gesture toward any forms of further implementation; moreover, the Spanish crown had no intention to penalize any of its subjects who engaged in the trade. The influence of "all those who have any connection with South America, or with the Spanish West Indian Islands," was very important at the court of Fernando VII.[15] To begin with, the preservation of Cuba as part of the Spanish Empire was a priority for the Spanish government in part because of its importance to planters, merchants, and investors, both Cuban and metropolitan, who had successfully projected the opinion that the abolition of the slave trade would catalyze pro-independence sentiments in the island.[16] Further, the tax revenue extracted from the "burgeoning export-led" sugar and coffee industries soon became indispensable to the crown in the context of the severe economic crisis precipitated by the ruinous Peninsular War and the almost as costly Spanish-American Wars for Independence.[17] As Murray has argued, "the main reason for the Spanish not to concede more was the risk of discontent in Cuba" and, as Wellesley reported to London in August 1814, the Spanish government was not even tentatively interested in entering into discussion about the economic compensation that the British government would pay for abolition; political stability in Cuba was a symbol of the King's authority in the Americas.[18]

The Anti–Slave Trade Declaration of the Congress of Vienna

British diplomatic pressure on the Spanish government continued after the signing of the Treaty of Alliance in 1814, moderated by the Foreign Office's reading of the Bourbon Restoration as a potential threat to Spanish political and economic dependency on Britain. The British government wanted to strengthen this relationship by conceding to Spain the financial support that the crown desperately needed.[19] However, as a result of the abolitionist campaign, the British parliament would not accept the provision of any support to Fernando VII without prior concessions from the Spanish monarch on the matter of the slave trade.

The Spanish secretary of state from May to November 1814, José Miguel de Carvajal, Duke of San Carlos (1771–1828), had a very keen disposition with regard to settling diplomatic relations with Britain on positive terms, and therefore to securing the continuity of the British subsidy—worth two million pounds a year—and to achieving an extra ten-million-pound loan.[20] In October 1814 the Duke of San Carlos formally proposed to the British government that Spain would commit to immediately abolishing the slave trade ten degrees north of the equator, and in its entirety after eight years.[21] The British government rejected this proposal and affirmed that it would not accept anything less than the slave trade being "immediately and entirely abolished."[22]

In its reply the Spanish government opposed an immediate abolition, and grounded its response on three main principles, which echoed the discourses advanced by the Cuban deputies at the Cortes de Cadiz: first, the small ratio of enslaved Africans in Cuba compared to those in Jamaica in 1807; second, the excessive immediacy demanded by the British authorities, by contrast to the time that the British parliament had dedicated to studying the issue; and third, the government argued that a sudden abolition of the slave traffic would endanger the safety and security of Cuba.[23]

The prevalence of these three ideas in Spanish political discourse is remarkable. They constitute, as Robert Paquette has demonstrated, the cornerstone of the official response of successive Spanish governments resisting the British anti–slave trade pressure until 1844.[24] Of the three, the reference to Cuba's security and stability was the most frequently invoked. This "threat" had first been put forward by the Cuban planters and slave owners and, as Barcia put it, was instrumental in their attempts "to lobby for privileges and concessions throughout the first half of the nineteenth century."[25] The colonial and metropolitan elites' argument was "in essence, . . . what might be called the "necessary evil" argument of the Southern slaveholders during the early stage of their ideological development."[26] They demanded time and independence to rule their own territories and raised the specter of a new revolution in the mold of Haiti, on Cuban soil. However, this new official discourse, developed from 1811 onward, tended to avoid defending the slave trade on moral grounds and publicly accepted that the traffic would have to end eventually.

After 1814 negotiations for the abolition of the slave trade entered into deadlock due to the Spanish refusal to accept the British demands. In these circumstances the debate moved from Madrid to the Congress of Vienna (1814–1815). This meeting of ambassadors of European states, chaired by the Austrian delegate, had the main goal of providing a long-term peace plan for the continent in the aftermath of the Napoleonic Wars.[27]

Following the popular antislavery campaign in Britain of 1814–1815, which produced 1,370 petitions, the British delegation pushed for a joint declaration from all the European powers regarding the immediate and global abolition of the slave trade.[28] This declaration was supported by Russia, Austria, Prussia, and France, and subsequently approved. Spain and Portugal, which had secondary roles at the conference, voiced their strong opposition. The Spanish delegate, Pedro Gómez Labrador (1772–1850), followed the same line of argument used by the Spanish government during the previous negotiations with Britain. He accordingly stressed the right of all nations to decide their own colonial policies and presented the issue as a matter of imperial sovereignty.[29]

The Spanish authorities introduced the concept of the defense of imperial sovereignty, against the interference of Britain, as part of the strategy to protect the slave trade. This discourse frequently highlighted the existence of what Gabriel Paquette identifies as a potent ideological stimulant for reawakening "a sense of patriotism and pride" in the context of intense imperial rivalries.[30] The Cuban oligarch Francisco Arango y Parreño, who was living in Paris while the Congress of Vienna was taking place, openly condemned in the press any foreign interference in Spain's colonial policy. From Madrid the representative of Havana's *cabildo* (city council), Claudio Martínez Pinillos (1782–1853), reported to his home institution that "the constant determination and efforts of the English [British] to stop this traffic, as the most direct way to destroy our agricultural industry" were welcomed at the international conference.[31] The colonial and metropolitan authorities denied British "philanthropic goals" and argued that the real objective of the British government was simply to ruin Cuba's economy. The idea of defending the slave trade as a patriotic struggle against the British Empire gained traction during the first half of the nineteenth century.[32]

Despite this opposition a declaration calling for the end of the slave trade was ratified by the Congress of Vienna, and the Foreign Office immediately requested that France, Spain, and Portugal legislate to these ends. France agreed to abolish the slave trade north of Cape Formoso, "in an attempt to gain British sympathies, during the Hundred Days."[33] Portugal, for its part, entered into negotiations with Britain to prohibit this traffic north of the equator. Since December 1814 the British secretary of state for foreign affairs, Lord Castlereagh (1769–1822), had encouraged the Spanish government, in different letters and conversations, to follow France and Portugal's examples and put into effect the declaration made by Fernando VII in the Treaty of Alliance of 1814.[34] In a letter to Castlereagh in July 1815, Labrador pointed out that any decision in this direction would be conditioned by the granting of a "very significant loan" and British support to "stop the rebellions in some of the Spanish American Provinces which had been promoted and protected by British merchants."[35] In other words, the Spanish government would stop the slave trade only in exchange for a significant amount of money and political support in the American crisis.

In August of the same year, Charles Richard Vaughan (1774–1849), in charge of the British diplomatic mission in Madrid, sent a copy of the treaty with France to the Spanish government and affirmed his "confident hope . . . that this fresh instance of liberality on the part of a great European Power . . . will influence the Councils of his Catholic Majesty."[36] In the letter he also tackled Spain's argument that this decision would be neither sudden nor negative to Spanish interests: "It has been urged in excuse for delaying the abolition of the slave trade, that that measure was not adopted in England until after many years had been spent in deliberation, but it should be recollected that all Europe was a party to those deliberations . . . and that the result of the experiment made by England is now before the world for the benefit of mankind in general."[37]

From the moment the agreement of Vienna was signed, the British government increased its naval activity against the slave traders operating along the African coasts and across the Atlantic, which became a major concern for the Spanish authorities. Days after the congressional declaration appeared in the British press, the Cuban Junta Consular, which represented the interests of Cuban merchant and planter elites, asked the Spanish king to demand that the British authorities "not disturb" the Spanish slave traders and compensate the owners of the vessels that had already been detained.[38] Labrador complained about the "tyrannical" British attitude that "considers everything they want to be their right," along with the British propensity to "fire on" and "board" Spanish and Portuguese slave trade vessels when, for Spain and Portugal, this traffic was perfectly legal.[39] Simultaneously, in Madrid, Wellesley presented several representations to no effect, and in July 1815 the Spanish secretary of state replied that the whole issue had been forwarded to the Council of the Indies for further consideration. The Spanish secretary of state needed time to define a new strategy agreed upon with Cuban and metropolitan planters, investors, and merchants. In October 1815 Castlereagh ordered that tension with the Spanish government be defused, and the issue remained unattended until mid-1816.[40] The deliberations of the Council of the Indies, however, would have an unexpected outcome.

The Council of the Indies' Anti–Slave Trade Reports of 1816

In February 1816, after a long process of information gathering from colonial and metropolitan authorities, the Council of the Indies presented its report on the slave trade.[41] The majority of the council recommended "that your Majesty may be pleased to command that the slave trade be forthwith perpetually abolished throughout your dominions."[42] They mainly focused on moral and religious reasons to argue in favor of the abolition of the slave trade and stressed the Christian character of the Spanish nation, and the evils of slavery itself: "When we consider the question with reference to morality, everyone must admit that the Christian maxims, and the mild character of the Spaniards, unite in condemning a Trade so execrable in itself, and by which a traffic is made in the blood of our Fellow Creatures. . . . In fact, how could a Traffic of this nature . . . be looked upon in any other light than with repugnance, by Spain, the center of the Catholic Religion? Not, indeed, because we think that Slavery, in itself, is opposed to the principles of the Gospel."[43]

In its report, the council highlighted the importance of "illustrious" and

"pious" British abolitionists such as "William Pitt" and "William Wilberforce," who "will be forever respected by all who feel and can appreciate the
high dignity of man."[44] They also tackled one of the main arguments of the
pro–slave trade advocates, arguing that the abolition of the slave trade would
create a safer and more secure society in the Spanish colonies: "the longer that
the People have lost their liberty, the stronger becomes in them their anxiety
to recover it."[45] Moreover, the characterization of the slave trade as a traffic
made "in the blood of our Fellow Creatures" recalls how Agustín de Argüelles
described it five years before at the Cortes of Cadiz, as a commerce "in the
blood of our brothers," and reinforces the notion of the centrality that Argüelles's proposal had in the construction of early abolitionist discourses in
Spain.[46]

The councilors rejected the idea that the British government was pursuing
the bankruptcy of the Cuban plantations. On the contrary, only "the principles of morality and policy equally" have driven their pressure on the Spanish
authorities: "the ardent zeal and endeavors of the [British] Cabinet . . . have
formed their object, to satisfy the minds of the English People, who, must be
naturally anxious for the abolition of the [slave trade]."[47] As a consequence,
the majority of the council advocated an "immediate" abolition of the slave
trade and stressed that in no way would this be a sudden determination, as
"sufficient time to provide themselves with the required number of Blacks"
had been given to the planters.[48]

This powerful conclusion overtly contradicted the government's official position on the slave trade, discredited Labrador's intervention in Vienna, and
even cracked opened a door that the Spanish and British governments stood
timidly on the threshold of the abolition of slavery in its totality. Surprisingly,
however, the report of the Council of the Indies has been consistently overlooked by the historians who have studied this part of the historical process.
Arthur Corwin only pointed out that "based on broad principles of humanity"
the council recommended abolishing the slave trade.[49] David Murray diminished the importance of the report based on its merely consultative character, and Julia Moreno, in her analysis of the Treaty of 1817, did not mention
its existence.[50] For his part, Fernando Armario Sanchez misinterpreted the
council's majority report and argued that it "was not very favorably inclined
towards the abolition of the slave trade," when it was exactly the opposite.[51]
This report is extraordinarily important in political and ideological terms. It
constitutes an unprecedented example of an anti–slave trade report produced
from within the absolutist regime. The laudatory rhetoric toward the British
authorities and the similarities with Argüelles's parliamentary speech directly
opposed the official line hitherto followed by the Spanish government, the
colonial elites, and the king himself.

A minority of the council, consisting of seven members, including Francisco Arango y Parreño, a representative of the Cuban planters, dissented and contrived a separate report.[52] In their statement, they acknowledged that Britain would eventually succeed in forcing Spain to abolish the slave trade, as had already happened in France. However, they aimed to secure a gradual abolition that would preserve the wealth of the colonial elites: "We admit that the Slave Trade ought to be prohibited . . . but by no means agree in the opinion, that the Slave Trade should be prohibited all at once."[53] The minority pointed out that a "sudden" abolition of the slave trade would "accelerate the injurious effects of the prohibition" and would "condemn thousands of landowners to lose a considerable portion of their incomes [and] spread sorrow and misery in Countries, where now reign prosperity and abundance."[54] The minority also asserted that abolition would have negative consequences for "those unhappy persons who are already slaves," because of the small number of female enslaved Africans living in the colonies: "without females whom they might marry, they would pass their sorrowful lives in forced and insupportable celibacy, and be forever deprived of the advantages and comforts which matrimony produces . . . particularly to the unfortunate."[55]

The opposing councilors proposed that Spain should claim an economic compensation from Britain, and that this money should be used "as an indemnification for the losses" caused to be given to the slave-owners.[56] They pointed out that there was no current threat to the security of the Caribbean colonies, that "the insurrections which have been occasionally excited by our slaves have been partial and momentary," and that the slave trade was not fueling in any way these slave revolts. But they warned the Spanish government that a sudden abolition "would be highly dangerous to risk in our possessions a repetition of those scenes of destruction and horror that occurred in the French colony of St. Domingo [Saint-Domingue]."[57] Finally, the minority of the council argued for an immediate abolition of the slave trade north of the equator and totally "after the 22nd of April 1821," accepting that ultimately abolition was unstoppable.[58]

The councilors who signed the majority report replied and submitted a short statement rejecting the ideas argued by the minority. They affirmed that there was no time to lose to put an end to this "repugnant practice . . . which has degraded the dignity of man": "We should no longer waste our time in discussions, as these have been exhausted; . . . We have only time sufficient left to us for putting an end to this traffic with a strong, firm and steady hand."[59] The majority of the council urged the king, once again, to abolish the slave trade totally and immediately.

Significantly, the minority of the council desisted in trying to contest moral arguments against the slave trade. As had happened at the Cortes of Cadiz, by characterizing the abolitionist report as hasty and radical, they aimed to avoid a debate on moral grounds, in order to move the discussion to when and how the abolition should take place, and to consider the complex network of interests at stake.[60] Argüelles's proposal of 1811 and British ideological and political influence had become central to defining the political ground on which the councilors on both sides of the argument were operating. Although these reports had an advisory character, and the Council of State and, ultimately, the Spanish government "had the choice of accepting either the majority or the minority position," they constitute fundamental evidence of the successful penetration of the abolitionist discourse defined at the Cortes of Cadiz five years before.[61]

The Anglo-Spanish Treaty of 1817

The position of Spanish absolutism with regard to the slave trade was not as monolithic as it appeared, and the British government hoped to take advantage of the complexity and conflict underpinning the council's policymaking. In March 1816 the British ambassador in Madrid, Charles Vaughan, managed to obtain copies of the reports of the Council of the Indies after winning "some confidence from the person appointed by the Council to draw [them] up" and immediately forwarded them to London.[62] The connection between Vaughan and, at least, one of the councilors who subscribed to the majority report proves that the deliberations of the Council of the Indies were not isolated from the political negotiations between Spain and Britain. Vaughan's subtle reference proves that the British diplomatic mission played an important role in the drafting of the majority report, and it is plausible to argue that they also circulated abolitionist publications among the councilors, as the African Institution had suggested in 1814.[63]

The reports of the Council of the Indies were sent to the Council of State on February 15, 1816, for further consideration. This upper council could accept either of the two proposals, and Pedro Cevallos advised the council that the abolition of the slave trade was a necessary concession to make to Britain, but only in return for very significant compensation.[64] Cevallos was willing to improve relations between the two countries, at a critical moment for the Spanish treasury, and endorsed the report signed by the minority of the Council of the Indies. As a result, the Spanish government circulated on March 27, 1816, a proposal to gradually abolish the slave trade in Spain. They agreed to prohibit the traffic immediately north of the equator, and in its entirety after five years. In return Spain would receive a compensation of £500,000 to cover the losses of Spanish slave vessels that had been captured by the British navy, and a second indemnity of £1,000,000 to finance the cost of sending a European workforce to Cuba to replace the enslaved Africans.

Additionally, Britain would support the Spanish efforts against the "Barbary States" (or Berbers) in the Mediterranean.[65]

In July 1816 Vaughan replied that Britain was not going to purchase Spain's abolition of the slave trade and would not consider an alliance to fight the "Barbary States," until Spain agreed to fully and immediately eradicate the slave trade.[66] Vaughan believed that the decision of the Council of State to support the report of the minority of the Council of the Indies was the result of the pressure leveraged by the "planters of the Island of Cuba" and the pro–slave trade position of Cevallos.[67] Vaughan argued that the inconsistency shown by the Council of the Indies proved that it was possible to change views held with regard to the slave trade within the court of Fernando VII, and that to do so Britain had to directly lobby members of the Council of State and the king. In October 1816 the British ambassador asked the Foreign Office for copies of Blanco White's *Bosquexo* to support his campaign in Madrid. Immediately, the African Institution provided two hundred copies of the abolitionist publication to be sent to Spain.[68] The replacement of Cevallos by José García de León y Pizarro (1770–1835) as Spanish secretary of state opened a new perspective for the negotiations and was welcomed by the British authorities.

At the international level the British government organized a conference in London between France, Austria, Prussia, and Russia in the winter of 1816–1817. The main reason for this meeting was to develop and expand the slave trade agreement signed in Vienna in 1815, and to force Spain and Portugal to negotiate an immediate abolition. Historians who have examined the resulting Treaty of 1817 have, however, downplayed this international meeting, with the exception of Julia Moreno, who has investigated Spain's diplomatic efforts to stymie British aspirations regarding abolition.[69] The failure of the conference, and the perception of Britain's international isolation arising from this meeting, explains Britain's subsequent strategy. From this point forward, the British government conceded some of its initial demands and accepted payment of "compensation" to Spain in return for an abolitionist agreement.[70]

The position of Russia had gradually changed since the end of the Congress of Vienna, and, as Cea Bermúdez, Spanish ambassador in Saint Petersburg, reported to Madrid, the British government would "not find an ally [in Russia] to its philanthropic plan."[71] He informed the Spanish government that "Alexander the Emperor will not assist Great Britain to force any other independent power to speed up the abolition of the trade in negroes, against their own interest."[72] Russia was skeptical about the role of the British government in Latin America and distrusted its motivations for encouraging other nations to abolish the slave trade. As has been shown, since 1815 the Russian authorities supported Spain in affirming that the abolition of the slave trade was a matter of "imperial sovereignty."[73] It can be argued, based on Cea Bermúdez's report, that the negotiations that Murray dated in 1817 had actually started months prior.[74] Russia thus became an important and ever-closer international ally of Spain against British pressure.

The positions of Spain and Britain remained distant until November 30, 1816, when events sped up and the negotiations, which had been in a state of paralysis since 1815, were resumed. That day Vaughan sent three reports to London in which he explained the sudden eagerness of Spain to reach a deal on the slave trade as soon as possible. The negotiation revolved around monetary compensation and an additional loan that Britain would grant in exchange for abolition. These negotiations led to the signing of an international treaty on September 23, 1817.

With the Treaty of 1817 (and the subsequent Real Cédula of December 19, 1817), the Spanish king prohibited Spanish subjects from being involved in the slave trade north of the equator immediately, and south of the equator after May 20, 1820.[75] Every vessel captain captured breaking the law would be imprisoned in the Philippine Islands, and the enslaved Africans on board would be declared free. Spain and Britain were authorized to search any vessels from both nations whenever there was a well-founded suspicion of them transporting enslaved persons. The crews of the captured ships would be taken before special tribunals established for this purpose. Two mixed courts, composed of an equal number of judges named by each nation, would be created in Sierra Leone and Havana. In return, the British government agreed to pay Spain £400,000 (35,559,684 *reales* and 12 *monedas de vellón* ["fleece coins"]).[76]

David Murray has highlighted two main reasons for Spain's sudden interest in signing the agreement.[77] One was the involvement of General Francisco Javier Castaños (1758–1852) in favor of a military alliance with Britain, and the other a parallel negotiation with the Russian government.[78] The money, the Spanish crown realized, could immediately be spent on the purchase of Russian warships to be used against the Mexican revolutionary armies. Vaughan suspected that these negotiations were taking place and reported to the Foreign Office that "a close connection with Russia is justified upon the grounds that Spain cannot look for naval assistance or money from England."[79] These secret negotiations with Russia show that the decision of the Spanish government to abolish the slave trade was driven only by military interest.[80] After the treaty was signed, Wellesley concluded that "the money, which they are to receive, [was] their principal motive for acceding to the abolition."[81]

In addition to the two factors suggested by Murray, the failure of the international conference in London the year before should also be considered.[82] British international isolation on this issue and Russian public support for

Spain's position motivated Britain to accept "compensating" the Spanish Empire for the abolition of the slave trade. Murray was right to suggest that the signing of the Treaty of 1817 essentially responded to the precariousness of the Spanish treasury and the need to patch up relations with Britain. However, Britain's decision to soften its demands should be interpreted as the result of the failure to build a unified continental abolitionist position and the growing pressure of its domestic antislavery movement.

In this regard British abolitionist leaders welcomed the treaty, hoping that it would restrain the slave trade due to the naval power of Britain. But they were aware of the real motives behind the position of the Spanish government. In October 1818 William Wilberforce wrote to Henri Christophe, king of Haiti, celebrating the signing of the treaty with Spain but also regretting that "it is not without the payment of a large sum of money that we have brought the Spanish cabinet to such conditions."[83] In a similar way, in 1819 the British member of Parliament and abolitionist James Mackintosh (1765–1832) recalled this negotiation in the House of Commons and counterposed the rationale of the Spanish king to the political determinations of Argüelles in 1811: "What Ferdinand had done for money, was spontaneously and gratuitously accorded by the insurgent colonies; that what Ferdinand reluctantly, and after long negotiation consented only partially to restrain, Argüelles prevailed on the Cortes instantly, universally, and forever to abolish."[84]

The Cuban colonial elite tried in vain to stop the signing of the international agreement and one of its foremost representatives, Francisco de Arango y Parreño, offered "a very significant amount of money" to the Spanish government as a counteroffer.[85] After the treaty was signed and introduced into Spanish law, the Cuban colonial elite did everything they could to avoid any British attempt to implement the measures established in the treaty. They consolidated a strong Anglophobic view in which the Spanish king was presented as a victim of British manipulations, and subsequently, defending the slave trade was glossed as a patriotic duty.[86] This narrative, which had already operated at the Cortes of Cadiz and during the deliberations of the Council of the Indies in 1816, would become a keystone of Cuban and metropolitan pro–slave trade strategies in the following years.[87]

Considering the ideological content of the exact wording used in the Treaty of 1817, it is apparent that a thread of proslavery rhetoric ran through the enactment. The Royal Order of December 19, 1817, which put the treaty into effect, stated that "the Negroes, far from suffering additional evils, obtained the inestimable advantage of a knowledge of the true God, and of all the benefits attendant on civilization."[88] The Spanish diplomatic missions abroad repeated this messaging, and in 1818 Luis de Onís (1762–1827), Spanish ambassador in Washington, informed the American secretary of state

John Quincy Adams (1767–1848) about the Treaty of 1817. In his letter Onís translated the Royal Order of December 1817 and explained that the agreement came about as a result of "the desire entertained by His [Spanish] Majesty of co-operating with the Powers of Europe," and that the course of action was made possible by a decline in demand for slaves within the Spanish colonial possessions. The ambassador argued "that the numbers of the Native and Free Negroes had prodigiously increased under the mild regimen of the government, and the humane treatment of the Spanish Slave Owners."[89]

The Spanish government did not earnestly pursue humanitarian or abolitionist ideas, nor did they have the will or even the necessary resources to implement the agreement. Nonetheless, the Treaty of 1817 constituted an important political victory for the British government. Although it would not have an effective impact in stopping the slave trade in the Atlantic, it wrenched into Spanish law the ethical principle that the slave trade was immoral on the grounds of its inhumanity. The signing of anti–slave trade treaties between Britain and Spain (1817), France (1814), Portugal (1815 and 1817), and later with Brazil (1826) established, in the opinion of Jenny Martinez, "a collective statement of agreement on the immorality of slaving," and the creation of two mixed commissions courts in Havana and Rio de Janeiro made it explicit that the slave trade was not only "contrary to the laws of nature" but also contrary to "the law of nations."[90] The Treaty of 1817 ratified Fernando VII's declaration of 1814 but also the anti–slave trade discourses at the Cortes of Cadiz. The Foreign Office succeeded in forcing Spain to legally accept that the traffic of enslaved Africans was wrong and had to be abolished for the sake of humanism.

The implementation of the treaty soon proved impossible, due to the weakness of resolve on the part of metropolitan and colonial authorities, and the lack of sufficient naval forces for surveillance of the expansive and inaccessible Cuban archipelago. The number of enslaved Africans introduced into Cuba increased exponentially until 1839, and then again in the 1850s.[91] In 1817 alone at least 25,448 enslaved Africans were introduced into Cuba.[92]

The Abolitionist Debate in Spain during the Liberal Triennium

On January 1, 1820, the lieutenant-colonel general Rafael de Riego led a revolution against the Absolutist Regime demanding the restoration of the Constitution of 1812 that soon spread to the rest of Spain. Fernando VII was forced to accept the demands of the revolutionaries on March 9 restoring a parliamentary system. The Liberal deputies that had been in exile or imprisoned since 1815 were granted amnesty in July 1820, and many of them had an important role to play in the new Cortes and its Liberal ministries. Until the elections of 1822, these institutions were controlled by a moderate faction of liberals, the so-called *doceañistas*. After this date, the parliament was controlled by a more radical sector of liberals, known as *exaltados*.[93] The establishment of the first Liberal government in 1820 was very welcome to the British antislavery lobby, which saw this situation as an opportunity to finally implement the neglected treaty signed three years earlier.

Wilberforce, Argüelles, and Toreno

As soon as the news of the formation of a new government reached London, William Wilberforce aimed to contact the new ministers and persuade them to implement the Treaty of 1817. He was keen to offer them advice and publications to strengthen their knowledge of the abolitionist cause. In April 1820 Wilberforce sent a letter to Lord Holland in which he acknowledged that "doubtless . . . Argüelles will be released from prison; and his influence cannot but be great with the new government."[94] The communication between Wilberforce and Argüelles and José María Queipo de Llano, Count of Toreno, constitutes the most significant attempt of the British abolitionist lobby to directly influence the Spanish political debate during the Liberal Triennium (1820–1823). This correspondence, most of which was hitherto unknown, has received no attention in the historiography but provides crucial clues to trace the evolution of anti–slave trade ideas in Spain in the years leading up to 1823.

On March 28, 1820, Wilberforce wrote to Argüelles highlighting his role in the promotion of abolitionist ideas and praised him as "dear to every lover of liberty, . . . and every friend of the Abolition of the slave trade."[95] Wilberforce expressed his relief concerning Argüelles's recent release from prison and congratulated him on his appointment as secretary of state for the interior in the new Liberal government in August of that year. Wilberforce did not hesitate to stress the remarkable importance of Argüelles's anti–slave trade commitment at the Cortes of Cadiz and credited his initiative as an important antecedent to the abolitionist treaty signed between Spain and Britain in 1817. "The disposition manifested by your country to join the other confederated powers in terminating the wrongs of Africa had probably been produced in no small degree by the force of your reasoning and the power of your eloquence."[96]

Wilberforce informed Argüelles about the details of the recent agreement between the two countries to totally abolish "the 20th May [1820] . . . a system which, under the name of commerce, includes in it whatever injustice and cruelty could perpetrate for the misery of its victims."[97] The British abolitionist concluded his letter asking Argüelles to be, once again, the voice of abolitionism in Spain: "It is by a singular ordination of Providence that it should be reserved for you, their advocate in the season of their misery and degradation, to pronounce the ordinance which is to declare admission to the rank of human beings, and to recognise the right which as our fellow-creatures they possess to the common claims of justice and humanity."[98]

On October 28, 1820, Argüelles replied to Wilberforce from Madrid. This letter constitutes the last known private document in which Argüelles expressed his opinion on the abolition of the slave trade. He informed Wilberforce that he had no "detailed knowledge of the status of the treaty . . . because urgent business issues have absorbed all [his] attention" but committed himself to its actual implementation: "The current Ministry will not, from this date onwards, hinder a convention aimed at the philanthropic relief of Africa, a convention that has benefited from your tireless efforts and determined policy over so many years. . . . I believe the time when the states of Europe agree in good faith to give up the slave trade is very near."[99]

Argüelles was concerned about the political crisis in Spain and the fears of invasion by foreign absolutist powers and asked Wilberforce to give his support to the Liberal government by comparing the struggle of the African slaves with the fight of the Spaniards, "who only aspire to be free and independent."[100] He asked him to "let your influence be no less powerful than it was in the cause of the Senegalese, who owe you so much, when you apply it to the Europeans."[101] Argüelles concluded that the same "philanthropic doctrine" that sustains abolitionism "upholds that the freedom of a nation is not incompatible with that of others."[102]

This first correspondence between Argüelles and the leader of the British abolitionist movement, one of the best-known political figures of the time, coincided, however, with the retreat of the former from the fight for abolition of the slave trade. This paradox can be explained as the joint effect of three factors: the profound Spanish political crisis that forced him to concentrate on domestic issues; the difficulties of holding any debate about the slave trade; and the gradual conservative turn of his political opinion, which distanced him from the more radical factions of Spanish liberalism. As Fradera put it, "many of the issues discussed in the Cadiz Cortes no longer made sense" and the big reforms ambitioned a decade before had been replaced by a "project adapted to [the] more immediate needs and possibilities" of the new Liberal administration.[103]

The Liberal government formed in April 1820, headed by Evaristo Pérez de Castro, inherited the approach to the slave trade defined by Fernando VII's administration prior to Riego's revolution. However, the pressure of the British diplomatic mission in Madrid motivated the official commitment of Pérez de Castro to full and honest implementation of the Treaty of 1817 and the establishment of the mixed commission courts in Havana and Sierra Leone.[104]

On May 30, 1820, the grace period stipulated by the treaty for the ending of the slave trade in the Spanish Empire drew to an end. Ten days before the deadline, the Spanish government formally requested of the British authorities "an enlarged extension of the term of five months."[105] They argued that the vessels already departed from Cuba to Africa to bring slaves before the cutoff should "be allowed to return unmolested, and hoping that England will not insist rigorously on keeping to the very letter of the Treaty, which is evidently in contradiction with the spirit of the original Agreement."[106] The period was not extended, but the slave trade continued with the consent and protection of the Spanish authorities in Cuba and Madrid. As Henry Theo Kilbee, British commissary judge, reported from Havana in November 1820, "on the 6th instant, the Brig *Tellus*, . . . entered this Port [Havana] with 178 Negroes from the Coast of Africa, and was admitted, and allowed to land her cargo." As Jennifer Nelson has recently found, Kilbee's report was ignored by the Spanish authorities in Cuba, "setting a precedent which was repeated throughout the court's existence."[107] It was only in 1824 that the first slave vessel was tried in Havana's Mixed Commission Court, the *María da Glória*, although it was ultimately acquitted. Later that year the *Relampago*, with 151 enslaved Africans on board, became the first ship to be condemned in the newly established tribunal.[108]

In terms of ideology, agitations made after the deadline—that is, under the new Liberal administration—in defense of the slave trade drew on discursive tropes typically used to defend the institution of slavery itself. Previous distinctions in the political uses of the arguments were smudged. To illustrate, a letter to the British ambassador from Pérez de Castro declared that the abolition of the slave trade in Spain was only the result of British pressure against Spain's interests. He affirmed that Spain was willing to fulfill its international commitments but also that it was "a known fact" that "the Spanish slave has ever enjoyed the immediate protection of a tutelary and philosophical code of laws."[109]

There were, however, significant exceptions to this consolidated pro–slave trade rhetoric. Between 1820 and 1821, Wilberforce and the Count of Toreno, who had been elected deputy in the new Cortes, exchanged at least two letters about the slave trade.[110] As Wilberforce had done with Argüelles months before, he aimed to persuade Toreno to pass legislation in the Spanish parliament to finally implement the Treaty of 1817 and take concrete steps toward abolishing the slave trade into the Spanish Caribbean dominions. In his response to Wilberforce, Toreno declared himself overwhelmed by the compliments and kind words received from the British MP and committed himself to the anti–slave trade cause: "Do not doubt that I will support you and that I will look for a way to become even more worthy of your admiration and among the friends of Africa in England."[111]

He assured Wilberforce that he would speak up for the issue of abolition as soon as he was in Madrid and asked Wilberforce to send to him "where I am [Paris] or to my country, the information that you want to share with me." Toreno concluded his letter in a laudatory tone, exhorting Wilberforce, "Let your light shine before me."[112] This correspondence, absent from histories of the episode, proves the direct involvement of the British antislavery lobby in influencing the Spanish MP and shows Toreno's commitment to ending the slave trade.

Soon after the Count of Toreno moved to Madrid, the British ambassador approached him to press the concerns of his government "upon the subject of the slave trade."[113] In March 1821 Wellesley reported to the Foreign Office, "[Toreno] assured me that he would take an early opportunity of bringing the question under the consideration of the Cortes," and that he would focus on "preventing by adequate penalties, the evasion of the treaty . . . for the entire abolition of this traffic."[114] Toreno requested from the British authorities more information about the Treaty of 1817 and other penal laws that had been enacted by the British parliament. He expressed his "greater alacrity since [promoting the eradication of the slave trade] would afford him an occasion of testifying his admiration of the British Nation and government."[115]

On March 23, 1821, Toreno fulfilled his promise and argued in the Cortes to stop "this shameful and inhumane traffic."[116] His proposal had the support of the chamber, and a special commission, chaired by Toreno himself, was appointed. Together with the deputies La-Llave, Martínez de la Rosa, Calatrava, and Ramos Arizpe, the commission drafted a law to stop the illegal slave traffic into Cuba and sent it to the Cortes.[117] The British ambassador was highly pleased with the result of this commission and reported to Castlereagh, "The Conde de Toreno has fulfilled in a most satisfactory manner the expectations which he had held out to me in the various communications which I had with him upon this subject."[118]

Toreno's anti–slave trade bill proposed using the threat of jail and economic sanction against any Spanish subject directly or indirectly involved in the illegal introduction of African slaves into the Spanish dominions. This included crew members, financial backers of the expeditions, slave buyers, and civil servants.[119] The project was sent to the Cortes in April 1821, but the proposal faced the strong opposition of the Cuban deputy Juan Bernardo O'Gavan, who successfully convinced a majority of the chamber to reject it. As Barcia has convincingly suggested, O'Gavan's main goal was to encourage the restoration of the transatlantic slave trade, following the instructions of Havana's local authorities. The Ayuntamiento of Havana argued that the Spanish king had been tricked by the British authorities and warned about the "dreadful consequences that this treaty . . . produced and will produce."[120]

The Cuban local representatives affirmed that if the treaty were not withdrawn, "the ruin of this island [would] be inevitable."[121]

O'Gavan's Reaction and Bowring's Response

In 1820 the Diputación Provincial, the Ayuntamiento, and the Consulado of Havana gave instructions to their representatives at the Cortes to formally propose the withdrawal of the Treaty of 1817, or at least to settle a grace period of six further years. The Diputación repeated the same line of argument used in the Cortes of Cadiz in 1811, contending that the resolution to abolish the slave trade was "hasty" and, further, that it contravened the "sacred laws" of property rights. However, they incorporated an additional line of attack in gesturing to the disadvantages shouldered by Spain in comparison with other countries with whom similar abolition treaties had been agreed. The Cuban representatives highlighted the more flexible approach that the British government had adopted with Portugal and Brazil and alleged that "the damage [caused by the treaty] was incalculable," and the compensation agreed with the British authorities was "very small and pretty much nothing."[122]

As had occurred in 1811, the Cuban colonial elite avoided defending the slave trade on moral grounds and tacitly accepted that abolition was inevitable. They aimed, however, to block its actualization for as long as could be afforded, and claimed, as they had done before, that the British only sought to provoke Cuba's bankruptcy: "We should not discuss the continuity of the commerce in slaves. The times have changed, let's talk about the general and total abolition, but cautiously, properly understood, and considering the public and particular interests."[123]

In March 1821 O'Gavan argued that his speech at the Cortes was not intended to justify slavery, but, in truth, it "was the closest imaginable thing to it."[124] He asserted that the slave trade had a positive impact on those brought to the Americas, allowing them to escape from a homeland of misery, barbarity, and stupidity. O'Gavan stressed that "our special laws highly favor the good treatment and the freedom of the blacks" and went on to describe that "these men, who would be indomitable wild beasts in Africa, learn and practice among us the precepts of the religion of peace, love, and sweetness, and become part of the great evangelical society."[125]

The stance of the Cuban deputy was deeply retrograde, repeating arguments that had already been abandoned even by those who defended the continuity of the commerce, such as Arango. O'Gavan "ignored what he knew was really happening just a few miles away from Havana" and "abandoned the thousands of souls that were daily whipped and shackled on his beloved island."[126] However, his opinion prevailed at the Cortes, and Toreno's comprehensive law proposal was rejected.

While the debate on the slave trade took place at the Cortes, O'Gavan published a pamphlet entitled *Observaciones sobre la suerte de los negros
del África, considerados en su propia patria y trasladados a las Antillas Españolas: Y reclamación contra el tratado firmado con los ingleses en el año 1817*. In this
work the Cuban deputy declared that the slave trade and slavery were essential for the "security and existence" of Cuba and warned the Spanish deputies
about the risks that the abolition of the slave trade would incur for the safety
of the island and the loyalty of the Cuban subjects to Spain:[127] "On this serious business depends essentially the happiness and even the existence of the
Island of Cuba. . . . Our interests have always been and are currently intimately intertwined with those of the Peninsula; and it would be painful if in-
appropriate laws were adopted. They would hinder the prosperity [of Cuba],
make them join the general movement that is shaking the American continent today, and adopt measures that are unfavorable to the union with the
European provinces."[128]

O'Gavan's "strongest argument" in defense of the slave trade "was Cuba's
possible loss to the Spanish Crown," and that Cuban merchant and planter
elites would contemplate the protection of the southern states of the United
States should Spain dare to implement the Treaty of 1817:[129] "There exists a
wise government, liberal in principles, powerful and active, which contrives
to extend above her [the Island of Cuba] a charitable hand and to attract her
by all means possible to its system of liberty and splendor, lavishing upon her
abundant resources for her agriculture and commerce."[130]

The truth is that "some of the Cuban representatives and institutions . . .
gave serious thought to breaking with the abolitionist treaty" of 1817 but did
not have enough support at the Cortes to simply withdraw from the agreement.[131] However, they were powerful enough to stop any proposal aimed at
its proper implementation.

The debate of March 1821 between Toreno and O'Gavan motivated the
unexpected participation of John Bowring, a collaborator of Jeremy Bentham
and future governor of Hong Kong. He had traveled to Madrid in the au-
tumn of that year and knew the contours of Spanish political debate from his
engagements with many of its key actors. He had "made many acquaintances
among the distinguished men of the time," including writers, historians, and
politicians such as "Argüelles, . . . Isturiz, Alcala de Galiano . . . , Count Toreno, [and] Don Francisco Martínez de la Rosa."[132] According to Gregorio
Alonso, Bowring was a member of a wider "group of political agents with personal links to leaders in the Mediterranean and across the Atlantic."[133] Led
by Bentham, these agents "played a leading role in the propagation of ideas in
both directions of the Atlantic that can hardly be exaggerated."[134]

In October 1821 Bowring presented himself to the British ambassador in

Madrid and expressed "his intention to organise a society for securing the effectual suppression of the slave trade" and "represented himself as a Plenipotentiary of the African Society, and having effected wonders at Paris."[135] The British ambassador was very concerned about Bowring's activism in Madrid and its potential to disrupt his diplomatic strategy: "The measure Mr. Bowring had in contemplation might succeed in France, as in any other country, but in Spain . . . any attempt of the kind would certainly lead to a most unsatisfactory and most unpleasant request. . . . For this reason, . . . I have signified to Mr. Bowring in the most unequivocal manner, my opinion that it will be highly expedient to desist at present from his purpose."[136]

Bowring, however, did not abandon his plan to influence Spanish public opinion and that same year published his *Contestación a las observaciones de D. Juan Bernardo O'Gavan, sobre la suerte de los negros de África y reclamación contra el tratado celebrado con los ingleses en 1817.*[137] In this short book, written in Spanish, Bowring rejected the arguments put forward by O'Gavan and aimed to convince "those willing to listen" that "philosophy cannot be twinned with the cruelty . . . [of those] who buy and sell human blood, who traffic in misery, tears and death."[138] Bowring vehemently countered the most oft-repeated ideas invoked by Cuban planters in defense of the slave trade. In so doing he appealed to the Christian feelings of the Spanish nation to abolish totally a trade so "opposed to all the most obvious principles of our holy religion" and to follow "the commandments of your religion, the feelings of your hearts."[139] Bowring rejected O'Gavan's idea that Britain was moved only by economic interests. Conversely, he argued that the abolition in Britain was moved only by "the most sincere, ardent, noble and disinterested philanthropy."[140]

Bowring's pamphlet has been paid a great deal of heed by historians who have examined this episode in the history of the Trienio Liberal (Liberal Triennium), including José Antonio Piqueras, Manuel Moreno Alonso, Jesús Navarro, Alberto Gil Novales, and Enriqueta Vila Vilar.[141] However, its importance in respect of the involvement of the British abolitionist lobby and its operations in Spain is typically overlooked. It is difficult to measure the circulation and impact of Bowring's publication in the Spanish political sphere, but it is reasonable to think that his work was, at the very least, accessible to most deputies.

The *Contestación* constitutes a very rare and exceptional example of British abolitionist activism operating in Spain without the support (and even against the instructions) of the British government. As Alonso has argued, the successive Liberal governments did not always follow Bowring or Bentham's advice, "but they and [the] Spanish Parliament did indeed bear in mind his works when codifying trade and penal matters."[142] In the context of the debate on the slave trade and the implementation of the Treaty of 1817, it is accurate to view Bowring's publication as confronting O'Gavan with a more earnestly humanitarian form of politics, a "philanthropic discourse" that had successfully operated in the Spanish public sphere since the Cortes of Cadiz.

As part of the strategy of the British abolitionist lobby during the Liberal Triennium, at least two antislavery works were published in London in Spanish: *Consideraciones dirigidas a los habitantes de la Europa sobre la iniquidad del comercio de los negros* and *Clamores de los africanos contra los europeos sus opresores, ó Exámen del detestable comercio llamado de negros*. The first pamphlet, signed by "Miembros de la sociedad de Amigos (llamados Cuakeros) de la Gran Bretaña e Irlanda" (Members of the Society of Friends [known also as Quakers] of Great Britain and Ireland), was published in 1822 in London by George Smallfield, and it is a canonical British antislavery manifesto directly addressed to "those who call yourselves Christians."[143] According to Juan Vilar, this work was reprinted in 1825 under the authorship of the Quaker Josiah Foster, in the London printing press of Harvey and Dalton.[144] The second pamphlet, published in 1823, was a translation of the book *Cries of Africa to the Inhabitants of Europe*, originally published one year before by Thomas Clarkson.

After the parliamentary defeat of Toreno's anti–slave trade law in March 1821, British diplomatic efforts focused on the drafting of the new penal code.[145] They wanted the Spanish deputies to include in the new code effective punishment for those involved in the slave trade, so they could possess sufficient legal powers—even without a new law specifically on the slave trade—to frustrate it. Lionel Harvey, secretary of the embassy in Madrid, and in charge of the diplomatic mission after the departure of Henry Wellesley, lobbied José María Calatrava and Francisco Martínez de la Rosa, who had been members of the commission that presented Toreno's anti–slave trade project to the Cortes. The three of them played a significant role in drafting the penal code and succeeded in including article 273, which referred specifically to the slave trade. This article prescribed ten years of forced labor and a fine for the "captains, ship mates and pilots of Spanish ships involved in the slave trade" and to free and compensate the enslaved Africans on board.[146] The British authorities did not request that the Spanish deputies declare the slave trade to be piracy, although the Foreign Office was starting to receive pressure from abolitionists and military authorities to cross this threshold. This was the case of Commodore George Collier, who in 1819 had already proposed to the Lords of the Admiralty that "the North Slave-trade shall be declared Piracy, and every one found engaged therein subject to all the penalties of Piracy."[147]

The article was more limited than the bill proposed by Toreno in 1821, but its incorporation into the penal code represented a success for the abolitionist ideas advanced by Calatrava, Martínez de la Rosa, and Toreno himself.

Fradera has downplayed the importance of the article and described it as a "pointless gesture" because it was never enforced.[148] However, such an assessment fails to give due credit to the ideological weight of inserting, for the first time in Spanish legislation, not only moral condemnation but actual concrete sanctions against the slave trade. Moreover, the main reason for its impotence did not lie in the article itself but in the lack of will on the part of successive authorities to enforce it. The article nevertheless was welcomed by the British authorities, and Lionel Harvey "happily" reported that the British government should be "chiefly indebted to Mr. M. Calatrava and Martínez de la Rosa for the insertion of this article in the Criminal Code."[149]

With regard to slavery in the Iberian Spanish territories, the Penal Code of 1822 also provided that all enslaved Africans purchased by Spanish subjects on the African coasts should be freed if introduced in peninsular Spain and the Balearic and Canary Islands. In March 1821, the slave María Flores, representing her fifteen-year-old daughter and herself, asked the Cortes to be freed from their master Bernando Guase. They were living in Ibiza, and the Cortes accepted their request. The legislative commission of the Spanish chamber also dictated that "as a general rule, in the Peninsula and the Balearic and Canary Islands, there will be no slaves; and any slave will no longer be so as soon as they set a foot in any of these territories."[150] The commission also dictated that the liberated Africans would have "the protection of the national authorities, so they will never be reclaimed or disturbed because of their former condition."[151] Although significant in terms of the advance of abolitionist legislation during the Liberal Triennium, this was not a radical maneuver. The reality was that "slavery had almost completely disappeared in the Spanish peninsular territories by this time," and therefore the number of enslaved Africans who could benefit from this measure was very limited.[152] Moreover, additional legislation to abolish slavery in peninsular Spain was not produced until 1836, which suggests that this resolution by the Cortes was not fully enforced by regional and local authorities.[153]

Varela's Reconciliation Project

After the elections of 1822, Cuba had three representatives in the Cortes during the Liberal Triennium: Félix Varela Morales (1788–1853), Tomás Gener Bohigas (1797–1835), and Leonardo Santos Suárez. Varela, a priest like O'Gavan, was also trusted by Havana's bishop, Juan José Díaz de Espada (1757–1832), and was elected deputy for the legislative period 1822–1823.[154] His parliamentary activity was characterized by its nonalignment with any group or party in the Cortes, and by his intense work on two issues: the slave trade and Cuban autonomy. In both cases his views differed from the Cuban colonial elite, who had given their vote to appoint him as deputy.[155]

Varela drafted a law proposal to gradually abolish slavery in Spain: *Memoria y Proyecto de Ley que muestra la necesidad de extinguir la esclavitud de los negros en la Isla de Cuba, atendiendo a los intereses de sus propietarios.*[156] The fundamental thesis of his work was a critique of the consistent disregard for the human dignity of enslaved Africans and free men and women of color (the so-called *libertos*) by the Cuban oligarchy. Varela argued that "it is only natural that these people [the *libertos*] try, in every possible way, to remove this obstacle to their happiness by liberating their equals."[157] He pointed out that it was unsustainable to keep a representative system that excludes its own free population: "Their inferiority compared to the whites has never been so conspicuous for them or so deeply felt as the day when they are deprived by the Constitution of their political rights, when the door available to them, is then almost closed on account of their nature, and they are even cut off from what constitutes the basis of the represented population, consequently they are Spanish but they are not represented."[158]

Varela defended a utopian model of conciliation between the desire for freedom for the enslaved Africans, on the one hand, and the interests of the oligarchy, on the other, presaging a bloody and unpredictable outcome if an understanding were not reached soon, as "frustration and despair will force them to choose between liberty or death." Wars of independence in America had upended the continent, and with the Haitian Revolution ever present in the Spanish consciousness, Varela concluded that "the first one to give the cry for independence [in Cuba] will have all those of African origin on his side."[159] The Cuban deputy thus reproduced the same ideas previously advanced by Arango and O'Gavan but with an opposite goal. Varela "formally attacked Great Britain and cited the fears of an invasion from the neighboring Republic of Haiti, and the risk of a major slave uprising in Cuba" to call the Cortes to gradually put an end to slavery.[160] Varela did not argue for a radical emancipation. He accepted the "legitimate interests" of the slaveholders and aimed to achieve the abolition of slavery with full respect for private property. He advocated freeing "the slaves in such a way that their owners do not lose the money invested in the purchase, . . . nor the free slaves under the enthusiasm produced by their new situation, go beyond the limits that must be set for them."[161]

In the *proyecto de ley* (law proposal) that Varela attached to the *Memoria*, he proposed a gradual abolition of slavery, emphasizing a model that reconciled the interests of the Cuban colonial elite and the enslaved Africans. He presented himself as the representative of the will of the majority of Cubans and argued that by "asking to free the African slaves made compatible with the interests of the landowners and with security and public order . . . I am merely demanding what the people of Cuba want."[162] However, nothing could be further from the truth: Varela's position on this debate was not representative of the interests and political position of the colonial merchant and planter elites.

Although Varela's project was fully drafted, he never submitted it to the Cortes. The sudden return of absolutism, and the subsequent shutdown of the Cortes, stifled any chance of moving his proposals forward. He was sentenced to death by Fernando VII but managed to escape, first to Gibraltar and from there to the United States in 1823, from whence he would advocate Cuban independence.[163] In April 1823 the absolutist regime was restored, and the Constitution and civil liberties were once again outlawed. Until the death of Fernando VII in 1833, the official policy of the absolutist regime on the slave trade remained the same. British political and diplomatic pressure focused on the implementation of the Treaty of 1817 in Cuba, with very little success. The Cuban authorities and economic elites, with the support of the metropolitan governments, ignored the international agreement and procured the continuity and development of the slave trade into the Spanish Caribbean dominions.

CONCLUSIONS

The fragmented development of abolitionist ideas in Spain becomes clear during this period. Between 1814 and 1823, anti–slave trade discourses were advanced both by a group of councilors from within the absolutist administration and by some Liberal deputies in an elected parliament. In both cases the endurance of Argüelles's contribution in 1811 is clear, but Argüelles himself had relinquished his prominent role. This chapter emphasizes the contradictions that arose from these varied positions against slavery and the slave trade. As stated, Spanish abolitionism "was never likely to unfold along similar lines" to the British movement, among other reasons because of the profound complexities and peculiarities of its political and institutional history.[164]

On the other side of the debate, abolitionist ideas and policies were effectively confronted by a well-organized opposition of Cuban planters and traders that linked the territorial integrity of the empire and their own loyalty to the continuity of the slave trade and the promotion of slavery. When "the empire was coming apart" and "the idea of a general reform" had been abandoned, abolitionism was seen as a dangerous tendency by some, and as unattainable by others.[165] A new colonial system was emerging that would define Spain's empire from that point on, to which slavery and the slave trade were essential. The idea, which was later taken on and repeated by Spain's elites, that "Cuba was everything" started here.[166]

3

Abolitionism, Exile, and the "Necessary Evil" Argument, 1823–1835

It is well known, that every river on the coast of Africa,
where slaves are to be obtained, still swarms with
slave-ships, bearing openly the flag of Spain.
—Lord Palmerston, March 26, 1831

In April 1823, some 95,000 French soldiers invaded Spain in response to the call for help made by Fernando VII to the so-called Holy Alliance of the Austrian and Russian Empires and the kingdoms of France and Prussia. The host commanded by Louis Antoine of France, Duke of Angoulême (1775–1844), wrested control of the country without significant opposition. The Liberal government sought refuge in Cadiz, but on August 31 the French army conquered the city. Fernando was restored as absolute monarch, the Liberal constitution of 1812 annulled, along with all ancillary civil liberties. Thousands of Spaniards sought political asylum abroad, in many instances resuming work for their previous causes—or new ones—from their new havens. This chapter addresses the absence of abolitionist discourse produced by Spanish Liberal exiles in London. Considering the actions of the refugees provides us with an insight into the fragility of the abolitionist discourse that had developed within the Spanish Liberal tradition. In addition, the chapter explores the breaks and turns in the construction of abolitionist and antiabolitionist discourses in the aftermath of the formal prohibition of the slave trade in Spain. It charts the state of the reactionary turn against enforcement of abolition and concomitant developments in the expression of pro–slave trade ideas. In its last section, the chapter unpicks the threads of various processes leading to the drafting of an anti–slave trade treaty in 1835 and the long-lasting and unexpected consequences this fresh agreement would have in consolidating the traffic of enslaved Africans into Cuba and Puerto Rico.

EXILES, PRESS, AND ABOLITIONISM: THE SECOND EXILE IN THE CONTEXT OF THE IMPERIAL CRISIS, 1823–1833

The early abolitionist discourse in Spain was shaped in its construction by the influence of the British government. The mainstreaming of the discourse owed to the scale of British involvement, both direct, in the diplomatic sphere, and indirect, in the ideological sphere. Analysis of the exile community in London allows us to test the durability of the discourse that was established, in the absence of any further direct political support from the British state. Far from their homeland, without a seat in the Cortes or a role in government, the key figures of Spanish liberalism continued to vividly express their opinions in newspapers, social gatherings, and private correspondence. This section shows, however, that abolitionist discourses slid from their political agenda and that the vehemence with which many of them had once defended the cause was to fade. The reasons for this encroaching silence will be explained by looking into two complementary factors: the fragmentation of the Spanish Liberal party and the absence, at this juncture, of an organized abolitionist movement. The experience of exile and the sense of political failure that followed the collapse of the constitutional regime fueled polarization within the Liberal party and a conservative turn among some former advocates of abolition.

Vicente Llorens has thoroughly studied the cultural and literary activity of the Spanish exiles in London between 1823 and 1834.[1] Tellingly, however, his research does not tackle the exiles' views on the slave trade or slavery. It provides the best analysis of the historical context for this study but contains no specifics pertaining to our object. Following in the steps of Llorens, Daniel Muñoz, Gregorio Alonso, and Juan Luis Simal have studied the political and cultural production of the Spanish exiles in London, their contribution to British public life, and the figure of the "émigré" on a transnational level.[2] However, their works also do not explore in any substance the (dis)continuities of abolitionist discourse within the exile community.[3] As Fradera has emphasized, "we need to explain the lengthy hiatus in open and effective abolitionist activity" between the earliest initiatives in the 1810s and the "tangible results" that were to be achieved in the late 1860s; and by focusing on the community of Liberal exiles in London between 1823 and 1836, this chapter does so.[4]

In September 1823 the Liberal exodus began. One thousand Spanish families sought and found asylum in London, and a further four hundred would also settle on the Channel Islands over the course of the decade.[5] In the English capital, most of them lived in the suburb of Somers Town, in the area of Euston-Saint Pancras, where a tightly knit community developed quickly. The majority of the refugees were military officers, but also among them were noted intellectuals, politicians, and skilled workers. Many were highly educated and put their minds to writing, translating, and publishing. Some of the most prominent Liberal politicians and essayists of the time—including José María Calatrava (1781–1846), José Canga Argüelles (1770–1843), Juan Álvarez Mendizábal (1790–1853), Francisco Javier Istúriz (1790–1871), Antonio Alcalá Galiano (1789–1865), Álvaro Flórez Estrada (1765–1853), and Agustín de Argüelles—were enveloped in a wave of new intellectual activity catalyzed by London's expeditious political and cultural life. During this time, London became a central hub for Spanish-speaking intellectuals from Spain and the Americas.[6]

Their presence attracted the attention of the British press. The *Times* reported on the situation of the refugees almost without interruption between 1824 and 1830, and some of them, particularly those who moved in the circles of Lord Holland and Jeremy Bentham, as Catherine Davies has studied, were well-known figures among the governing classes.[7] This was the case of Agustín de Argüelles, who was in touch with Lord Holland, but also, as has been shown in the previous chapters, with other towering figures, notably William Wilberforce. Argüelles's escape from Spain together with Galiano, Calatrava, and Gil de la Quadra, via Gibraltar, was reported by the *Times*.[8]

According to the British press, the Spanish exiles were warmly welcomed by the British public. The *Times* referred to them as "the friends of constitutional government," and the British government gave pensions to some of them in reward for their fight against Napoleon.[9] Nevertheless, the majority of the exiles became poor and depended on the charity of organizations like the Spanish Committee Fund, established in 1824.[10] Repeated attempts to reignite the spark of revolution in Spain, including such initiatives as the conspiracy of José María Torrijos y Uriarte (1791–1831)—in which he lost his life in December 1831—were met with repeated failure. The period of the London exile would end in 1830 with the decision of most in the community to relocate to France following the July Revolution. Those still alive would later return to Spain, granted amnesty in 1834 by the new queen regent, María Cristina.

The Spanish exiles published seven newspapers between 1824 and 1829, but only two of them enjoyed some degree of permanence: *El español constitucional*—which had been initially established during the previous Liberal exile in London (1814–1820)—and the new *Ocios de los españoles emigrados*.[11] *El español constitucional* restarted as a monthly publication from March 1824 until June 1825, under its previous editors Pedro Pascasio Fernández Sardino and Manuel María Acevedo (1769–1840). According to Llorens, and in reference to this second period of the publication, *El español constitucional* was "the most spirited of the Spanish publications in London" and came into conflict with *Ocios de los españoles emigrados*.[12]

The references to the slave trade in *El español constitucional* during the second exile were, as in the first exile, scarce. In 1824 the newspaper translated the speech of February 3, 1824, given by King George IV in the House of Lords, in which he called upon the assembled peers to act "calmly and cautiously" when grappling with the matter of the "amelioration" of the conditions of enslaved Africans in the West Indies. The king wished to underline that slavery was "an old and complicated system in which the fortunes and security of many of H.M.'s subjects were involved."[13] The editors made no comment on this speech.

In March 1824, *El español constitucional* published six letters between the Russian emperor and Fernando VII, originally written between 1817 and 1818, in relation to the negotiation of the anti–slave trade treaty of 1817.[14] These letters, originally published by the *Morning Chronicle* in December 1823, exposed, in the eyes of the editor of *El español constitucional*, how dishonest the Spanish crown had been. The correspondence documents a parallel negotiation between Fernando VII and the Russian emperor for the hiring of Russian warships to fight in Mexico. The Spanish king stated his intention to use 400,000 pounds given by the British government "for abolishing the slave trade" to pay for this operation.[15] The editors of *El español constitucional* criticized Fernando VII's conduct but made no comment on how the king's actions trivialized negotiations toward abolition of the slave trade.

Ocios de los españoles emigrados, for its part, was published monthly from April 1824 to October 1826 and then reappeared as a quarterly magazine from January to October 1827. The brothers Jaime (1765–1824) and Joaquín Lorenzo Villanueva (1757–1837), along with José Canga Argüelles, founded it some months after they arrived from Spain. After the death of Jaime Lorenzo in 1824, Pablo Mendíbil (1788–1832) replaced him.[16] *Ocios de los españoles emigrados* represented the voices of the moderate or even conservative wing of the Liberal refugee community in London.

Ocios de los españoles emigrados was able to count on the collaboration of Liberal politicians, including Agustín de Argüelles and Alcalá Galiano, among others. It was almost entirely written by Spanish immigrants in London and incorporated foreign contributors only in its quarterly phase from January to October 1827. The newspaper had extensive international circulation and was read and commented upon in Mexico, Colombia, the United States, France, and Germany.[17] The Foreign Office and the Mexican Embassy in London financed the newspaper, which influenced the editorial line of the publication. Vicente Rocafuerte, secretary of the Mexican diplomatic mission in London from 1824, ordered a monthly subscription of two hundred copies on behalf of the Mexican government and established a close relationship with Joaquín Lorenzo Villanueva.[18]

Throughout the entire span of the newspaper, there were almost no references to either the slave trade or slavery. This omission becomes especially percussive when viewed in light of the political and popular agitation that preceded the 1833 abolition of slavery in the British Empire, and the abolitionist ideas that some of the authors of *Ocios* had advanced in Spain in previous years. The effect of the paper's abdication from the debate in which some of its key figures had cut their teeth constituted a deafening silence.

Thinkers and political leaders who had openly defended the abolition of the slave trade had very little to say about it during this period. Argüelles's attitude is emblematic in this regard. In his works published in London, *Apéndice a la sentencia pronunciada en 11 de mayo de 1825 por la Audiencia de Sevilla contra los 63 diputados de las Cortes de 1822 y 1823*, written in 1827 and published in 1834, and *Examen histórico de la reforma constitucional*, published in 1835, the Spanish politician did not deign to mention the subject.[19] Argüelles maintained a close relationship with Lord Holland while in London. But in their correspondence and meetings, they seemingly never discussed any aspect of the slave trade or the abolition of slavery that was being debated in the British parliament.[20] It is thus reasonable to think that the abolition of the slave trade was one of the causes that Argüelles would, later in 1836, bunch under the somewhat pejorative label of "philanthropic theories"—in short, causes he no longer saw practical to advance.[21] He became a more conservative thinker during and after exile, as a result of his sense that the constitutional project in Spain had failed. Argüelles's newfound concerns represented a diversion in the Spanish Liberal discourse that would precipitate a radical change in the approach of the *doceañistas* to colonial policy. This new view would advocate the restriction of political and civil rights available to the colonial population, a growing militarization of colonial rule, and the maintenance of the status quo in the colonies.[22]

Analysis of the Spanish Liberal community in London is necessary to understanding the interruption of Liberal abolitionist discourses post Liberal Triennium. That said, the editors of both *El español constitucional* and *Ocios* never defended in their pages the continuity of the slave trade or slavery. Nor did Argüelles publicly change his mind or regret his previous advocacy of the abolition of the slave trade, but the abolition of slavery and the implementation of the anti–slave trade treaty of 1817 did not constitute political priorities for him. This lacuna further illustrates the fragility of early abolitionist discourses in Spain and the absence, at this point, of a committed Spanish abolitionist movement.

ABSOLUTIST POLICIES IN THE AFTERMATH OF THE ABOLITION OF THE SLAVE TRADE, 1823–1834

Back in Spain, the picture was very different. In the aftermath of the restoration of the absolutist regime in 1823, the Spanish government was forced to implement some of the provisions agreed on in the Treaty of 1817. This section explores the ideological and political consequences of the establishment of the Mixed Commission Court in Havana and the legitimization strategies developed by antiabolitionist sectors in Spain and Cuba to protect and even promote the slave trade into the empire's Caribbean dominions. Nationalist Anglophobia and a rhetoric of the trade as a "necessary evil" fed the antiabolition discourse after its agreed-upon outlawing. This ideological development prepared the ground for the settlement of a new status quo in the attitude of the empire to its colonies.

"Spain Is Only Yielding to Circumstances": Havana's Mixed Commission Court and Anglophobic Narratives

The establishment in 1820 of the Mixed Commission Court in Havana constituted a milestone in the arduous process of implementing the Treaty of 1817 as part of the British strategy to fight against the slave trade in the Spanish Empire. British judges operated as abolitionists on the ground and, more importantly, as a persistent reminder of the legal obligations of the authorities with regard to the slave trade. The establishment of Havana's Mixed Court stirred a very powerful Anglophobic rhetoric among antiabolitionist sectors in the context of heightening imperial rivalry between the Spanish and British governments.[23] This outcome, together with the weakening of the British authorities' ability to promote anti–slave trade perspectives in Spain, contributed to the reinforcement of a Spanish narrative of self-victimization and ultimately to the consolidation of the slave trade in the Spanish Empire.

As Nelson has described, "despite their limitations, and a nominal ability to undermine slave traders' livelihoods, the courts represented an alternative abolitionist voice, which was considered potentially subversive."[24] For Spain, however, the Mixed Commission Court undermined its imperial sovereignty and was described by the Cuban authorities as an "inquisitorial tribunal of foreigners."[25] David Murray has convincingly argued that the court's "unpopularity" among Cuba's white population was the result of two factors: the "belief that the prohibition of the slave trade was a measure which Britain forced on Spain under a cloak of philanthropy, but really as a means of hitting at Cuban prosperity, and the extensive participation in slave-trading ventures by Cubans of all classes."[26] In fact, the slave trade in Cuba was a very profitable business. Although illegal from 1820, it was tolerated, and even promoted, by the Spanish authorities.[27] Robert Jameson, the first British commissioner in Cuba, between 1819 and 1820, reported in August 1821 that shares in slave-trade expeditions were "eagerly sought for by clerks in public and mercantile offices, petty *caballeros* [lower nobility] or gentry . . . and shopkeepers, overseers, etc."[28] Involvement in the slave trade was transversal across a wide spectrum of the colonial population, including metropolitan economic and political elites alike, and according to the Cuban intellectual Domingo del Monte (1804–1853), it was criticized only by "the poor," referring to the only ones that did not directly benefit from it.[29]

Even the British West Indian squadron showed some tolerance of the slave trade in the first months of the prohibition. No slave trade vessel was taken to Havana by the British navy until 1823.[30] The British judge in Havana's Mixed Commission Court, Henry Kilbee, reported that "British naval commanders . . . hesitated to risk unpopularity and loss of lucrative cargoes capturing Spanish slavers."[31] The commander of the West Indian Squadron, Admiral Halsted, rejected Kilbee's accusations and five slave-trade Spanish vessels were captured between 1825 and 1826 alone. Fifty-five vessels were captured and tried by the Mixed Commission in Havana between 1824 to 1854, and forty-eight of them were condemned.[32]

The Spanish officials in the Mixed Commission did their best to obstruct the works of the court, restrict their powers, and, in short, to protect the interests of the slave traders. The colonial authorities acknowledged that stopping the slave trade would deeply damage Cuba's prosperity and therefore that it was their duty to protect its continuity. In this regard Captain General Francisco Vives reported to Madrid in 1825 that he "concealed the existence of the slave trade and the introduction of slaves as much as is possible given the treaty obligations," as he was "completely convinced that if the lack of slave labor continues the Island's wealth will undoubtedly disappear within a very few years."[33]

The first Spanish representatives at the Mixed Commission in Havana were Alejandro Ramirez y Blanco (1777–1821), as a judge, and Francisco de Arango y Parreño, as arbitrator, later replaced by Claudio Martínez de Pinillos (1782–1853). Arango had been the key ideologue for and spokesperson of the slaveholders and their associate traders at the Cortes of Cadiz and the Council of the Indies, and, together with Martínez de Pinillos, played a frontline role in defending the continuity of the slave trade. However, as Nelson pointed out, "the slaveholding notoriety of the next two judges seems not to have caused consternation except privately amongst the British."[34]

British commissioners knew that the abolitionist cause was a very complex task to fulfill in such a hostile context. They were aware that their work in the Spanish colony was seen from the beginning as a direct attack on Spanish imperial sovereignty and as a threat to the constituted power and economic status quo in Cuba. British judge Henry Kilbee and his successors carried out an efficient and steady job of providing data about the slave trade in Cuba to the Foreign Office to bolster its case for the Spanish authorities to further tighten its ordinances. The British authorities failed, however, to undermine the dominance of pro–slave trade sentiment in Cuba or, as Kilbee would later put it, to "correct the public opinion of this Country upon the subject of the slave trade."[35] Despite the work of the Mixed Commission Court, the number of enslaved Africans introduced in Cuba from 1820 to the late 1830s grew exponentially, together with the exportations of Cuban sugar (Figure 3.1).

The Council of State resolved, in May 1822, that more than just "philanthropic sentiments" motivated British anti–slave trade policy.[36] Anglophobic messages operated as a recurrent argument within the Spanish administration to justify the steps that the king was taking "against his real will" to prohibit the slave trade. The Spanish authorities openly doubted Britain's humanitarianism and believed that the British could jeopardize prosperity and peace in Cuba, for their own imperial gain. These ideas had circulated on the island from the beginning of the nineteenth century and reinforced a mixed sentiment of victimhood and patriotism. As Nelson has rightly claimed in this regard, "in such climate the Mixed Commission and its British representatives had become convenient scapegoats."[37]

In January 1829 Commissioner William Sharp Macleay reported to the Foreign Office that the slave trade had drastically increased in Cuba in the past years despite efforts of the Mixed Commission Court, and that the Spanish government was effectively promoting the slave trade by protecting the traders. Macleay protested that the traffickers knew that "the Spanish laws will never be put in execution against them," and this contributed to the settling of a pervasive Anglophobic sentiment on the island:[38] "It is however easily seen, that, while it would be difficult for the Local Government to avoid carrying the Decrees of the Mixed Commission into effect, they need have no reluctance in executing them, since by letting the Spanish Laws relating to the prohibited traffic remain a complete nullity, they make the Slave traders believe that, with respect to the Mixed Commissions, Spain is only yielding to circumstances it cannot control; and thus contrive to throw all the popular odium on the British Government and its Agents."[39]

Anglophobia was enhanced by rumors circulating in Cuba suggesting the imminent sale of the island to Britain by the Spanish government, or even a possible invasion of Cuba by British forces after encouraging the enslaved Africans to revolt against their masters. In some cases this excuse was used by the Spanish authorities to justify authoritarian measures and reiterate the notion of Cuba's vulnerability to British machinations. The possibility, however, of a British takeover of Cuba was not entirely remote during the nineteenth century, and the idea was contemplated by London's governments. One early insinuation appeared in a report by Lionel Hervey, secretary of the embassy in Spain, to Castlereagh in June 1822, in which he stated, "If it should ever enter into the contemplation of His Majesty's Government to give up Gibraltar, I apprehend that there would not be much difficulty in obtaining the

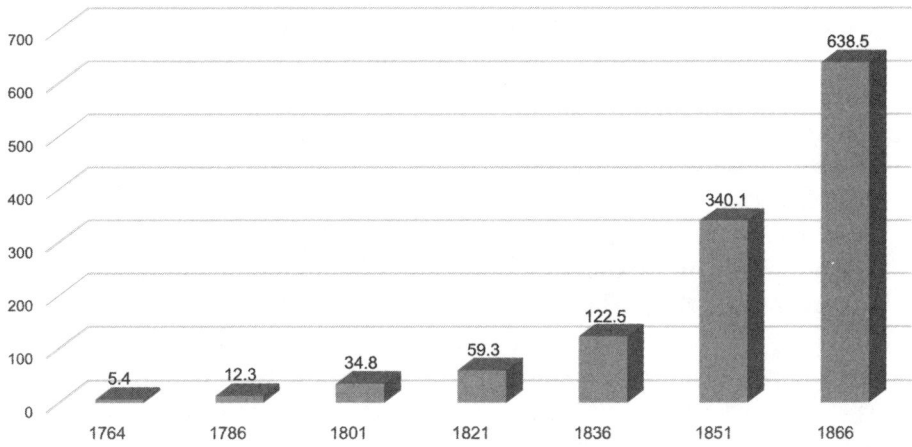

Figure 3.1. Cuba's sugar exports (1764–1866) in millions of metric cubic tons. (Data from Marrero, *Cuba: Economía y sociedad*, vol. 12. Madrid: Editorial Playor, 1984–1987, p. 109)

Island of Cuba in exchange."[40] This negotiation never took place, but the idea that Cuba could be a bargaining chip between the two states in the context of Spanish imperial disintegration was entertained.

Only a few months later, in March 1823, the Spanish ambassador to the United States, Joaquín de Anduaga, informed Cuba's intendant, head of Havana's Finance Department, of the publication of an inflammatory proclamation to the Spanish and Cuban people in an American newspaper. The document urged, on the one hand, the Spanish people to rise against absolutism, and on the other, for Cubans to claim independence from Spain. The text also propagated the idea that the island could "be ceded to the British" and called on the Spaniards and Cubans to "resolve, and resolve quickly; liberty and independence, or submission to the British yoke."[41] It concluded: "They may destroy the constitution, give unlimited power to King, and rivet chains on the people, but they never will subdue their brave spirit; neither will the descendants of *Pelayo*, the *Cid*, and of *Padilla* be unmindful of the glory and the chivalry of their ancestors."[42]

In a similar vein, in July 1827, the Spanish ambassador in London reported that there were activists "weakening the spirit of the people of Havana and rousing public opinion in favor of England."[43] According to the ambassador, a double process of Liberal revolution in Spain and an uprising in Cuba would have the support of the British government: "[The Cubans] would spontaneously call the English for help, who would intervene this way without colliding with the United States, and . . . after a new revolution in the Peninsula, . . . a Spanish general would come to the Island of Cuba promising freedom but without independence from Spain."[44]

This political tension affected the United States and France; both countries also entertained the possibility of taking control of Cuba as a way of extending their influence in the Caribbean.[45]

Britain's reaction to this turbulent new political weather came in the shape of an offer to the Spanish government in May 1824 to support Spanish sovereignty of Cuba on the condition that Spain accepted the independence of its mainland territories in the Americas, an offer that Spain, however, declined. In 1825 the British government promoted an international agreement between the United States, France, and Britain to guarantee that these powers would not invade Cuba. As secretary of state for foreign affairs, George Canning very frankly stated in a letter to the United States ambassador in London in 1825, "You cannot allow that we should have Cuba; we cannot allow that you should have it; and we can neither of us allow that it should fall into the hands of France," and therefore the easiest solution was to defend a Spanish Cuba.[46] Although it is impossible to determine how plausible a British annexation of Cuba would have been, it is undeniable that this possibility played a major role in the political and ideological context of the first half of the nineteenth century. It deepened and promoted an Anglophobic view within the Cuban population and weakened British anti–slave trade influence, which was seen by colonial elites and the Spanish administration as another destabilizing and subversive initiative.

So, while the Havana Mixed Commission Court succeeded inasmuch as it relayed accurate information to the British on the slave trade in Cuba—while constantly needling the colonial government to fulfill its treaty obligations—the work of the commission stoked Anglophobic zeal among elite sectors of the Cuban public. This second consequence was deeply counterproductive, solidifying the pro–slave trade positions of these sectors by daubing abolitionist ideas with the red mark of foreign incursion.[47] A steep rise in the polarization of the political debate on slavery was one barrier to the emboldening of British efforts against the slave trade, compounded by moves by the US and France—as well as Britain—to extend their dominion into Latin America, which undermined diplomatic efforts. The association of abolitionism with the upended Liberal Triennium was a further barrier. The British authorities confined themselves to encouraging Spain to fulfill the provisions established in the Treaty of 1817. By 1830 British diplomacy and the British antislavery movement had failed to do in Spain what they had achieved in Britain: to persuade the public of the benefits of abolition and to define a positive postabolition scenario.

"A Matter of Self-Preservation": The Equipment Article and "Necessary Evil" Rhetoric

In the aftermath of the second restoration of Fernando VII as absolutist king, British diplomatic pressure to effectively stop the slave trade into Cuba increased, and the Spanish authorities gradually adopted a new antiabolitionist stance that defined the traffic as a "necessary evil." This section explores the British demand for new legal instruments to fight against the slave trade and how the Spanish government adopted a nonconfrontational response aimed at protecting the trade and avoiding a diplomatic crisis.

Only a few days after the reestablishment of the absolutist regime, in May 1823, the Spanish Council of State sat to discuss the British proposal to add an article to the anti–slave trade treaty of 1817. This additional article would enforce the prosecution of any vessel that was found to be fitted out with the equipment needed to participate in the traffic of slaves, fixing definitions of these technical elements in law. The British government would request the new stipulations time and time again, without success, when the negotiations for a new treaty did finally commence. "Nothing short" of the additional equipment article, according to the British commissioners in Sierra Leone, could effectively stop the "arrival of Spanish vessels at . . . the Rio Pongos, Rio Nunez, and Gallinas."[48]

The Council of State resolved in May 1823 that it would not be "political or convenient to just reject the article proposed by the Minister of Her Britannic Majesty" and elaborated a legal analysis of the difficulties that the implementation of such new provisions would imply.[49] The council was clearly not enthused by the idea but was also aware of the difficult position adopted by the Spanish government, which risked being seen to run roughshod over its own international commitments and laws.

The former secretary of state, Pedro Cevallos, submitted in May 1823 a dissenting vote to the council's report, based on economic and moral arguments. Cevallos relied on the traditional insistence that the British demand was too sudden and questioned Britain's humanitarianism. He argued that Jamaica was in a much better position than Cuba when the slave trade was abolished in the British Empire and affirmed that the "superabundance" of enslaved Africans made the British colony more competitive in the production of sugar.[50] Cevallos elaborated a pro–slave trade argument on moral grounds, which reiterated themes found in O'Gavan's disquisitions in 1821. He wrote that ending the slave trade would not have a positive impact in Africa, as those people who were not captured by slave traders faced an even worse life in their homeland. Cevallos rejected the addition of any new article to the 1817 Treaty and concluded, "The powerful interest of humanity in the disappearance of the traffic in Negroes is very equivocal, or at least it is not so positive, since it will cause the inevitable sacrifice of agriculture and trade in Cuba and Puerto Rico, without which its inhabitants will fall in the most disastrous misery; and Spain will be devoured by the pain of having sacrificed so many victims to a misunderstood virtue or the hypocrisy of humanity."[51]

Cevallos replicated O'Gavan's justification of the slave trade and reproduced his idea that the eradication of the trade in slaves "would hinder the prosperity [of Cuba]," as upon the traffic depended "essentially the happiness and even the existence of the Island of Cuba."[52] Cevallos also reinforced Anglophobic rhetoric in his statement, which had proliferated in Cuba since 1811. In this regard Macleay wrote that this idea had "always in some degree prevailed in the Island of Cuba, that Great Britain, in her anxiety to extinguish the Slave-trade, has only been actuated by a desire to protect the interest of her own sugar Colonies."[53] Cevallos's views, however, were not publicly shared by the Spanish government, and moral justification of the slave trade would become more and more infrequent in official correspondence. The report of the Council of State had no immediate effect on Spanish policy, and the British demand was not accepted.

The British diplomatic mission in Madrid continued to repeatedly request the introduction of the equipment article and to report on the exponential rise of the slave trade in Cuba. The establishment of Mixed Commission Courts in Havana and Sierra Leone allowed the British Foreign Office to obtain firsthand information on the number of enslaved Africans and slave vessels that arrived in the Spanish colony, and they used this information to gradually increase the pressure on Spain. In April 1828 George Bosanquet, British ambassador in Madrid, expressed his concerns to the Spanish secretary of state, Manuel González Salmón, on the growing number of enslaved Africans illegally transported to Cuba. Based on the reports of the British commissioners in Havana, Bosanquet denounced the fact that the slave trade was "being carried out more notoriously, if possible, than ever before" and insisted that it was "morally impossible that the public authorities of the Island ignore what happens every day in front of their eyes."[54]

After this communication the Council of State was required to deliberate once again on the information presented by the British authorities. The council affirmed two main ideas in its report. First, slavery was essential to the prosperity of the colonial economy, and therefore the slave trade had to continue as a "necessary evil." Second, the council questioned the philanthropic motives of the British authorities, using Anglophobic rhetoric, and moving the debate from a legal or moral dispute into a conflict of imperial rivalries.

The council pointed out that "if the entry of new Negroes in the Island of Cuba was absolutely forbidden, the decline of its rural industry will be a certain and so visible consequence that it will be possible to point out the day in which crops would disappear . . . because the introduction of European colonists [as a substitute workforce] is a chimera."[55] The slave trade was presented as an economic necessity while Spain's coffers grew more dependent on Cuba's contribution. The Cuban market, which was fully dependent on the slave trade, was the focus of a thriving trading network between the Iberian peninsular ports of Santander, Cadiz, Malaga, Alicante and Barcelona, and Havana. The prosperity of the Cuban market determined the economic stability of the whole Spanish market, and "from the 1820s until 1837, the greatest arguments in favor of tolerating slavery [and the slave trade] in Cuba were unquestionably economic."[56] Significantly, however, the council did not seek to justify the slave trade on moral grounds and concluded that slave owners in Cuba, "compelled by the strong need of self-preservation" had acted against "their own opinion" and "put in risk their own interests."[57]

The "necessary evil" doctrine, as defined by David Ericson for the US case, is articulated around the idea that "the institution was evil on deontological grounds but . . . that its continued existence was necessary on consequentialist grounds."[58] To exemplify its meaning, Ericson quotes Thomas Jefferson when he expressed this position in the wake of the Missouri crisis: "We have the wolf by the ears, and we can neither hold him, nor safely let him go. Justice is in one scale, and self-preservation in the other."[59] The absence of a moral defense of the slave trade, or even the attempt to argue for the "mild conditions" of slavery in Cuba, as the Spanish authorities used to do, inaugurated a new antiabolitionist discourse that focused on stressing the vital necessity of continuing the slave trade as a "self-preservation" strategy, a "necessary evil" that portrayed slave owners, traffickers, and colonial authorities as "victims" of a system they had not chosen, and "patriots" against the machinations of a foreign nation that militated tirelessly against their prosperity.

The Council of State, following the trend identified in the previous section, also defended its antiabolitionist position on the basis of openly Anglophobic discourse, or as Murray put it, "once again Britain was the villain."[60] The members of the council argued that the Treaty of 1817 was the result "not so much of generosity and love of their fellowmen, but of the particular and commercial interest" and was pursued by Britain only to "strengthen even more the monopoly of India." According to the council, it was Cuba's patriotism and its "desire to keep their property acquired with great effort" that eventually turned the treaty into a dead letter: "[The Cuban people] used first-class ships equipped as in wartime, avoiding English surveillance, and frustrating the plans of Great Britain, which cannot see without jealousy the amazing prosperity of Cuba."[61]

The council opposed the addition of an equipment article, because this would have allowed the British navy to become a "sea-police, as they have always aspired to be," and "then, under any pretext, they would stop the vessels, diverting them from their true destiny and paralyzing the mercantile operations, which would ruin their owners."[62] They also blamed the British government for the rise of "bloody piracy" in the Caribbean Sea, because, the council argued, the Treaty of 1817 forced "four thousand sailors" into poverty, who had then resorted to piracy as a means of survival.[63] Therefore, they recommended that the Spanish king "dissemble without being unfaithful to the treaties. . . . Since we cannot obtain what is desirable, the suspension of the damaging treaty of 1817, at the very least we will refuse any new restriction or addition to that convention" until Cuba could achieve the level of prosperity of Brazil.[64]

The Council of State tended to have a conservative and antiabolitionist approach, while the Council of the Indies had a record of openly upholding abolitionist principles and a more positive view of the British campaign against the slave trade across the Atlantic. This continued to be the trend after the restoration of Fernando VII in 1823. The proposal on the equipment article was also sent to the Council of the Indies for their consideration. A majority of the council agreed to propose, in January 1830, that all Spanish vessels traveling from Cuba or Puerto Rico to the African coast should be inspected before their departure and that any ships arriving without evidence of previous inspection would be seized and its officers imprisoned.[65]

The Spanish cabinet considered both reports and decided to reject Britain's proposed equipment article. Following the advice of the Council of State, the Spanish government insisted on its "faithful" commitment to ending the slave trade. In the instructions sent to the captain general of Cuba, Dionisio Vives, a few weeks later, the government reiterated its official position in a very dramatic and rhetorical way. They ordered Vives to "let the orders given to the effect be observed and comply with the greatest scrupulosity. H. M. wants to stop, by all possible means, a shameful and inhuman trade that disgusts the generous feelings of his magnanimous heart and avoid the impunity of those who dedicate themselves to it in contempt of the laws."[66]

The reality, however, was very different to these ostensibly impassioned instructions. The Spanish government, by insisting on the moral condemnation of the slave trade and reaffirming its commitment to fight against it, was adopting a tactical position that would prove successful in the long term. This simulation of a nonexistent commitment avoided a diplomatic crisis with the British government and was supported by the colonial elites who felt implicitly protected by the metropolitan authorities. David Murray interpreted this situation as a consequence of "lacking an essential policy decision from the higher authorities" but, in fact, the strategy of the Spanish government was consistent and successful in protecting the slave trade.[67] It was the deliberate response of a second-class empire that could not openly defend the slave trade anymore but was doing everything to protect, promote, and intensify the introduction of enslaved Africans into its colonies.

Between 1830 and 1833, British diplomatic pressure calling for more, and more effective, legislation against the slave trade increased. Even the tone of this pressure became gradually more hostile as the evidence gathered by the British commissioners in Havana and Sierra Leone showed the continuity of the trade and the collusion, if not direct involvement, of the Spanish authorities. British diplomats repeated, "time and time again," as Henry Unwin Addington, British ambassador in Madrid, put it, their demand for new legal instruments against the slave traffic, "until such time as a favourable combination of circumstances may arise for compelling attention to them [the Spaniards]."[68]

In February 1831 Addington insisted on his government's request for the insertion of the equipment article to the 1817 Treaty and denounced that "open and barefaced violations of the Treaties . . . are continually being practiced" at Spanish ports. The British ambassador pointed out, based on information provided by the British consul in Cadiz, that in this port it "is publicly known" that Spanish vessels "make preparations for [their] speedy departure from Cadiz, with the view of procuring a cargo of negroes."[69] The ambassador insisted that the slave trade into Cuba, far from stopping, had "actually increased."[70]

British pressure not only increased during this period but also took a more belligerent tone toward the passive attitude of the Spanish. In March 1831 the secretary of state for foreign affairs, Lord Palmerston, instructed the British ambassador to intensify the pressure on the Spanish government and accused the Spanish authorities of acting in collusion with the slave trade and even of actively working to promote it: "It is well known, that every river on the coast of Africa, where slaves are to be obtained, still swarms with slave-ships, bearing openly the flag of Spain; while vessel after vessel sails for that coast from the Havana, returns laden with these slaves, of whom even the number on board is publicly known, lands them unmolested at the back of the Island of Cuba, re-enters the port of the Havana in ballast, and is again fitted up, rapidly and without impediment, for a fresh expedition in this prohibited traffic."[71]

Palmerston directly pointed to the Spanish navy, "whose Commanders ought to have been instructed to detain slave-vessels, and send them to the Havana for condemnation, have actually sailed from that harbour in company with vessels fitted up for the slave-trade expressly for the purpose of convoying such vessels on their way."[72] The secretary of state concluded that the Spanish cabinet had the "evidence before them, not only that this traffic is carried on by Spanish Merchants, supported by the Spanish Navy, and in the very presence of Spanish Authorities, but that it is conducted with all those aggravating circumstances of outrage and lawless violence."[73]

In his letter Palmerston proposed three main measures to the Spanish government and ordered his ambassador to lobby the Spanish authorities to such an end: first, to declare the slave trade piracy; second, to adopt the equipment article; third, to create a regulation for the Spanish officials in Cuba so that they observed their judicial and executive duties.[74] The Spanish government simply ignored Palmerston's proposals and did not even give an official answer to the British ambassador's notes of August 1831 and January 1832.[75]

The British ambassador insisted at least two more times, in April and May of 1832. In the latter communication, he introduced a new argument to try to convince the Spanish cabinet. Henry Addington argued that the slave trade was not only immoral and illegal but also increasingly dangerous to Cuba's own safety:

> I would also ask whether the Spanish Government, for the sake of a temporary, and rather apparent, than real advantage, are prepared to risk the eventual convulsion, or even loss, of their splendid Colony of Cuba, by the daily and most impolitic increase of the negro population; which, in the event of any foreign attack, or civil disturbance in that Island, would inevitably side with the invaders or insurgents, in order to overthrow all vestige of Government, and make themselves masters of the Colony.
>
> This is no ideal apprehension. The picture of the painful scenes which have lately passed in Jamaica, may well be held up to the Possessors of other Colonies, and to Spain in particular, as a warning of the danger to be apprehended from a disproportioned negro population, when once excited to acts of resistance, however strong and vigilant the Government, to which they are subject, may be.[76]

Addington echoed in his letter a notion that was not new but which had cautiously become more widespread in Cuba. As early as 1802, Antillón had expressed that Spain should not rely on the "dangerous and unreliable enslaved African labor" as the British and French had done.[77] In 1823 the Cuban deputy Felix Varela wrote that "frustration and despair" would eventually force the enslaved Africans "to choose between liberty or death," and that "the first one to give the cry for independence [in Cuba would] . . . have all those of African origin on his side."[78] The British ambassador repeated this warning, which would become the cornerstone of José Antonio Saco's antislavery doctrine in 1837. The idea of an imminent "racial war" opened the door to racist anti–slave trade rhetoric, which will be analyzed in the following chapter.

Increasingly, the only Spanish response to British pressure was to officially encourage Spain's colonial authorities to fulfill its legal obligations. The British strategy of "the exhibition of the whip," as later described by the British ambassador in Madrid, kept the issue of the slave trade in the diplomatic correspondence between the two countries but obtained few if any tangible results.[79] In summer 1833 Prime Minister Francisco Cea Bermúdez (1779–1850) decided to appoint a three-member commission to examine, once again, the British proposal for an equipment article, following the advice of his secretary of state. Cea Bermúdez's aim was to ease the growing diplomatic tension with Britain, for fear of an imminent civil war in Spain, and the commission gave him exactly that. In October 1833, days after the death of Fernando VII, the commission concluded that the end of the slave trade would cause the loss of Cuba and suggested giving to the British authorities "a very diplomatic refusal." The commission successfully recognized "the intractable nature of the problem it was called on to solve," but more importantly, it delayed the controversy and reinforced Spain's strategy of doing nothing.[80]

The virulent combination of a new state-sanctioned Anglophobia and the concomitant adoption, by Spanish authorities, of the "necessary evil" argument marked a new juncture in the strategy of those sectors—metropolitan and colonial—that resisted abolition. The establishment of Havana's Mixed Commission Court threw fuel on the flames of an already-burning Anglophobia—in both metropolitan and colonial public opinion—leading to a conservative reconfiguration of slave-trade discourse around notions of patriotic duty and foreign invasiveness. Paired with the gradual excision from official rhetoric of normative moral defenses of the slave trade, the doctrine of the traffic as a "necessary evil," needed to preserve Cuba's economic and political stability, won out.

From a "Very Diplomatic Refusal" to the Treaty of 1835

The death of Fernando VII in 1833 did not alter the policies of the crown. The Spanish authorities continued to block the enforcement of both the anti–slave trade treaty of 1817 and any of the additional commitments made to the British since.[81] Among the metropolitan and colonial authorities, the idea of preserving Spanish rule in Cuba necessarily meant preserving the slave trade; it was on this basis that a consistent, robust, and negative response developed on the part of these authorities to British diplomatic and political pressure. The strategy of successive Spanish governments was put under stress in 1833, when important international and domestic factors forced the cabinet of Martínez de la Rosa to concede, at least on paper, some of the demands that the British authorities had been advocating for a long time. The Anglo-French Convention of March 22, the abolition of slavery by the British parliament on

August 28, the outbreak of a new civil war in Spain, and a widespread cholera epidemic in Cuba, destabilized the strategy through their impact on the
Spanish slave-trade debate.[82]

The Revolution of July 1830 in France saw the ascension of Louis-Philippe
I to the French throne and the establishment of a constitutional monarchy. As
part of a wider colonial reform policy, the new regime advocated the eradication of the slave trade and a gradual transition to the total abolition of slavery in its colonies. To these ends, in March 1831, the French government introduced a more restrictive law against slave trading, and further still, in the
Anglo-French agreements of November 1831 and March 1833, France acceded to a mutual right of visit for vessels suspected to be involved in trafficking. British diplomacy "achieved . . . what it [had] been pursuing since 1815,"
advanced its strategy of creating "a collective statement of agreement on the
immorality of slaving," as Jenny Martinez described it, and contributed further to the portrayal of Spain as a rare anomaly amid the "civilized world," for
the fact that the trade persisted in its possessions.[83]

Also in 1833 the British parliament formally abolished slavery throughout
the British Empire.[84] This was the result of a long process beginning in 1807
with the abolition of the slave trade, which set off a complex political and
social struggle led by figures such as William Wilberforce and Thomas Fow-
ell Buxton. The British parliament decreed a gradual process of emancipation,
which it called "apprenticeship," to last until 1838 and established an unprecedented economic compensation for slave owners.[85] From this point onward,
British authorities continued to encourage other countries to abolish and
eradicate not only the slave trade but also slavery itself. The political agitation
that carried the process of abolition in the British Empire also led the British government to strengthen its diplomatic pressure on Spain. Interestingly,
this meant a gulf in strategy emerged "between the anti-slavery activists and
the anti-slavery state" in Britain.[86] From 1833 to 1844, "the successive British
governments were anxiously desirous to see the slave trade put down and the
condition of slavery abolished in every part of the world," as Palmerston put
it, to the point of now gradually distancing themselves from the traditional
pacifist approach of the British abolitionist movement.[87]

In Spain the death of Fernando VII opened a succession crisis between
his brother Carlos María Isidro and the political guardians of his daughter,
the three-year-old Isabel of Bourbon, commencing a civil war. Carlos María
Isidro, who stood for the return of absolutism, had strong support from the
rural and lower Catholic clergy, conservative sectors of the Spanish elites, and
vast sections of the rural population. Isabel and her mother, María Cristina
of Bourbon-Two Sicilies (1806–1878), who acted as regent due to Isabel's
infancy, sought the establishment of a moderate monarchy and attracted the

support of urban and economic elites as well as that of the Liberal politicians and intellectuals.[88]

Each faction sought and received significantly different international support. On the one side, Carlos María Isidro was supported by Russia, Prussia, Austria, and the Portuguese Miguelists. On the other hand, Isabel relied on the help of Britain and France. The international dimensions of this conflict elevated its significance for the development of slave trade politics in Spain. The alliance between Britain and the Spanish Liberal government would enhance the influence that London's cabinet had in Madrid and bolstered its demands for both more and more effective Spanish action against the slave trade. The war lasted until 1839, when the Liberal army eventfully defeated the remaining forces loyal to Carlos María Isidro.[89]

Also in 1833 a cholera epidemic caused thousands of deaths in Cuba, predominantly among the population of enslaved Africans. The catastrophe shrank the labor pool, sparking a sudden and dramatic increase in demand for new Africans to be brought to the island to replace those lost to the outbreak.[90] As Kenneth Kiple is right to have argued, the epidemic—which "continued to flow into Havana until 1836"—and its consequences for the supply of labor likewise had a destabilizing effect on Spain's slave trade policy. Mariano Ricafort Palacín y Abarca (1776–1846), Cuba's captain general, exaggerated the number of enslaved Africans who had died, and reported in August 1833 that fifty-five thousand had lost their lives as a direct result of the epidemic. According to Adrian López Denis, in actuality around twenty-five thousand enslaved Africans (still 9 percent of the 1825 slave population) died from cholera during this period, and, as Kiple and Franklin Knight conclude, it is probable the magnitude was overstated by the Cuban authorities "to claim that most of the *emancipados* [emancipated Africans] had died, whereupon they were 'hurried away into the interior' and re-enslaved."[91] Cuban slave owners "hoped with news of massive slave mortality from cholera to tip Madrid on to their side," to further outweigh British pressure.[92]

All these factors codetermined a new political scenario, both domestically and internationally, that drastically impacted the negotiation of the antislavery treaty of 1835 and opened a new chapter in the development of abolitionist policies and antiabolitionist ideas in Spain's empire, lasting until the 1860s.

The Abolitionist Treaty of 1835

After the decision of Cea Bermúdez's appointed commission to suggest "a very diplomatic refusal" of the British proposals in 1833, the Spanish government was determined to keep holding back British demands for additional action against the slave trade. In March 1834 George Villiers (1800–1870), the new British ambassador in Madrid, complained bitterly to Palmerston about the Spanish attitude, with the foreign secretary insisting on the importance of maintaining strong pressure in this regard.[93] David Murray has very positively described Palmerston's stance during this process and stressed his persistence.[94] However, if we look at the outcomes of the diplomatic campaign that began in 1823, the result was repeat frustration for the British government and relative success for the Spanish authorities, who managed to play their cards very effectively. As Villiers put it, Britain's "serious sacrifices" against the "infamous traffic" were "without the sincere co-operation of Spain, . . . even worse than useless."[95] Over twelve years after formal abolition, the slave trade to the Spanish colonies was prospering as never before.

After the outbreak of a civil war in Spain, the government of Francisco de Paula Martínez de la Rosa (1787–1862) managed to keep control of Madrid and was recognized as legitimate by Britain and France. De la Rosa's cabinet, loyal to the claim of Isabel, desperately needed the military and economic support of its international allies to win the war against the Carlist faction. In this new context, the Spanish government could no longer downplay British demands for an equipment article. In July 1834 Villiers informed Palmerston that the Spanish government would eventually sign the equipment article but stressed that it would be a mistake to assume that "Spain is sincere in wishing to put down the slave trade."[96] The negotiation, however, faced the direct opposition of the Cuban colonial elite and the hesitations of Martínez de la Rosa himself, who had to perform a very complex balancing act. On the one hand, he needed to secure British military support against the *Carlistas*, and, on the other, he needed to maintain Cuba's stability. Villiers toughened his language and, in April 1835, threatened the Spanish government with "those measures that the public opinion would force the British government to adopt as a consequence of the infraction by the Spanish authorities of a solemn agreement" if Spain did not show a real commitment to negotiating a new treaty.[97]

Finally, the negotiations commenced on June 28, 1835, concluding with the signing of a new bilateral agreement. The Spanish government, even during these negotiations, cut a strategy to distance itself from the content of the treaty, largely by portraying it as part of the war effort. The government hoped that, in this way, "the people and settlers in Havana, who will be displeased by these stipulations" would understand "that Spain [had] been requested [to accept these conditions . . .] in a critical moment, and [would] see the need to comply."[98]

The treaty of 1835 was more comprehensive and politically ambitious than that of 1817. The agreement proclaimed that the slave trade was "totally and finally abolished in all parts of the world" (art. 1).[99] The treaty acquiesced to the demands of the British government for an equipment article, establishing the "seizure and condemnation of vessels carrying specific equipment for the slave trade, even [if] slaves were not on board at the time of the capture" (art. 10).[100] It also ruled that Spain should approve, within two months, legal penalties against the slave trade (art. 2) and established the reciprocal right of visit by war vessels of suspected ships (art. 4).[101] The agreement also included a new regulation for the mixed commission courts and for "the good treatment" of the *emancipados*.[102]

In sum, the treaty of 1835 introduced new legal instruments to effectively fight against the slave trade and bring it to a halt. The critical economic, political, and social situation Spain was going through at the time largely explains this British diplomatic success. As had occurred in 1817, the Spanish government agreed to sign a treaty it had no real intention or motive to enforce. The British authorities were aware of this but hoped that its military superiority and diplomatic capacity would suffice for ending the trade even without the collaboration of Madrid. However, the Spanish cabinet had different plans, and even before the negotiations on the new treaty had begun, the appointment in June 1834 of Miguel Tacón as the captain general of Cuba demonstrated the unfailing support of Spain to the continuity and protection of the slave traffic. His appointment was a coded message of reassurance to the colonial and metropolitan elites that the commerce would continue unabated.[103]

The news about the new anti–slave trade treaty had a double effect in Cuba. On the one hand, some expeditions were cancelled, and insurance companies showed hesitation in protecting the voyages of slave traders, accepting only to cover the return from Africa.[104] On the other hand, the idea that perhaps the slave trade was actually going to be stopped this time caused a drastic rise in the number of enslaved Africans introduced in 1835 (24,959) and 1836 (23,414). The abolition of slavery in the British colonies of Jamaica and Barbados, the rise in the price of sugar, and the cholera epidemic of 1833 all fostered unprecedentedly high numbers since the deregulation of the slave trade in the Spanish dominions.[105]

Although the equipment article became an effective legal instrument for the British African Squadron to capture more slave trade vessels, the Treaty of 1835 soon proved to be fundamentally ineffective in stopping the slave trade into Cuba. Three main reasons explained this situation: (1) the support and involvement of the Spanish authorities in the slave trade; (2) the capacity of the slave traders to quickly adapt their practices to the new legal framework, sailing their vessels through loopholes in the new legislation; and (3) the failure of the British authorities and antislavery activists to successfully challenge the pro–slave trade consensus among the Cuban white population.

Regarding the first factor, the appointment of Tacón to the post of captain general, months before the signing of the new treaty, indicated the support and promotion of the slave trade by the Spanish government. He was close to Martínez de la Rosa's administration and part of the new Liberal elite who were supporting the regency of María Cristina against Carlos María Isidro. However, his political behavior in Cuba very soon became authoritarian, corrupt, and conservative, perhaps reflecting the weight of the pressures brought to bear on the Office of the Captain General by the island's elites. Tacón strongly believed, as David Murray has shown, that the main reason for the Spanish Empire's collapse was having "conceded political rights to her colonists which made them equal to Spaniards living in the peninsula," allowing them to become politically organized and foment resistance to Spanish rule.[106]

From the beginning of his mandate in Havana, Tacón was aligned with the planter elite, whose economic interests he defended while promoting the repression of political dissent against their monopoly. Tacón defended the exclusion of colonial deputies from the new parliament opened in Madrid in 1836, and he opposed the expansion of the new political and civil rights established by the new Madrid government—like freedom of the press—to Cuba. With the implicit approval of the Spanish crown and government, Tacón resolutely supported the continuation of the slave trade, embracing a strongly imperialist, Anglophobic rhetoric to frame abolitionist pressures as foreign aggressions or the contrivance of imperial rivals. According to the Cuban historian Juan Pérez de la Riva, the new captain general was accused of receiving bribery payments for each slave illegally introduced into Cuba, of up to a total of 450,000 pesos. Tacón also relied on the money and political support provided by prominent slave traders such as Joaquín Gómez and Julián de Zulueta, and slave trade investors like Francisco Marti y Torrens.[107] Although this type of corruption "did not cause loss of official revenues," since this was an illegal trade, the entry "of slaves to Cuba, oiled by the bribing of authorities, caused social and human harm for the personal gain of a few, and it placed Spain's diplomatic prestige and foreign credit at stake"; furthermore, it normalized and gave official sanction to an inhuman practice.[108] In 1844 Tacón openly recognized in a private letter his support, as captain general, for the slave trade in the aftermath of the signing of the treaty of 1835: "The general opinion being positive about the importation of Africans, and as a result of the big earnings that the traffic produced, . . . no slave trade vessels were ever captured by the Spanish Navy and every time that the British commissioners denounced to the Captaincy General that any of these had arrived to the ports after disembarking the Negroes . . . instructions were given to build a case in favor of those that had been accused."[109]

The second reason for the ineffectiveness of the Treaty of 1835 was the capacity of the slave traders to work around the new legal framework. The nonexistence of equivalent agreements between Britain and Portugal and the

United States with respect to the right of visit opened a loophole that the Spanish slavers consistently used after 1835.[110] By sailing under the colors of the Portuguese, American, Austrian, or Russian flag, among others, Spanish slave trade vessels evaded inspection by the British navy, who had no rights to attend to the vessels of these countries. According to British commissioners' annual reports, between 1835 and 1840, of all the suspected slave trade vessels leaving the port of Havana, 42 percent were Spanish, 40 percent were Portuguese, and 18 percent were American.[111] The practice was protected by the Portuguese, American, and French diplomatic authorities in Havana. The appointment in the spring of 1837 of José Fernández, "a notorious slave dealer," as Palmerston put it, as Portuguese consul in Havana illustrates the support for this illegal traffic and the power of the slave trade lobby in Lisbon.[112] British commissioners also denounced the collusion of Nicholas Trist (1800–1874), US consul in Havana, with the Cuban slave traders. The US government ordered an investigation and concluded that it was "a matter of public notoriety" that the US flag had been consistently used to stymie the Treaty of 1835 and imputed Trist as a facilitator of this fraud. The US consul was dismissed from his post in Havana but in the end did not face prosecution.[113] Likewise, in 1840 Gaspard Théodore Mollien (1796–1872), French consul in Havana between 1831 and 1848, was accused by the British abolitionist activist David Turnbull (1793–1851), of protecting a French slave-trade vessel, which "re-entered the port, after landing no less than 500 negroes on the shores of the Island."[114] Moreover, the involvement of British subjects and capital in the slave trade persisted long after 1833. This also arguably included officials, like Charles David Tolmé (1792–1865), British consul in Havana from 1833 to 1844, who was accused by James Kennedy (1789–1859), British commissioner between 1837 and 1851, of "being too entwined with slave trading interests."[115] As David Eltis has pointed out, "as long as the slave trade existed anywhere and as long as the British remained dedicated to the goals of laissez-faire and civilizing the world through trade, it was impossible to prevent British involvement."[116]

Together with the use of foreign flags, the collusion of foreign authorities, and the support of international investors, Spanish slave traders also developed new strategies to avoid prosecution under the new laws.[117] The British commissioners in Havana reported to London that in the years that followed the signing of the new treaty, Spanish traders had established new factories in the west coast of Africa to facilitate the more efficient boarding and capture of new slaves; started to use smaller, faster vessels; and organized their expeditions in groups of three or more ships so they could reduce the risk of confrontation and capture.[118] Cuban slave traders were able to "develop new skills and capabilities" by "fostering an extensive and personalised network of agents," reducing "their risks through diversification" and introducing "technological innovations into their business operations," all despite "constant British surveillance."[119]

David Murray has pointed out that "neither British diplomats nor British abolitionists had so far succeeded in eliminating the slave trade to Cuba" and that "the main reason of course was Spain's refusal to co-operate."[120] However, what Eltis described as the "self-congratulatory tone of the British authorities" also had the effect of undermining Britain's humanitarian stance, aided the case for Anglophobic rhetoric, and ultimately consolidated a pro–slave trade consensus among Cuba's white public.[121] British "moral superiority," which gradually hardened into arrogance, was "not likely to induce cooperation," and therefore Murray's disclaimer of British responsibility should be critically revised.[122] As Richard Huzzey has argued, it would be mistaken to suggest that Britain's "humanitarian intentions" were simply false, and that "formal legal imperialism" was the tool that the successive British governments had used "to spread anti–slave trade laws around the globe."[123] It is, however, important to take into consideration the negative repercussions of Britain's "whip strategy" in polarizing the debate and consolidating antiabolitionist and Anglophobic discourses in Spain and Cuba.[124]

British authorities were unjustifiably confident that they could put an end to the slave trade even without the support of any foreign government, the political and intellectual leaders of the country, or its public opinion. In 1831 Commodore John Hayes asked for permission to "capture every vessel carrying slaves or fitted for the carrying of slaves without any regard to country or flag and I will answer with my commission that in three years there shall be no slave vessels to be found on this Coast."[125] In a similar vein, Edward Villiers, brother of the British ambassador in Madrid, published in 1836 an article in the *Edinburgh Review*, following instructions from his brother, in which he highlighted the importance of the recently signed treaty because "it does not depend for its fulfilment upon Spanish co-operation. All is left to the regulations of the British Government, and the activity of British cruisers."[126]

Hayes's and Villiers's sense of imperial superiority made them believe that they could achieve the end of the slave trade in spite of or even against the involvement of other incumbent political actors, and in so doing they further reinforced Anglophobic and antiabolitionist discourses. Pro–slave trade sectors of Spanish public opinion depicted these ideas as foreign aggressions and linked the protection of, and even involvement in, the slave trade, to an idea of Spanish patriotism and national pride. The British "whip strategy" undoubtedly contributed to the continuity of the slave trade in the Spanish Empire.

CONCLUSIONS

Discontinuities and fractures characterized the construction and development of abolitionist and antiabolitionist ideas in Spain in the last decade of Fernando VII's reign. The complexity of these processes proves the ineffectiveness of adopting an evolutionary approach and stresses the need for a comprehensive understanding of all the actors involved. After 1823 the Liberal thinkers and political leaders exiled in London who had openly defended the abolition of the slave trade changed their attitude. The anti–slave trade agenda was advanced only by the British authorities in Spain, who time and again demanded a bona fide commitment from the Spanish government to put an end to the slave trade flourishing on Cuban shores. In this context, two movements became central in the construction of antiabolitionist discourses: the "necessary evil" discourse and the pervasive national sense of victimhood culminating in Anglophobic rhetoric. The deep political changes that started in 1833 with the death of the monarch and ensuing civil war forced the hand of Madrid in the signing of the Treaty of 1835. However, the support of the Spanish authorities for the continuity of the slave trade, the rapacity of the slave traders in their quick adaptation to the new legal framework, and Britain's failed "whip strategy," consolidated and even strengthened the trade of enslaved Africans into the Spanish colonies.

4

Political Exclusion, Racism, and Abolitionism in the 1840s

In vain are my efforts to arouse any repugnance in myself at the thought that a man of color might sit at my side on these benches.
—Domingo María Vila, 1837

By 1833 Spain was a very different country from the one that had resisted the Napoleonic invasion. The independence of most of the American territories, the civil war, the repression and the long exiles of some of its key Liberal political figures had created a much darker political climate, in which many pledged to preserve what was left of a shrinking empire at any cost—even if for some, like Agustín de Argüelles, this meant arguing against what they had passionately fought for twenty-five years before. The new regime restricted the liberties and rights of colonial subjects, excluded their representatives from the parliament, and ignored those "philanthropic theories" that had inspired the debates of Cadiz. All in the name of the preservation of what was left: Cuba, Puerto Rico, and the Philippines.

In this context, new antislavery activism and voices emerged. But not all of them came about in an attempt to protect the dignity of the enslaved Africans. A new anti–slave trade discourse, articulated by key Cuban intellectuals, emerged as a political response to Spain's inertia. José Antonio Saco publicly advocated the eradication of the slave trade in Cuba as a necessary first step to "whitening" the island, promoting its economy, and advancing political rights for its white population. Saco's racist anti–slave trade ideas were to become the most successful strain of abolitionism to operate in Cuba during the 1840s.

This chapter explores the construction of abolitionist and antiabolitionist discourses following the proclamation of the Constitution of 1837, the impact of Britain's "abrasive" diplomatic strategy, and the reaction to the political and military repression that followed the conspiracy of La Escalera.

CUBANS "STAND ATOP A VOLCANO": EXCLUSION AND SLAVERY AT THE CORTES OF 1836

After the death of Fernando VII in 1833, his wife, María Cristina, assumed the title queen regent, holding power on behalf of their daughter Isabel, with the support of reformist sectors of the court. In 1834 Francisco Martínez de la Rosa, who had been in exile in France since 1823, was appointed prime minister with the support of the conservative and moderate Liberals. Under his presidency, the regent sanctioned the Estatuto Real of 1834, a *charte octroyée* inspired by the French one proclaimed in 1814. The Estatuto was strongly contested by radical and progressive Liberals, who in 1836, after the military uprising known as the Motín de La Granja de San Ildefonso, proclaimed the restoration of the 1812 Constitution of Cadiz.[1] The difficulties in implementing it led the new prime minister, José María de Calatrava, to call for the formation of a Constituent Cortes to write a new constitution with the consensus of Conservative and Progressive parties.

The resulting Constitution of 1837 reestablished a representative monarchy in Spain but determined that Cuba, Puerto Rico, and the Philippines would be ruled by special laws, restricting the access of colonial subjects to the civil rights proclaimed in the new constitution and withdrawing the colonies' political representation from the Cortes. The colonial territories would be governed directly from Madrid, and their tax revenues would remain under the opaque jurisdiction of the central Hacienda (central Treasury).[2]

In the aftermath of the severe territorial and economic contraction of the Spanish Empire, the new constitution aimed to preserve the last remaining overseas dominions. The fear of pro-independence ideas being disseminated if political liberties were granted, combined with the demographic "heterogeneity" of these colonies, justified, in the eyes of the peninsular deputies, the need for "special treatment" by the Madrid government. The debate on this point took place between March 7 and 11, 1837, and brought the opinions of several deputies led by Vicente Sancho (1784–1860) and Argüelles, on one side, and Domingo María Vila, on the other, into conflict.

The debate on the exclusion of the colonies from the new constitutional provisions was based upon certain historical justifications, fiscal and tax control, and a renewed emphasis on the "singularities" of the colonial territories.[3] The strategic importance of slavery in Cuba's economy and the fact that the enslaved and free Africans and Afro-descendant people represented a majority of its total population (with possible electoral consequences), as José A. Piqueras has stressed, inclined Cuban slave owners and planters to oppose constitutional exclusion. The report of the parliamentary commission that suggested the exclusion of Cuba, Puerto Rico, and the Philippines from the constitutional provisions praised the "carefulness" with which the absolutist governments had administered Cuba, the success of its thriving economy, and concluded that it was "not possible for a homogeneous law to rule upon such heterogeneous elements."[4] The new colonial regime would have the support of the Cuban colonial elite, who, as restitution for a drop in their direct representation in the metropolis, were assured of Spain's role in protecting "internal social order" as a "necessary accomplice" in the protection of the illegal slave trade.[5] This solution "provided a nexus of strengthened colonial dependency" that was welcomed by both parties.[6]

Argüelles argued passionately for the exclusion of the colonial deputies and the necessity of "special laws," different from the constitutional provisions, for preserving the colonies as part of Spain's empire. Argüelles's idea of "American disloyalty" to the Constitution of 1812 characterized his parliamentary intervention.[7] He affirmed that the "philanthropic theories" that he had advocated in 1811 had had a harmful effect in the Spanish colonies and therefore he asked the deputies not to commit the same mistake twice, and to subordinate those noble maxims to the preservation of the remaining territories.[8] He argued that those "special laws" would protect the prosperity of the colonies and the security of the Cuban subjects who were not fully aware of the fragility of their own safety. Argüelles also emphasized that the colonies would enjoy the liberties of the peninsula when "it would be compatible with the circumstances of those countries." However, the deputy believed that in the current demographic state, such freedoms were "a dangerous germ," as Cubans "stood atop a volcano."[9] He further argued that "there [in Cuba,] gentlemen, there is a race that believes itself irreconcilable, and that aspires to the destruction of the other inhabitants, as the only way to obtain its freedom; however, the treatment that the Negroes have in the Island of Cuba is the least bad that is given in any country."[10]

Argüelles was using the same arguments that Andrés de Jáuregui and Francisco de Arango y Parreño, representing the slave traders' interests, had used in the Cortes of Cadiz in 1811. The fear of sparking a racial war, which would replicate "the horrors" of Haiti's Revolution, plus the "mild conditions" of the Spanish slavery regime were in his mind sufficient to justify this "necessary evil."[11]

The deputy Vicente Sancho, in a similar vein, defended the exclusion of the overseas deputies and the necessity of "special laws" to rule those provinces. For Sancho, the Constitution of 1812 committed the mistake of according the same rights to "the Spaniards of both hemispheres" when this was simply not possible. Sancho perfectly understood the contradiction "between universal rights (applied to the white population) and the heterogeneity of civil and racial status that such unlimited equality could hide."[12] Sancho argued that a

Constitution was a legal instrument to provide "freedom and equality" to men, but "in those countries [Cuba and Puerto Rico], those words, that sound so nice to our ears, are words of extermination and death."[13] Sancho concluded that "if the Island of Cuba is not Spanish, it will be black, necessarily black, and everybody knows that."[14] Sancho, as Argüelles had done before, weaponized this "Black fear" to sanction the political repression and militarization of Cuba that would protect "the whites, our brothers, from the dagger of the Negroes."[15]

It is revealing to observe how the same rhetorical figure, "our brothers," that Argüelles had adopted in 1811 to advocate the abolition of the slave trade was now used by Sancho as a racist attack to protect slavery and defend the need for repressive policies in Cuba. To "brothers" had been added the silent qualifier of "white."[16] Sancho opened the door to "the theory of racial superiority and inferiority to Spanish parliamentary rule" and fed the notion that political freedom should be subordinated to imperial integrity. For Sancho and Argüelles, slavery was no longer up for debate, and even the continuity of the slave trade, which they both avoided mentioning, was not publicly condemned anymore. Without the support of the metropolis, Cuba's white male "effeminate and corrupted" population, as Sancho described it, would be destroyed. Any change in the colonial status quo, they believed, would irreversibly lead to Cuba's ruin.[17]

The deputy Domingo María Vila rejected Argüelles's and Sancho's arguments and warned the Cortes about the potential consequences of depriving the colonial population of their political and electoral rights. Vila, a member of the Progressive Party, had been in exile in Britain after the end of the Liberal Triennium.[18] During his exile he established a close relationship with Quaker circles, and in 1833, when the scientist and abolitionist leader William Allen (1770–1843) visited Madrid, Vila was his first contact in the Spanish capital. As Allen himself wrote, Vila had "just returned from England, and [was] acquainted with Friends [Quakers]."[19] As García Balañà has pointed out, Vila knew the Americas well and had traveled to Rio de la Plata and Brazil as a representative of the Spanish government in 1820. The Catalan deputy highlighted the complexity of Cuba's society and the existence of a "separationist germ" among the *criollo* elite but declared,[20] "If the Cortes close the door . . . to the deputies that have been elected by the Overseas provinces, the consequences in my view will be fatal; if these doors are closed, the interpretation will be malicious, the results disastrous, and all your good faith, gentlemen, will not be enough to convince anyone of the truth of your ideas."[21]

Vila also tackled the provocative assertion advanced by those in favor of exclusion that giving electoral rights to the Cuban population would eventually result in the election of a Black deputy. Vila responded to this fear that "in vain are my efforts to arouse any repugnance in myself at the thought that a man of color might sit at my side on these benches" and proclaimed that "intelligence also lies under a skin less white than ours."[22] Vila's antiracist discourse went beyond the demands of the Cuban Liberal elites and advanced the idea that a Liberal constitutional regime not only was capable of ruling over a "heterogeneous" community but could also strengthen its internal cohesion. Vila's speech relied on an implicit antislavery discourse because, as Balañà has suggested, he was perfectly conscious that "the recognition of the free blacks' political rights would announce the beginning of the end of slavery."[23] In other words, slavery was fundamentally incompatible with Vila's notion of Liberal constitutionalism.

Freedom and political rights were the answer, according to Vila, to the secessionist question. Granting political rights to the *criollos*, *pardos*, and liberated Africans was, for Vila, the antidote to the "supreme command" and praetorianism of Cuba's captains general.[24] Contrary to Argüelles's and Sancho's belief, Vila considered that political repression would only exacerbate pro-independence aspirations and ultimately fail to preserve Cuba as a Spanish territory.[25] Ultimately, on April 16, 1837, 150 deputies voted in favor, and two against, that the overseas provinces should be ruled by "special laws" and excluded from the constitutional provisions. In a different vote, ninety deputies voted for the exclusion of the colonial deputies from the chamber, and sixty-five opposed it.[26]

The exclusion of Cuba, Puerto Rico, and the Philippines from the constitutional provisions "followed the script" defined by the new Liberal regime established in 1834. The increasing militarization of Cuba's politics and the *criollo* elite's restricted access to the enjoyment of political rights had characterized the peninsular agenda since the appointment of Miguel Tacón as captain general.[27] In the following years, Domingo del Monte and José Antonio Saco were to become the most important Cuban dissident voices against imperial power. To their mind the eradication of the slave trade was a fundamental first step in reclaiming their political rights.

A THIRD ANTI–SLAVE TRADE VOICE: RACIST ABOLITIONISM FROM CUBA

Cuban intellectual José Antonio Saco, one of the elected colonial representatives excluded from the Cortes in 1837, publicly protested against this decision in his pamphlet *Examen analítico del informe de la comisión especial nombrada por las Cortes*, published in Madrid that same year.[28] Saco claimed that the demographic and economic reasons given by the parliamentary commission to exclude the overseas provinces from the constitutional provisions were imprecise or erroneous. The Cuban argued against the disenfranchisement imposed by Madrid and asserted that only a Liberal government would be able to tackle the political challenges that the island faced, concentrated around slavery: "At all times we are reminded . . . of the formidable example of Santo Domingo. I did not participate in that terror . . . we are intimately persuaded that a Liberal government in Cuba, far from reprising the calamities of Santo Domingo, will be the best method of avoiding such a catastrophe."[29]

Saco belonged to a new generation of Cuban thinkers and writers who pursued a new spectrum of political demands, using a more outspoken and radical public discourse. Saco, Domingo del Monte, José de la Luz y Caballero (1800–1862), and Félix Tanco (1797–1871), among others, led a generation of intellectuals characterized by the vindication of political liberties and civil rights for the white population in Cuba, and the articulation of a nationalist Cuban discourse, strongly influenced by Francisco de Arango y Parreño and Felix Varela.[30]

For all of them, slavery and the slave trade constituted central issues in their analysis of Cuba's political and economic situation. All of them argued for the abolition of the slave trade, but only Tanco advocated the radical abolition of slavery as well. Saco defined a new racist anti–slave trade discourse that was to become the most significant contestation of the slave traffic produced in Cuba. In 1832 Saco published an article in the journal *Revista bimestre cubana*, in which he condemned "the horrendous traffic in human flesh" and accused all those involved in the trade of putting their homeland at risk: "men who pretend to be patriotic when they are no more than *patricidae*, who flood our territory with chained victims . . .; We will not stop repeating: let us save our motherland, let us save the motherland."[31] In this article, Saco presented the central idea that inspired his abolitionist discourse: the instrumental necessity of stopping the slave trade in order to obtain political and civil rights for the white Cuban population. For Saco, the United States represented a successful model, in which "liberal principles are fully developed" and in which "some states, political rights are limited to the white race."[32]

In another work, *Memoria sobre la vagancia en la Isla de Cuba*, published in 1832, Saco blamed the enslaved Africans for restraining Cuba's economic prosperity, as they had "turned our white population away from the arts [. . . and] in such a deplorable situation, it was no longer expected that any Cuban white man would devote himself to the arts, because if he does, he seems to have renounced the privileges of his class."[33] Embracing an orthodox Liberal discourse, Saco characterized the slave trade as an uneconomic activity and argued that the eradication of the slave trade into Cuba, far from having a negative impact, would create a more competitive environment, sugar production would increase, and new settlers would "be dedicated to the branch of industry that offers the most advantage to them."[34]

For Saco, the slave trade and the repressive policies imposed by the Spanish governments were the true enemies of Cuba, and they were closely intertwined. In his opinion, however, slave owners were not to be blamed, as they represented the most dynamic, prosperous, and entrepreneurial group on the island. In his work *Paralelo entre la Isla de Cuba y algunas colonias inglesas*, published in 1837, Saco commented on the economic advantages of following the British example in stopping the slave trade and praised the contribution of the slave holders and planters to Cuba's economy:[35] "I will not blame the Cuban who buys them [the slaves]. His farm requires arms and not being able to find any others to use, will he have to lose his property? Should this sacrifice be demanded of a family man? I do blame and accuse the government, which being able to extinguish the infamous African contraband, tolerates, consents and authorizes it in violation of treaties, with contempt of the laws and scandalizing public and private morals."[36]

The solution for Saco, as he wrote in 1837, was a white recolonization of Cuba and the gradual substitution of enslaved Africans for free white workers.[37] He believed that white workers were "more intelligent" and more productive than enslaved Africans, and he consistently equated the Black population with "wild animals."[38] Saco's "racialist and racist" ideological framework, as Piqueras described it, constituted the cornerstone of his political discourse: "It is true that the African, in the manner of other savages, knows how to run and jump, and also to beat his fellows and wild beasts; but when the cries of hunger cease and the fury of their passions is extinguished, then they indulge in the deepest and most stupid indolence."[39]

Saco stressed two main arguments, previously put forward by Cuban and Spanish pro–slave trade elites, to defend the eradication of the slave trade and the "whitening" of the island. First, the Cuban thinker argued that the security of the island was in peril and that the preservation of the white population of Cuba was balanced on a knife edge. In his work *La supresión del tráfico de esclavos africanos en la Isla de Cuba, examinada con relación a su agricultura y a su seguridad*, published in Paris in 1845, Saco stressed that for the first time, the number of white people was smaller than that of the "African race" and that both groups were "essentially the opposite" and "irreconcilable enemies."[40] Second, Saco stated that Britain, "the most powerful" and "skillful" nation, would achieve its purpose of ending the slave trade one way or another, and that it was in the interest of the Cuban people to stop the slave trade by their own means.[41]

Saco was not alone in his analysis. In a similar vein, Domingo del Monte, a Cuban Liberal intellectual, defended in his work *La Isla de Cuba tal cual está*, published in New York in 1836, that the slave trade and slavery represented the most important obstacle to Cuba's economic and moral prosperity.[42] Del

Monte collaborated with the British officials Richard Madden (1798–1886) and David Turnbull in the abolitionist cause during the late 1830s and early 1840s, and in the years before had publicly denounced Captain General Miguel Tacón's praetorianism and accused him of accepting bribes from slave-traders and planters:[43] "It is public and notorious . . . that a slave ship does not disembark on the Island its cargo of beast-men, without being charged half an ounce of gold by His Excellency [Tacón] for each slave. In this past year of 1835, those who traffic in this infernal business calculate, that 19,000 Negroes have entered through the ports of this province, which is to say, His Excellency has received 9,500 ounces, or 3,830,000 *reales.*"[44]

Del Monte, as well as Saco, compared the "*negros*" with wild animals and consistently characterized them as "vicious, stupid and immoral" and naturally inferior.[45] In 1848 Del Monte argued in a letter written from Paris to "J. in Havana" that Cuban problems had their origin in "the slavery of the black race," and consequently he exhorted all the Cubans "of noble and healthy patriotism" to fight to end the slave trade first, "then to suppress slavery, without shaking or violence; and finally, to cleanse Cuba of the African race."[46]

Another member of this generation of Cuban Liberal thinkers was José de la Luz y Caballero, philosopher and scholar, who also advocated the abolition of the slave trade. He agreed with Saco that the slave trade was negative for Cuba's prosperity and supported British action to achieve its eradication. For Luz, slavery was at the root of the problems that Cuba faced at the time.[47] On May 30, 1836, Luz wrote a long letter to Saco to congratulate him on his election as Cuban deputy and invited him to fight against the Cortes' decision to exclude the colonial deputies from the chamber. In this letter Luz endorsed Saco's anti–slave trade position and advised him to be pragmatic and to do whatever was needed to convince the Cortes to stop the slave trade in Cuba, even blaming the British: "Appeal to your own writings, and holding them, blame the English. This is the question; ignore if [the slave trade is] good or bad, disregard justice or injustice, and focus only upon the facts: the English, the Christian world, all at once, are committed, and are interested in, abolishing slavery: what shall we do?"[48]

Saco's and Del Monte's racist abolitionism contrasted with the progressive view advanced by the Cuban writer Félix Tanco. In 1837, in the context of the debates about the exclusion of the Cuban deputies from the Cortes, Tanco argued in a letter to Del Monte that slavery should be abolished in Cuba, giving the Spanish deputies no excuses to limit civil and political rights on the island: "Destroying then this premise [slavery] and forming a new one properly, such should be the great goal of our legislators."[49] For Tanco, everyone seemed to repeat "that it is a necessary evil to own men as property to produce sugar," but he believed that "this is the sophism that must be refuted."[50] He affirmed

that Cuban colonial elite, represented by Saco in Madrid, only pursued political power for themselves, and "to keep things as they are: power, gambling,
slaves, trade, taxes, etcetera, etcetera,"[51] and concluded: "Stop it; patriotism is
an exotic plant that currently doesn't grow in this land. . . . The only thing that
some or all would like would be for the Creoles, and not the Spaniards, to
rule; reducing the issue to the people and nothing more."[52]

The opinions and works of Saco, Del Monte, Luz, and Tanco are important
in the development of anti–slave trade discourse, as they represented a third
way between the Spanish political class and British abolitionists. However,
the attempt to identify these men as spokesmen for their generation, as David Murray put it, is problematic.[53] First, because the ideological differences
between them, as has been shown, are important and the political future they
wanted for Cuba was just as uneven. Second, because their actual capacity to
influence a wider audience in Cuba and Spain was unclear.[54] As Tanco himself argued, in Madrid Saco primarily represented the interests of slave owners
and planters who, between 1820 and 1837, had illegally introduced more than
273,500 enslaved Africans into Cuba. As Jorge and Isabel Castellanos have
argued, "many historians insist on considering Saco as the main leader of the
Creole bourgeoisie of his time [. . . but] with regard to the suppression of the
slave trade, he never was."[55] The reality is that Saco, Del Monte, Tanco and
others failed to convince important sectors of the Cuban colonial elite of the
alleged dangers of the slave trade and the benefits of stopping it.

Saco, always in need of financial backers, dedicated his work *Mi primera
pregunta* to "the landowners of the Island of Cuba," but this responded more
to his yearning to attract the powerful Cuban planters to his side than to the
fact that he was speaking in their name at the Cortes.[56] Saco's capacity to influence the political debate has often been overstated, partly because of the
credibility and importance that the Spanish authorities and British officials
on the island gave to his contributions. William Sharp Macleay (1792–1865),
British Mixed Commission judge in Havana, reported in 1834 to London
"that Tacón dreads the effect of Saco's writings against the Slave Trade and his
influence on the opinion of the rising generation."[57] Similarly, David Turnbull,
British consul in Havana, reported that "many of the most enlightened Creole
landowners . . . express their genuine and sincere feelings, comparable to Wilberforce or Clarkson's ones, in wishing . . . the immediate, total, and irrevoca-
ble suppression of the slave trade."[58]

In this last example, Turnbull strategically overestimates the reach of Saco's
thesis among the Cuban colonial elite to convince the British government and
the abolitionists that all the effort put into changing Cuban public opinion
was starting to bear fruit, and that his role in Havana was more important
than ever before. However, there was very little ideological confluence between

Saco and Wilberforce, or Del Monte and Clarkson. As Murray pointed out, "their co-operation could never be close," and "certainly there could not be any fusion into a unified abolitionist movement combining Cuban creoles and British abolitionists."[59] The struggle of Saco and his colleagues for the eradication of the slave trade, built upon racist rhetoric, was merely instrumental.

As María del Carmen Barcia and Murray have rightly argued, although Madden and Turnbull obtained information from Cuban intellectuals, their relationships were "superficial," and Turnbull, out of personal interest, generalized the aspirations of only a few individuals to "the whole class."[60] Referring to a Cuban abolitionist movement in the 1840s would be an overstatement.

Madden, Turnbull, and a New Abolitionist Strategy

Between 1835 and 1843, six different captains general governed Cuba: Miguel Tacón (1834–1838), Joaquín de Ezpeleta (1838–1840), Pedro Tellez Girón, Prince of Anglona (1840–1841), Jerónimo Valdés (1841–1843), Francisco Javier de Ulloa (1843), and Leopoldo O'Donnell (1843–1848). All of them faced growing diplomatic pressure from the British authorities, amid concern about the cargo of abolitionist activism and propaganda from the British West Indies and the United States, and the emergence of dissident voices, from Cuba and places of exile, in favor of more autonomy for the island or its annexation by the United States.[61]

The 1836 Liberal uprising of Manuel Lorenzo in Santiago de Cuba, and the increased frequency of Black armed movements throughout the western part of the island during the 1830s, contributes to explaining the decision to exclude the Cuban deputies from the Cortes.[62] The authoritarian response from the colonial authorities in the aftermath of this decision consolidated the gradual militarization of Cuban society during Tacón's tenure. The captain general surrounded himself with prominent slave traders and slave owners such as Joaquín Gomez and the Catalan Francisco Martí y Torrens, who became his "principal partners and advisers" in relation to the slave trade.[63] As discussed, during his mandate Tacón advocated the protection and preservation of the slave trade as a strategic activity in Cuba.

For the Spanish colonial authorities, Cuba's stability and security were in jeopardy, and—as Captain General Joaquín Ezpeleta, successor to Tacón, would describe it—the arrival in Cuba of abolitionist activists and propaganda put at risk the very foundations of Cuba's "slavery architecture."[64] The fear of abolitionist ideas making headway in Cuba was not a new phenomenon. Since the Haitian Revolution, the Spanish authorities had been concerned about the dissemination of antislavery propaganda, activists, and even rumors on the island.[65] However, during the 1830s and 1840s, the idea that this was the result of an international campaign led by Britain gained ground.[66] Since the beginning of Tacón's governorship, concerns about the circulation of abolitionist propaganda in Cuba had increased.

In November 1835 an abolitionist poster with a reproduction of a famous design by British potter Josiah Wedgwood—*Am I Not a Man and a Brother?*—was discovered on a road near Havana, alarming Tacón, who reported the incident to Madrid.[67] The proximity of Jamaica, Haiti, and the United States was seen by both Tacón and the captains general who preceded and followed him as a constant and direct threat to Cuba's political tranquility. In May 1836 Tacón sent his secret agent, Captain José Ruiz de Apodaca, to Jamaica "with the purpose of infiltrating the [abolitionist] societies [. . . and] to gain an exact idea of the Methodist Society."[68] One year later, Antonio Brosa, Spanish consul on the British Island, informed Tacón that there was a serious risk of "suspicious people being introduced [into Cuba]; and as I have some news that the Methodists and Anabaptists are trying to send some agents to the province of Cuba (I am afraid some of them are introduced already) in order to see if they can induce the Negroes to revolt."[69]

Some months later, in February 1838, Brosa warned Tacón that he had been informed of the economic support that abolitionist activists in Jamaica had received from England with the intention of "sending from this island to that one [Cuba] commissioners with money and incendiary papers, to try to encourage the Negroes to revolt and emancipate them."[70] In December 1836 the Spanish ambassador in Washington, Ángel Calderón de la Barca, drew the attention of the Spanish government to the "alarming progress being made by societies that aim to abolish slavery [in the United States . . .] and the consequences that their success would have,"[71] and some months later, in July 1837, Calderón insisted on repeating his concern about the "associations for the abolition of the Negro slavery."[72]

The arrival of abolitionist activists from different religious sects and institutions also worried the colonial authorities. In 1837 George Davison, a Black British subject, was arrested for "having disseminated pernicious doctrines among slaves on this island."[73] In April 1839 the presence of a "subject of His Britannic Majesty" who was found "spreading the maxims of the abolition of slavery" in Matanzas was also reported to the captain general.[74] The following month "five Baptist individuals" arrived in Trinidad and were accused of belonging to the "Anti-Slavery Society of Jamaica."[75] The presence of these agents was perceived as a direct attack on Cuba's sovereignty and was linked by the colonial authorities to an international attempt to instigate a massive slave revolt. This series of incidents "had convinced both the colonial and metropolitan governments that British abolitionists, supported by the British government, were intent on destroying Cuban slavery."[76]

The Foreign Office, headed by Henry John Temple, Lord Palmerston, developed a new diplomatic strategy to deal with Cuba between 1836 and 1842, which was more abrasive and direct, in which Richard Robert Madden and David Turnbull played key roles. The British government adopted this approach, rightly convinced that the Spanish authorities were protecting the slave trade. The social and political mobilization that preceded the abolition of the apprenticeship system in 1838 and the preparations of the Anti-Slavery Conference of 1840 in London, gave Palmerston the domestic support required to strain relations with Spain.[77]

As part of the bilateral agreement between Britain and Spain in 1835, a British official had to be appointed to arrange the transfer of Africans liberated by Havana's Mixed Commission Court to British dominions. In 1836 the Foreign Office appointed Madden to this end, as the first "superintendent of liberated Africans." Madden held this post until 1839, and his time in Cuba defined the beginning of a drastic deterioration in the diplomatic relationships between the two governments and a growing anti-British sentiment in Cuban public opinion. Madden was "unwelcome . . . to say the least" in Havana. His appointment represented an unprecedented decision to put an abolitionist activist at the heart of the most profoundly slave-based society in the Caribbean. Madden was an Irish physician with experience in the region as a magistrate in Jamaica, where he had been in charge of implementing the British Emancipation Act, facing great opposition from the planters. After his short stay there, he returned to Britain where he published the book *A Twelvemonth's Residence*, in which he criticized the newly established apprenticeship system in the British West Indies and advocated its abolition.[78]

Tacón described Madden as "a dangerous man from whatever point of view he is considered, and living on this Island he will have far too many opportunities to disseminate seditious ideas directly or indirectly, which not even my constant vigilance can prevent," and argued for the immediate withdrawal of his appointment.[79] The vagueness of the accusations of the captain general, however, had nil effect, and Madden remained in his post until 1839, when he resigned. The appointment of Madden, "a committed abolitionist," confirmed the worst fears of the Spanish officials and "added to the credibility of the Cuban belief in a British abolitionist conspiracy."[80] It fueled anti-British sentiment, reinforced the self-victimization narrative of the Spanish government and the Cuban colonial elite, and consolidated the protection of slavery and slave trade as a matter of national sovereignty and security.[81]

In 1837 the British government requested Spain's authorization to harbor a vessel, the HMS *Romney*, in Havana's port to accommodate the hundreds of Africans freed from slave ships condemned by the Mixed Commission Court, before they were sent to British territories. The presence of these liberated Africans, or *emancipados*, was seen by the Spanish authorities as a threat to the city's safety; therefore, the British proposal was quickly accepted.[82] As Jennifer Nelson has pointed out while discussing the *Romney* as well as the HMS *Crescent*, which was placed in the Bay of Guanabara in Rio de Janeiro for similar purposes, "although the receiving ships were only bare "hulks" and were not in a position of being galvanized to carry out any sort of military attack, they had a symbolic relevance which seemed to go beyond the physical threat which they encapsulated."[83] Some Black soldiers were part of the contingent on the vessel, which contributed to reinforcing the idea in Cuba that the HMS *Romney* was not only a vivid icon of British imperial strength but a direct provocation.

For Cuba's Captain General Ezpeleta, the presence of Black British soldiers in Havana "will just by their words and dress arouse in those of their race a strong desire for freedom at any cost and in defiance of all danger," affirming that its impact would be more psychological than diplomatic or political, as "the very sight of those soldiers presents serious difficulties which are easier to perceive than to describe."[84]

This growing diplomatic tension between the two countries was seen as unnecessary and even detrimental by James Kennedy, British judge of the Mixed Commission Court in Havana between 1837 and 1851. He believed that the decision to harbor the HMS *Romney* in Havana was "an unnecessary incurring of dislike" and advocated its removal. Kennedy represented a moderate figure in the escalating tension between the two governments.[85] He requested a more cautious approach, as he understood that adopting a position of superiority by Britain would contribute to anti-British sentiment and the self-victimization discourse on the island. Palmerston, however, opposed withdrawing the *Romney*, and the vessel remained in Havana until 1851. Its symbolism operated in two directions: it became an icon of Britain's abolitionist commitment in Cuba and, at the same time, a blatant demonstration of its imperial superiority.[86]

The impact of the *Romney* would have undoubtedly been less significant without the concurrence of a wider strategy to drive the Spanish government into a corner and compel it to stop the slave trade. David Turnbull played a central role in this strategy. Turnbull was a Scottish journalist who worked as a correspondent for the *Times*, covering continental Europe. In 1832 he was sent to Madrid, where, according to Manuel Llorca-Jaña, he collaborated with the British ambassador George Villiers during the negotiations of the Treaty of 1835.[87] Between 1838 and 1839, he traveled to the Caribbean and visited Demerara, Barbados, Trinidad, Jamaica, Port au Prince, and Cuba. As a result of this trip, in 1840 he published the book *Travels in the West: Cuba; with Notices of Porto Rico and the Slave Trade*, in which he denounced the involvement of "British capitalists" in the slave trade and directly accused the British consul in Havana, David Tolmé, of collusion with slave traders.[88] In August 1840 he became a member of the British and Foreign Anti-Slavery Society (BFASS), created one year before to foment the worldwide abolition of slavery and the slave trade.

Soon after its creation, the BFASS became the most influential abolitionist institution in Britain. It was led mainly by Quakers, and the pacifist convictions of this religious group permeated the whole organization and structured its political strategy. The abolition of the slave trade was seen as a moral crusade, and its achievement would result from success in persuading other nations of the brutality and intrinsic evil of slavery.[89] It would thus require close collaboration with other abolitionist groups across the Atlantic, and to this end the BFASS called for the celebration in London of the World Anti-Slavery Convention of 1840. Delegates, mainly from Britain and the US, gathered in the English capital to define and coordinate the political strategy of the abolitionist movement worldwide.[90]

In the absence of Spanish delegates, the information presented by David Turnbull about the Spanish Caribbean colonies and his opinion on how to fight against the slave trade in Cuba were highly influential at the convention.[91] Turnbull proposed a legalistic approach that would discourage Cuban planters from buying new enslaved Africans and would ultimately put an end to the slave trade. He argued that if the Mixed Commission Courts were given the necessary capacities to challenge the lawful ownership of the enslaved Africans introduced into Cuba after the prohibition of the slave trade in 1820, it would prevent the slave owners from carrying on purchasing slaves in Africa. He believed that the "simple extension of the powers of the court" could not be rejected by the Spanish government that so many times had expressed its "*earnest* desire to abolish the traffic."[92]

Turnbull pointed out that the main obstacle to his plan was that the Spanish government considered "the maintenance of the traffic . . . as a sort of political necessity." However, Turnbull believed, in line with Saco's widely spread message, that abolitionists could count on the support of the "Creoles of Cuba," who had "neither the wish nor the interest . . . to continue the practice of the slave trade."[93] He admitted that for many years abolitionist legislation had been passed in Spain with no effect, but he was confident that his proposal would face no "serious opposition" and would eventually "produce a radical and practical change in the legal condition of the imported Africans."[94]

Turnbull's confidence in Britain's persuasive power was, however, challenged by members of the British government who had been dealing with the Spanish government on this issue for many years. Far from seeing his plan as "easy, cheap and almost immediate," as Turnbull presented it, James Bandinel, head the slave trade division in the Foreign Office, stressed the flaws of the initiative.[95] Similarly, MacGregor Laird, a Scottish merchant who advocated West Africa's colonization as the best way of stopping the slave trade, argued that Turnbull's plan would "shake to its foundations, if not destroy, the whole social fabric in Cuba"; and, as Murray put it, considered the notion that "Spain would ever agree to such plan was utterly naïve."[96]

Turnbull nevertheless achieved the decisive support of the BFASS and of Palmerston, who after two decades of ineffective diplomatic efforts, agreed to explore his proposal. In August 1840 he was appointed British consul in Havana, replacing Tolmé; and, in December that year, Palmerston instructed Arthur Ingram Aston, British ambassador in Madrid, to present to the Spanish government the proposal of a new treaty, by which all the enslaved Africans illegally introduced into the Spanish dominions after 1820 would be declared free.[97]

The arrival of Turnbull in Havana was interpreted as "characteristic disregard for Spain" on the part of Palmerston's Foreign Office and a direct threat to the island's safety by the Cuban planters and colonial authorities.[98] The long reviews of his *Travels in the West* published in the British press circulated in Cuba and contributed to the characterization of Turnbull as a radical abolitionist and a dangerous foreign agent. On November 1, 1840, Captain General Pedro Téllez Girón informed the Spanish government that Turnbull's appointment was contrary to "every feeling in my soul" and that he would do everything in his power to preserve "the peace of this country that is under my vigilance."[99] In a similar vein, the Junta de Fomento de Agricultura y Comercio of Cuba, an institution dedicated to the promotion of Cuba's economy, reported to Madrid the feeling of "sorrow" that the arrival of Turnbull had caused and the fear that "our sons will be under the power of the Negroes."[100] Cuban economic and political elites energetically protested Turnbull's appointment and the proposal of the British government to inspect the plantations and free the enslaved Africans introduced after 1820. They believed that this decision would be an abuse of power and a direct attack on Spanish national sovereignty, as it would cede judicial jurisdiction to a foreign authority on Spanish soil.[101]

In December 1840 the publication of a letter from the Spanish thinker and politician Ramón de la Sagra, in the Spanish newspaper *El Corresponsal*, arguing for the eradication of the slave trade as the first necessary step in the abolition of slavery in Cuba, generated even more political tension in the colony. The Tribunal de Comercio of Havana, a provincial court of business appeals, and the Junta de Fomento, Agricultura y Comercio of Cuba condemned the article and argued that the Spanish press should not be allowed to discuss the issue of slavery or the slave trade. Sagra's publication was the result of the meeting that he had held with a delegation of the BFASS in

Madrid.[102] Two members of the society, George William Alexander and Benjamin Barron Wiffen, "visited some of the principal towns in that country," including "Barcelona, Madrid, Valentia [sic], Seville, and Cadiz," in 1840. In Barcelona they met with the publisher Antonio Bergnes, "who was already acquainted with the question of Negro slavery," and "F. Delamere," "another friend to our cause." In Madrid, during the meeting with Sagra, the BFASS delegation also met the Usoz y Rio brothers, Luis and Santiago.[103] Luis Usoz y Rio was a Spanish religious scholar who had been in exile in Britain during the 1820s. Also in the Spanish capital, they met Manuel Marliani, who they hoped would champion their "views . . . in the Spanish Cortes," and Agustín de Argüelles, who had "years ago advocated the abolition of the slave-trade by Spain."[104]

The abdication of María Cristina as Spanish regent in the summer of 1840 led to the political rise of General Baldomero Espartero (1793–1879), supported by the Progressive Party, and a tentative rapprochement between Britain and Spain.[105] The new Spanish government rejected the British proposal to investigate and liberate illegally introduced enslaved Africans but agreed to adopt a truly committed attitude against the slave trade. The appointment in 1840 of Jerónimo Valdés, a personal friend of Espartero, as captain general of Cuba was seen as an attempt to ease the political tension with Britain and implement the antislavery treaty of 1835. The selection of Valdés was the political response of the Spanish government to the complex situation created by the appointment of Turnbull and, more generally, by the new diplomatic strategy defined by Palmerston in 1836.[106]

In the years following his arrival in Cuba, Valdés was committed to the scrupulous observance of the existing anti–slave trade legislation. He conceded to the slave traders "a six-month period to end the illegal slave traffic," after which he consistently opposed the introduction of new enslaved Africans and freed those captured.[107] In December 1841 Valdés reported to Madrid that he had liberated seventy-eight individuals that year, and his stance persisted in 1842.[108] That year the number of enslaved Africans introduced into Cuba was three times lower than the year before, and the lowest since 1823.[109] However, the new political attitude on the Spanish side did not lead to an improvement in the relationship between the new captain general and the British consul.

Turnbull's political activity in Cuba was not limited to the persecution of the slave trade and the protection of the *emancipados* but was also strongly committed to the promotion of abolitionist ideas and ultimately to the eradication of slavery on the island. To this end he started an energetic informal campaign, meeting important personalities within the Creole elite, such as Domingo del Monte, as well as free Black Cubans and slaves.[110] His main purpose was to identify common goals that would bring together the interests of the Black population and some young Creoles who advocated the extension of civil rights and political freedoms. Turnbull, however, as has been shown, failed to achieve his objective, and the aspirations of both groups remained irreconcilable.

The relationships between Turnbull and other members of the British mission in Havana were also prone to conflict, no more so than with James Kennedy, who was accused by Turnbull of keeping enslaved Africans.[111] "Turnbull's abrasive approach," as described by Murray, caused a serious confrontation with Kennedy, who called for a more constructive relationship with the Spanish authorities, and made an effective collaboration between the consul and the commissioner impossible.[112] The charges and countercharges volleyed between the two officials "provided ammunition for what became a Spanish campaign against Turnbull."[113] But it also reinforced the notion, widespread among the Spanish authorities and landowners, that they were the victims of Britain's arbitrary radicalism. Kennedy's approach proved more effective in the long term, becoming a "bitter opponent" of the repressive policies of the Spanish colonial authorities from the 1830s, as Manuel Barcia has suggested.[114]

Turnbull's public calls for the abolition of slavery also distanced him from those within the Cuban colonial elite with whom he agreed on the necessity of stopping the slave trade, like Saco or Del Monte, but who thought slavery essential for the prosperity of the island. His radical abolitionist position bred further anti-British sentiment among the planters, for whom Turnbull's informal activities were placing at risk the security of the white population. This Anglophobia opened the door to a more positive representation of the United States and encouraged annexationist aspirations. In March 1841 Gaspar Betancourt Cisneros, who later became a passionate annexationist, advised his friend Domingo del Monte not to collaborate with the "sinister designs" of the British, in reference to Turnbull's antislavery activities.[115]

The informal negotiations of the British consul were viewed by the Spanish authorities as illegal and a threat to Cuba's safety and security, and gradually led to a generalized feeling of fear, "verging at times on hysteria."[116] In July 1841 the Spanish government informed the British ambassador in Madrid that "the government knows that these [abolitionist] ideas have gained some ground, thanks to the constancy with which the secret agents in charge of promoting the revolution have been working for many years."[117] In November, Valdés informed the Spanish government of the fears that Cuban landowners had about Turnbull's activities, the spread of abolitionist ideas, and the way in which Spanish newspapers openly discussed slavery. He proposed the transfer of Havana's Mixed Commission Court to Puerto Rico and the removal of Turnbull from Cuba.[118]

The resignation of the British prime minister—William Lamb, Lord Melbourne—and his cabinet led to the replacement of Palmerston by George Hamilton-Gordon, 4th Earl of Aberdeen, as new foreign secretary, in September 1841. Aberdeen was appalled at the aggressive Atlantic policies that had resulted from the Palmerston Act of 1839 and was determined to improve diplomatic relations with Spain, to which Turnbull was the principal obstacle.[119] The initial commitment of Valdés against the slave trade gave the Spanish government solid ground to denounce the activities of the British consul as illegal and contrary to the international agreements signed by both states. In February 1842 Turnbull was removed as British consul but kept his position as superintendent of liberated Africans. This decision was received with disappointment by the Spanish authorities, who continued to argue for his complete removal from Cuba. Turnbull eventually left the Spanish colony in August 1842, following Aberdeen's decision to abolish his remaining office.[120]

Turnbull's ideological and political legacy in Cuba's collective memory is remarkable. As the key actor in Palmerston's diplomatic strategy to hold the Spanish authorities' feet to the fire until the end of the trade in Cuba, Turnbull caused unprecedented political tension between the colonial authorities and the British mission in Havana. The Spanish government's decision to appoint Valdés and to adopt a truly anti–slave trade policy was directly influenced by Turnbull's appointment. However, in the long run, the work of the British consul consolidated an anti-British sentiment among the Cuban colonial elite that reinforced the victimization discourse of the Spanish authorities. As Murray has rightly argued, "the panic engendered in Cuba in 1841 bedeviled future British attempts to suppress the Cuban slave trade."[121] Turnbull's activism and passion are undoubtedly admirable, but his "abrasive approach" ultimately failed to achieve its main goal, helped to justify the militarization of Cuba's public life and the authoritarian practices of future captains general, and therefore hampered the diplomatic work of his colleagues on the island.

JERONIMO VALDÉS: FROM "FULFILLING HIS DUTY" TO THE ESCALERA CONSPIRACY

Captain General Valdés's political commitment against the slave trade during the first years of his mandate gave the Spanish government an unprecedented moral high ground from which to question Turnbull's activities with the British Foreign Office. However, Valdés also faced a great deal of opposition to his political activity. Slave owners and political authorities in the peninsula argued in concert against Valdés's anti–slave trade policies. Some Spanish *diputaciones* (regional administrations), headed by the Diputación of Santander, accused

Valdés of being manipulated by "agents of a foreign nation" and adopting "the unfair and unwise demands advanced by those who desire the ruin of those precious dominions."[122] Valdés responded to these accusations by arguing that he was simply "fulfilling his duty" and that no one should request that he violate the law.[123] He stressed that the slave trade "that was done here in violation of the treaties was so poorly hidden, that in the very entrances of this capital [Havana] barracks destined to the sale of human flesh are located for all to see."[124] The Spanish government backed Valdés's initial anti–slave trade zeal and commended that he had "acted with the determination and energy" asked of him by the crown.[125]

Valdés's political legacy in Cuba is seen in the colonial government's increasing interventions into the island's public life, the colony's gradual militarization, and his unprecedented commitment to stopping the slave trade and the promotion of better living conditions for the slave population. He strongly defended the government's censorship of the press and the control of every cultural, political, and educational institution in order to prevent the circulation of ideas that could represent a threat to "the security and tranquility of the country."[126] During the first year of his tenure, Valdés sent a questionnaire to some of the island's most influential planters requesting information regarding the life and working conditions of their enslaved Africans. Valdés's "questionnaire was not well-received by many planters, who once again complained that a new set of regulations would entitle slaves to rights that they would later want to exercise."[127] Sebastián de Lasa, José María de Jesús de Herrera, José Manuel Carrillo, Wenceslao de Villaurrutia, and Domingo Aldama, among others, opposed "any direct intervention of the government" that could undermine their authority and raise the aspirations of the enslaved Africans.[128]

Valdés, however, dismissed their claims and, in November 1842, published a new version of the *Código negro* (Black Code), with which he intended to improve the conditions of the slave population with the twin goal of increasing the reproductive rate and discouraging slave revolts.[129] According to Valdés, the abuses of some slave owners went "against the reproduction of the serf and [had] increased the need for new slaves, perpetuating the illicit trade in human flesh."[130] In other words, consolidating the current slave population and promoting their natural reproduction would eventually render the slave trade unnecessary. As Barcia has concluded, "the planters' premonitions and fears were proved right," and just after the promulgation of the "Black Code," "several slave uprisings broke out in the western part of the island, culminating in the discovery of an extensive conspiracy in December 1843."[131]

During the first months of his mandate, Valdés developed a truly committed anti–slave trade policy to duly comply with the agreements arrived at with

Britain. Despite this, the actual prosecution of the slave trade did not constitute a top priority for his administration. As Jennifer Nelson has rightly argued, "it was unclear to the British whether he was genuinely against the slave trade, or willing to make concessions through anti–slave trade activity to protect against British intervention viewed as overzealous."[132] Valdés never articulated humanitarian grounds for the abolition of the slave trade, confining his nonetheless real commitment to a matter of public duty. As he admitted in 1849, he was aware of more slave ship arrivals than the British commissioners reported to him, but that never constituted a priority for him.[133] However, this does not alter the fact that, relative to three years prior to Valdés's arrival, the number of enslaved Africans introduced into Cuba was reduced by approximately 45 percent, and around 1,215 liberated Africans were issued their final letters of emancipation, "which was quite substantial in comparison to the 1,367 freed in the preceding 15 years."[134]

Valdés's policies did not develop in isolation. It can be argued that the Palmerston Act of 1839 and the intensification of British naval action against the slave traders on the African coasts drastically stemmed the flow of enslaved Africans trafficked to Cuba. But it is undeniable that, at least for a few months in 1841, the captain general of Cuba worked earnestly to stymie the slave trade and comply with the agreements Spain had reached. For the first time, it became clear to slave traders and their financiers on each side of the Atlantic that the Spanish authorities were no longer turning a blind eye to their operations.[135] However, this genuine fervor on the part of Valdés did not last long, and by October 1841, British commissioners reported that their hopes in Valdés had vanished, and that he had caved to bribery.[136]

In March 1843 enslaved Africans from the plantation Alcancía, in the region of Bemba, revolted and marched through the Camino Real after killing a group of white people. Some months later, in November 1843, "the biggest slave revolt ever seen on the Island" took place on the plantations of Triumvirato and Ácana (Matanzas), the so-called Escalera Conspiracy.[137] In December, the arrested enslaved Africans were brutally tortured and questioned by the colonial authorities, who discovered that they were faced with the "biggest conspiracy in the history of Cuba," in which "black, mixed race and white, men and women, slaves and free people" were involved.[138] The reaction of the colonial authorities was ferocious.

In Manuel Barcia's words, "the subsequent repression of free colored people and slaves who were involved in the plot was the bloodiest episode in nineteenth-century Cuba until the first war of independence in 1868."[139] Hundreds of enslaved Africans and free Black people were detained, tortured, and killed. In March 1844 the attorneys of the Cuban Military Commission also started arresting white and foreign people accused of involvement in the conspiracy.[140] In April 1844 the captain general ordered the expulsion of all foreign free Black subjects from Cuba, and in June the mixed-race poet Gabriel de la Concepción Valdés, better known as Plácido, was executed, accused of being a leader of the conspiracy.[141] In his death sentence, published in the *Diario de la Habana*, the judges linked the conspiracy with the activities of Turnbull and the British diplomats, and pointed out that "by himself or with others of his colleagues, he was the one who conceived the destructive idea."[142]

These accusations, together with the arbitrary arrest of British subjects and the expulsion of all foreign free Black people, led to unparalleled tension between the captain general and Britain's diplomats in Havana, now led by Joseph T. Crawford, successor of Turnbull. Contrary to Turnbull, Crawford pursued a very efficient strategy focused, during the repression that followed the Escalera Conspiracy, on protecting his fellow subjects and protesting against the authoritarian practices of the Spanish administration. According to Barcia, both Crawford and Kennedy "were the firmest critics of O'Donnell's repressive policies[, and] they questioned their decisions in a brave and almost reckless manner."[143]

Nevertheless, the impact of the Escalera Conspiracy goes beyond the violent repression employed by the colonial authorities. It also had an extraordinary and long-lasting ideological effect on Cuba's population. For many whites on the island, the conspiracy proved the fragility of their security and reinvigorated their oldest fear of "a second Haiti." Self-victimizing, anti-British, and racist discourses found confirmation in the conspiracy. It uncovered "the narrowness and racism inherent in the Creole definition of political liberty," as Murray put it, and significantly contributed to justifying and enhancing authoritarian practices on the part of the colonial authorities, and the restriction of civil rights.[144]

The rise and fall of Valdés was linked to the tenure of General Espartero. In July 1843 the regent was forced into exile in London by the military uprising of General Ramón María Narváez (1800–1868). The new Moderate government dictated the demotion of Valdés in September of that year and decreed the appointment of Leopoldo O'Donnell.[145] The new captain general protected the slave trade during his tenure and surrounded himself with some of the richest and most important slave traders on the island. O'Donnell, who openly believed "that the slave trade was vital" for Cuba's prosperity, "was more known as an accomplice than as an opponent of the traffic."[146] Together with the reinstatement of the Count of Villanueva as the intendant of the Treasury of Cuba, the two most important authorities on the island were now open supporters of the slave trade.

During the tenure of Valdés, British attempts to persuade the Spanish government to pass new legislation in accordance with the Treaty of 1835 had been consistently rebuffed. However, in the aftermath of the Escalera Conspiracy, the British government aimed to capitalize on the Cuban colonial elite's fear and demanded from the Spanish authorities new legal instruments to halt the trade. The appointment of O'Donnell, his overt support for the slave trade, and the political repression carried out on his orders in the aftermath of the conspiracy, exasperated Aberdeen, the new British foreign secretary, and led him to demand "in every proper manner" the removal of O'Donnell.[147] Aberdeen instructed the British ambassador in Madrid, Henry Bulwer, to insinuate to the Spanish authorities that Britain was ready to break diplomatic relations with Spain if O'Donnell remained in post: "I really can see no other result if they should preserve in maintaining O'Donnell at Havana. Let them make him Captain-General of Madrid or anything they please; but let them only send a man who is determined to execute the Treaty [of 1835], and who is able to resist the bribes of the slave dealers."[148]

British diplomatic pressure failed to achieve O'Donnell's removal, as he had the support of the Spanish regent and the newly appointed Spanish minister of foreign affairs, Francisco Martínez de la Rosa. Aberdeen's pressure, however, was not totally ineffective, and the Spanish government acceded to the negotiation of a new penal law for the suppression of the slave trade. This "face-saving compromise for both countries" provided a solution to the diplomatic crisis and allowed Aberdeen to show some progress in negotiations with Spain to his own public.[149]

Martínez de la Rosa presented to the Spanish Cortes a draft bill on December 22, 1844, based on the recommendations made by a commission headed by former captain general Jerónimo Valdés. The bill aimed "to radically stop the introduction of slaves" into the Spanish colonies, protect the property rights of the slave owners and reassure the slave owners of Cuba against "new threats and disturbances."[150] The draft law proposed a maximum of six to eight years of imprisonment, fines, and exile for senior officers, owners, and investors involved in the illegal introduction of enslaved Africans into the Spanish colonies. The rest of the crew would be subjected to half of this punishment. The draft bill also determined the destruction of condemned vessels, and specific punishments to be applied if the enslaved persons had been tortured during the voyage, and gave the Spanish authorities the right to intervene in the event they suspected a slave landing or the departure of a slave expedition.[151]

For Martínez de la Rosa, speaking on behalf of the government, the continuity of slavery was unquestionable, "because this issue is on fire and no one would dare to touch it, much less the government." He stated that stopping the slave trade was the best way "to appease" the people in Cuba and "to protect the right of property over slaves that currently exists.[152]

Opposition to the penal law proposal was headed by the deputy from Cadiz, Francisco Javier Istúriz, who argued that it would have disastrous economic consequences for his region and would ultimately lead to the abolition of slavery and the loss of the colonies. Cadiz was part of the trading network between Havana and some key peninsular ports, and the wealth of the Spanish Iberian market rested upon the economic stability of Cuba's.[153] Istúriz proclaimed that "the prosperity of the Island of Cuba . . . is solely the result of the work of the Negroes" and that, if the bill were passed, "the region of Cadiz, and particularly the city of Cadiz, would suffer a lot."[154] He demanded that the government "find a way of reconciling [humanitarian] principles with the salvation of the Antilles."[155] Istúriz concluded that the abolition of the slave trade could not be separated from the abolition of slavery, and the first event would "irretrievably" lead to the second.[156]

This rehashing of pro–slave trade discourse in the Spanish Cortes left a big impact on the *Times* correspondent in Madrid, who described it as "intolerable [and . . .] even disgusting to hear men who talk so glibly and so fluently of the oppression under which they themselves groan, attempt to resist the effort now made to put a stop to the abominable traffic in human beings."[157] During parliamentary discussions of the draft bill, two amendments were accepted against the wishes of the government. These changes in many ways "nullified its effect," as Murray has argued.[158] The first amendment limited the investigative capacity of Spanish officials to occasions when the suspected slave expedition had come directly from Africa, while the second prohibited the colonial authorities from inspecting the plantations and therefore precluded the possibility of investigating the origin of any slave who was already on the island.

The Spanish Cortes passed the Penal Law on February 27, 1845. The new law failed to stop the slave trade into Cuba, and after its adoption more than 180,000 enslaved Africans would be illegally introduced to the island in violation of Spain's international treaties with Britain.[159] The Penal Law would also be used from this point forward as "unequivocal proof" of the Spanish government's commitment to ending the slave trade, and the strongest shield against British diplomatic pressure for more effective measures.

CONCLUSIONS

The constitutional debates of 1836 and 1837 represent a milestone in the way Spanish Liberal parties reflected on how the remaining colonial territories of a collapsing empire should be ruled. The consolidation of political liberalism and the reestablishment of representative institutions in Spain were not linked to the eradication of the slave trade or to the strengthening of abolitionist ideas and discourses. On the contrary, key Liberal ideologues, such as Argüelles, started developing a perspective that contemplated the slave trade and slavery as a "necessary evil" in order to maintain Spanish imperial control of Cuba.

This chapter has also considered the importance of a new racist construction of anti–slave trade discourses, set in motion by José Antonio Saco, who authored the most influential abolitionist ideas produced in Cuba until the 1860s. However, Saco's racist abolitionism failed to persuade many of his own compatriots. Spanish and Cuban political elites remained convinced of the need to protect, in one way or another, the slave trade and slavery on the island. The political and military repression following the conspiracy of La Escalera, and the sea change in British Atlantic policy after the Palmerston Act of 1839, together made many fearful and, undoubtedly, darkened the tone of the debate, but pro–slave trade discourse continued to bear fruit in this period and beyond. Far from producing a structural change, these episodes of the first half of the 1840s had only limited and quite temporary consequences.

Finally, this chapter has analyzed the impact of the British government´s new "abrasive approach" with regard to the Spanish slave trade and the role that Madden, Turnbull, and the BFASS played until the publication of the Penal Law of 1845. This strategy of escalation had the inverse effect. Far from achieving the demise of the slave trade, it invigorated the self-victimization discourse perpetuated by the Spanish authorities to sanction their inaction. The deepening of anti-British sentiment ultimately consolidated the institution of the slave trade by further elevating the matter to one of national sovereignty and security.

5

The End of the Slave Trade
in the Spanish Empire

Horrible slavery! . . . Who in righteous anger does
not burn? / Who, heartbroken, does not groan / and
to God and the world cry for their help?
—Concepción Arenal, 1866

The end of the slave trade had been regarded for decades as inevitable.[1] The political efforts of slave owners, abolitionists, and authorities
had concentrated on the question of just how long the trade could persist,
rather than contestation of whether it could be tolerated indefinitely. In the
two decades leading up to the 1860s, the forces opposed to abolitionism had
profited from a general atrophy in this debate, and as such the Spanish slave
trade of the late 1850s was as profitable and dynamic as ever before. There
was little hope in the abolitionist camp of seeing a sudden end to the "odious
commerce."

This chapter traces the impact of US annexationism with regard to Cuba in
the debates on the continuity of the slave trade and the construction of Spain's
"balancing-act strategy," by which the Spanish authorities managed to disregard British demands for more effective legislation against the slave trade and
simultaneously succeeded in persuading London against the pursuit of unilateral action. This chapter also tackles how "national dignity" and a "sense of
honor" characterized a new phase in the anti–slave trade discourse that operated within the Spanish colonial administration during the 1850s and 1860s.
Finally, this chapter charts the international and domestic factors leading to
the end of the slave trade and how the Spanish political actors reassessed their
position and built a new narrative that stressed the need for change in order
to preserve what was left of a decaying empire.

"Cuba Is Everything": US Annexationism and Spain's "Balancing-Act Strategy"

Until 1865 the Penal Law for the Repression of the Slave Trade of 1845 provided the only legal instrument with which the Spanish authorities could contest the operation of the trade. Article 9 of the law, which prohibited the colonial authorities from inspecting the plantations, severely blunted the instrument, making it fundamentally ineffective. By restricting the power of the Spanish authorities of searching the plantations and identifying recently introduced slaves, the law virtually legalized the status of all slaves as soon as they had set a foot on a plantation, no matter how or when these people had been introduced to the island.[2]

The 1845 law also played a central role in the political strategy followed by Spanish governments for preventing Britain from adopting unilateral measures against the slave trade into Cuba. In the context of the growing resonance in the Spanish colony of the notion of absorption by the United States, the Penal Law represented for the Spanish authorities the "unquestionable" Spanish commitment to ending the slave traffic. In this sense it operated as a powerful argument against any possible "warlike" actions by the British government, similar to the Palmerston Act of 1839 against the Portuguese slave trade or the military pressure mounted against the Brazilian traffic in 1850.[3]

Initially, however, the Spanish government was truly concerned only with the negative effect that the implementation of the Penal Law could have on Cuba's economic prosperity and social stability. According to the Spanish cabinet, by no means should the new legislation produce any actual discomfort to the Cuban planters or cause a decline in sugar production on the island.[4] To measure the possible impact of the law and suggest solutions to the lack of a workforce in Cuba, the Spanish government appointed a commission of experts in 1846, which included former captain generals Jerónimo Valdés and Joaquín Ezpeleta.[5] The conclusions of the commission insisted on the malign nature of British diplomatic pressure against Spain and affirmed the special circumstances of Cuba's economy with reference to conditions in the United States and Brazil. The commissioners agreed with Captain General O'Donnell about the disastrous consequences that ending the slave trade into Cuba would have for the island's economy and unashamedly suggested that "if some slaves were introduced there would be a hidden relief of the fear that now afflicts Cuba."[6] The commission also prioritized the importance of introducing new free workers from China to compensate for the shortage of labor in the growing economy, and the importance of maintaining a minimum ratio of four white people to every six Black people, in order to make more difficult any slave revolts.[7] To achieve this they advocated either expulsion from the island or forced labor on the plantations for every free Black worker under the age of fifty.[8]

The conclusions of the commission provided a timely reminder of the continued pervasiveness of anti-British sentiment and the "necessary evil" discourse within the upper echelons of the Spanish administration. Moreover, it evidences the lack of any real commitment toward the even and effective implementation of the Penal Law of 1845. This was also confirmed by the Spanish intention to introduce enslaved Africans from other American territories, such as Brazil, a conceit made possible through an extremely lax interpretation of the Treaty of 1835, and the Penal Law itself.

According to the Spanish authorities, this legislation would be understood as referring only to the slave trade from Africa, and therefore the transportation of slaves from other territories, like Brazil, would be legally acceptable. The response of the British government was immediate and, as to be expected, emphatically against the Spanish position. London argued that Spain had agreed to stop the slave trade worldwide and that this was incompatible with setting up new regional routes of traffic. Spanish and British diplomats fervently debated this issue between 1847 and 1848, when Spain severed diplomatic relations with Britain.[9]

The outbreak of the French Revolution of 1848 was watched with great concern by the government of General Ramón María Narváez, who had been appointed president of the Council of Ministers for the second time, in October 1847. Between March and October, revolutionary riots in Spain were brutally repressed by the authorities in Madrid, Barcelona, Valencia, and Seville. Simultaneously, in June 1848, Ramon Cabrera, the leader of the Carlist faction, entered Catalonia with the intention of reorganizing the Carlist forces for the conflict that would become known as the Second Carlist War (1846–1849). The government accused Britain of giving support to the Carlists and broke off diplomatic relations with London.[10]

Relations were not normalized until 1851, and in this three-year period, Federico Roncali, Count of Alcoy (1809–1857), who had been appointed captain general of Cuba in February 1848, rejected all claims from the British authorities with regard to the slave trade; the new controversy concerning the introduction of slaves from other territories remained unresolved until relations were reestablished. Between 1850 and 1851, while the diplomatic tension between Spain and Britain was ongoing, the British Foreign Office adopted a new diplomatic and military strategy against the Brazilian slave trade that would have important repercussions in the Spanish Empire.[11]

Palmerston's second term as the head of the Foreign Office, beginning in

1846, saw the diplomatic trouble between Brazil and Britain reach "a new level" of severity, as Leonardo Marques put it.[12] On April 22, 1850, Britain adopted a new, stronger interpretation of the anti–slave trade Aberdeen Act of 1845. This legislation authorized the British navy to search and capture any slave trade vessels under the Brazilian flag or without any nationality, but, for the first time, the Foreign Office advised the Admiralty that these laws allowed for no restriction in terms of where these actions could take place and therefore authorized the British naval forces to operate "within the Brazilian waters as well as on the high seas."[13] This apparently minor change in the British interpretation of the law "had far reaching consequences which at the time were perhaps not entirely foreseen."[14]

Exactly two months later, on June 22, the British government ordered its warships to enter Brazilian territorial waters and ports to seize any vessels suspected of being involved in the slave trade. This unprecedented decision, more aggressive than any previous action against Brazilian territorial sovereignty, forced the Brazilian government to propose to the Chamber of Deputies a new anti–slave trade law, which would eventually be passed on August 13. Under this new legislation, the Brazilian government deployed all its military and police capacity against the slave traders and its supporters.[15] After the passage of this law, "slave traders operating in Brazil did not abandon the business immediately," expecting the trade to restart, as Marques has shown.[16] Contrary to what the Brazilian government had expected, the British government maintained its "warlike acts," as described by the Brazilian minister of foreign affairs, Paulino Soares de Sousa (1808–1866), until 1852, by which point the slave trade had virtually ceased in Brazil.[17]

In the wake of the end of the Brazilian slave trade, some prominent traffickers from West Central Africa immigrated to New York, "heralding a new era" in the history of the slave trade "dominated by the United States, West Central Africa and Cuba," as John Harris has shown.[18] As they had in 1835, slave traders adapted to the new reality by tailoring "their investment patterns . . . to limit risk" in an increasingly hostile commercial environment for slave traffickers. Merchants, slave owners and investors from Cuba, West Central Africa, and New York "reached across the Atlantic World, forging alliances, pooling capital and attempting to counter the risks from suppression."[19]

The Brazilian government tried to present the eradication of the slave trade as the result "solely and exclusively" of its own commitment—stating that Brazil could no longer, according to Paulino, "resist the pressure of the ideas of the age in which we live."[20] For the British authorities, however, "nothing would or could have been done by the Brazilian government alone."[21] As Bethell has concluded, both sides claimed credit for putting an end to the slave trade in Brazil, and both "exaggerated the extent of their own responsibility."[22]

For Palmerston, British "gunboat diplomacy" had achieved in a few months what forty years of diplomatic negotiations had not. According to the British foreign secretary, "persuasion seldom succeeds unless there is [behind it] compulsion of some sort."[23] Palmerston was willing to direct this more aggressive form of strategy toward Spain, and, as soon as diplomatic relations were reestablished in 1851, he sent an ultimatum to the Spanish government demanding "a faithful and honourable fulfilment of the Treaty engagements" and stating that they would be solely responsible for "any consequences which may arise from a longer continuance of the breach of faith in this respect."[24] The foreign secretary made clear that "Great Britain will no longer consent to be baffled in regard to the Spanish slave trade as it has hitherto been" and accused the Spanish authorities in Cuba of "systematically and notoriously [. . . violating the] stipulations of the Treaty and . . . the enactments of law."[25] Palmerston concluded that "this system of evasion should cease."[26] The British government thus sharpened its tone, emboldened by its success in Brazil, but there were still two main obstacles that played to the advantage of Spain's "balancing-act strategy": the notion that Spain was not comparable to a "second-class" government like Brazil and the rise of US annexationism in Cuba and Puerto Rico.

For the British, Brazil, Portugal, and the Spanish American republics, among others, were "half civilized governments," a second-class type of nations against which the British Empire could interfere in its own interest.[27] Palmerston believed that these governments "require a dressing down every eight or ten years to keep them in order," as "they care little for words and they must not only see the stick but actually feel it on their shoulders."[28] Therefore, the general interest of ending the slave trade justified a certain degree of violence in the eyes of the foreign secretary. This stark display of "legal imperialism," to again use Richard Huzzey's term, operated in a less audacious way in the case of Spain.[29] Although its military capacity and political influence had dramatically decreased during the first half of the nineteenth century, the Spanish Empire was still perceived as a "civilized government," and a military intervention against it, like the one against Brazil in 1850, was inconceivable. The activities of David Turnbull and the episode of the HMS *Romney* in Cuba were as far as the British government could go without openly declaring war on Spain.

The second reason for the British government's avoidance of a more aggressive approach against Spain was the rise of US expansionism and Cuban annexationism.[30] Palmerston believed, as did many others in Britain, in the inevitability of American Manifest Destiny, or, as he put it in 1857, that "the

Anglo-Saxon Race will in process of time become the masters of the whole American continent, North and South, by the reason of their superior qualities as compared with the degenerate Spanish and Portuguese Americans."[31]

However, Palmerston also believed that it was Britain's duty "to delay [such a result] as long as possible."[32] By 1850 British aggressive intervention in Cuba could lead to Cuba's independence, or even worse in the eyes of Britain, to "the American annexation of the island."[33] This climate of increasing international tension fundamentally contributed to the success of Spain's political strategy to protect the slave trade, a situation that would change only with the outbreak of the US Civil War in 1861 and the beginning of the second government of the Unión Liberal in Spain in 1863.

The interest of the United States in acquiring Cuba was historical. "A presumption of ownership" over Cuba, as Lars Schoultz put it, had characterized the US approach since John Quincy Adams stated that Cuba and Puerto Rico were "natural appendages to the North American continent" and that "annexation of Cuba to our federal republic will be indispensable to the continuance and integrity of the Union itself."[34] Thomas Jefferson stated in 1809, in the context of Napoleon's invasion of Spain, that France would accept the US annexation of Cuba "to prevent our [US] aid to Mexico and the other provinces," and that the United States should "immediately erect a column on the Southernmost limit of Cuba and inscribe on it a 'Ne plus ultra' as to us in that direction."[35] In 1822 Jefferson suggested that Cuba's "addition to our confederacy is exactly what is wanting to round our power as a nation," but—as mentioned—in 1825 the British government had sued successfully for an international agreement between the United States, France, and Britain to mutually guarantee that none of them would invade Cuba.[36] Expansionism, however, continued to be a major driving force of American foreign policy, and in 1848, following the United States' victory against Mexico, President James K. Polk formally presented to Spain an offer of one hundred million dollars for the purchase of Cuba. The offer was rejected by Spain; Cuba was worth far more as its core colonial territory.[37] However, the offer of a price for annexation was not without precedent on the part of the United States, which in 1803 had acquired the Louisiana Territory (828,000 square miles) from France, while in 1819 Spain itself had ceded Florida to the United States through the Adams–Onís Treaty.

In the summer of 1848, Narciso López (1796–1851) led the annexationist conspiracy of La Mina Rosa Cubana, in the region of Manicaragua.[38] The plot was dismantled by the Spanish authorities in July 1848, but López managed to escape to New York, before settling in New Orleans. Between July and August 1849, the US government gave support to the first unsuccessful military expedition of López in his attempt to free Cuba from Spain, but the newly elected US president, Zachary Taylor, oriented the country's expansionist policies away from the island and refused to provide further support to López during Taylor's federal administration.[39] In 1850, however, López attempted a second expedition with the support of the governor of Mississippi, John A. Quitman, and six hundred German and Hungarian mercenaries from the states of Louisiana and Mississippi. This second attempt was also repelled by the Spanish colonial authorities, and López escaped to the United States once again. Then, in 1851, he coordinated a third attempt with the support of 420 volunteers under the command of William J. Crittenden, nephew of the then-incumbent president Millard Fillmore, Taylor's successor. This expedition also failed. Third time unlucky, López was captured, sentenced to death, and publicly executed in Havana on August 31, 1851.[40]

Under the presidency of Franklin Pierce (1853–1857), a pro-South Democrat, expansionist voices again called for the acquisition of Cuba as a new slave state for the Union. The appointment of Pierre Soulé (1801–1870), a pro-southern and proslavery politician, as the US ambassador in Madrid, was interpreted as Pierce showing his strong commitment to Cuba's annexation.[41] Soulé was born in France, the son of one of Napoleon's generals. Jailed during the Restoration for his radical politics, he immigrated to the United States, arriving in New Orleans in 1826. Starting virtually penniless, he quickly built a career in the Democratic Party, filling a vacancy as senator for Louisiana in 1847, and then serving a term from 1849 to 1853, before President Pierce appointed him ambassador to Madrid. A consistent advocate of freedom for the peoples of Europe, Soulé was also an ardent expansionist with a particular interest in the acquisition of Cuba. In Madrid his primary goal was to find a way to make Cuba American.[42]

In 1854 Secretary of State William Marcy authorized Soulé and the US ambassadors in Great Britain and France, James Buchanan and John Y. Mason, to draft a strategy to purchase Cuba from Spain. The ambassadors met secretly at the Belgian city of Ostend and wrote what was later named the Ostend Manifesto of 1854. They declared that "Cuba is as necessary to the North American Republic as any of its present members, and that it belongs naturally to that great family of states of which the Union is the Providential Nursery," and urged an American intervention to stop what they believed would be an imminent slave insurrection that could "spread like wildfire" to the southern United States: "We should, however, be recreant to our duty, be unworthy of our gallant forefathers, and commit base treason against our posterity, should we permit Cuba to be Africanized and become a second St. Domingo, with all its attendant horrors to the white race, and suffer the flames to extend to our own neighboring shores, seriously to endanger or actually to consume the fair fabric of our Union."[43]

The document was sent to Washington in October 1854, arguing for the American purchase of Cuba from Spain and that the United States "shall be justified in wresting it from Spain" if the purchase was again denied.[44] Against the will of Pierce's administration, the minutes of the meeting were leaked to the press, and four months later the opposition to the president in the House of Representatives forced the American government to publish the document in full.[45] The manifesto was strongly criticized. On the one hand, the northern antislavery opposition saw it as an attempt to extend slavery in the United States. On the other, the Spanish, British, and French governments presented the document as a threat to Spain's national sovereignty.[46] The disclosure of the Ostend Manifesto debilitated the US expansionist project and reinforced the narrative of self-victimization adopted by Spain in its dealings with Britain.

The expression of expansionist sentiment in the United States found a parallel response from Cuban intellectuals who developed an annexationist strategy both on the island and in the United States.[47] As Leonardo Marques has argued, "many Cuban Creoles saw annexation to the United States as the best way to keep slavery alive" and provided support to Narciso López's expeditions.[48] Annexationists, as Chaffin has rightly argued, "called themselves soldiers of liberty and republicanism, yet they had no intension of extending liberties to Cuba's 436,000 enslaved blacks."[49]

In December 1847 the Count of Alcoy reported to Madrid that "inside the Island of Cuba some bad Spaniards join their efforts and their intrigues to the efforts and intrigues of the foreigners, to snatch the Island from their metropolis."[50] The Count of Alcoy characterized annexationist ambitions as "a false liberalism" that wrongly proclaims: "Cubans [live] oppressed under a despotic yoke, exposed in their businesses and properties to all the arbitrariness of absolute power, and overwhelmed by hateful taxes that have no other goal than to enrich their masters. [The Cuban people] look forward to the day when the Republic of the Union has to open its arms, inviting them to take a seat among the peoples of the American Confederation."[51]

This group of "bad Spaniards" had the support of an important community of Cuban exiles living in New York, New Orleans, and Florida. Gaspar Betancourt Cisneros, José Aniceto Iznaga, Cristóbal Madán, Domingo Goicuría, and the Count of Pozos Dulces, among others, organized political opposition to the Spanish control of Cuba and actively defined and promoted annexationist discourse. Since its first manifestations at the beginning of the 1840s, the advocates of annexation generally argued in favor of slavery in Cuba.[52] Fully convinced that Britain would eventually force Spain to liberate all the slaves illegally introduced to the island after 1820, Betancourt Cisneros told José Antonio Saco that "the annexationist revolution was indispensable to save us."[53] Saco, who was living in exile in France at that time, responded that the desire for annexation was the result of the "weakness" of Cuban planters, who, "unable to resist the seductive temptation to buy Negroes . . . and to avoid the claims of England, seek the opportunity to break their oaths and covered with the American flag, . . . surrender without scruples and with debauchery to the traffic of human flesh."[54]

In January 1848 a group of annexationists linked to Betancourt Cisneros founded in New York the newspaper *La Verdad* as the main propagandistic platform for disseminating their political agenda.[55] In their pages they advocated annexation to the United States as the best and only viable way to protect slavery from the machinations of the British, who promoted "the freedom of all slaves and *emancipados*."[56] The newspaper was embroiled in a public controversy with José Antonio Saco, for whom the preservation of slavery on the island was also indispensable, but who believed that the annexationists were putting Cuba's safety and prosperity at risk. He argued that an annexationist revolution would be followed by a general slave revolt. In 1848 Saco published *Ideas sobre la incorporación de Cuba a Estados Unidos*, in which he appealed to Cubans' national pride and the fear of a massive slave uprising to reject the case for annexation by the United States: "Once the war begins, . . . either of the two sides if they feel the need to, but above all the Spaniards, will they not call our most formidable enemy to their aid? Will they not raise the magical cry of freedom and reinforce their legions with our own slaves? Even if none of the two belligerent parties called for such dangerous support, they [the slaves] will not remain calm. . . . The day the thunder of the cannon separates them, that day the horrors of Santo Domingo could be repeated in Cuba.[57] Saco argued that, with the outbreak of war, the slaves would have the support of "the abolitionist groups, which will not miss the precious occasion" to put an end to slavery in Cuba. Saco believed that sparking a revolution against the Spanish authorities would have unpredictable and tragic results for the white population of the island.[58]

The annexationists responded to Saco in the pages of *La Verdad* in June 1851. They argued that the preservation of slavery and the avoidance of a general slave revolt were a priority for the annexationist movement and that the Spanish authorities, even in the context of war, would never instigate a slave revolt, because "although some *peninsulares* and part of the army are enemies of the annexation, they are not of the race to which they belong and they would never lend to the Negroes such criminal and inhumane support."[59] The authors of *La Verdad* concluded that ultimately the revolution would be supported by the United States, which "will embrace the cause" and guarantee "liberty and property" in Cuba.[60] Underlying this debate was the wider question of which "white culture," the Anglo-Saxon or the Latin, was better equipped to rule the island. Saco argued that the Spanish monarchical culture should prevail, while the annexationists believed that the American republican tradition would bring greater prosperity to Cuba.[61]

In spite of these arguments, the failed expeditions of López in 1850 and 1851 proved that the annexationists had grossly overestimated both their support on the island and the reluctance of the US government to break the Neutrality Agreement of 1818 with Spain.[62] The assurances that Narváez's government gave to the Cuban slave owners, and the failure of the French Revolution of 1848, reduced the interest of the Cuban oligarchy in annexation by the United States; however, as Romy Sánchez has concluded, this was "only a temporary appeasement of an explosive situation."[63]

Annexationism played a central role in the successful construction of Spain's rhetoric of victimhood, as it proved in the eyes of the international community how "vulnerable" Spain's sovereignty over the island was, and how "dangerous" any colonial reform would be in such a volatile political context. Spanish officials frequently referred to annexationist fears to confront British demands and diplomatic pressure. In 1858 the first secretary of the Spanish embassy in London, Augusto Conte (1823–1902), wrote to the British government about this.[64] Stressing the difficulties that the Spanish government faced in implementing any reform in Cuba, he argued that "in the case of a colony so close to the United States, the metropolitan government cannot take there certain kind of measures that would produce discontent among its inhabitants."[65] Conte affirmed that, despite the efforts of the Spanish colonial authorities, certain "wealthy and important people had forged a horrific conspiracy for the emancipation of the Island."[66] He also argued that the "fanatic" recent declarations of Lord Brougham and Samuel Wilberforce, Bishop of Oxford, demanding a more aggressive strategy against Spain, would only result in "the United States [becoming] the owners of our colony."[67] Conte concluded his communication expressing the ideological importance that possession of Cuba had for the Spanish collective thinking, and the consequences of adopting a similar approach to the gunship diplomacy used with Brazil: "What is Cuba for Spain? Cuba is everything; it is what remains of the shipwreck of our fortune, it is the future of our trade and navy. . . . Do you want, as a result of pursuing at all costs and suddenly the suppression of the [slave] trade, to terrify the Island of Cuba? It would be the same as setting the Island on fire or abandoning it to the United States."[68]

In conclusion, annexationist and expansionist discourses, together with Spain's international stance, which dissuaded Britain from adopting unilateral measures, significantly contributed to the success of the Spanish strategy of protecting the continuation of the slave trade into Cuba. A careful "balancing act" was performed, based on the false premise that the Spanish authorities were doing everything they could to put an end to the slave trade and were committed to its international obligations. The reality, however, was that the Spanish government consistently avoided the drafting of effective anti–slave trade legislation, instead dedicating great effort to dissuading Britain from adopting a unilateral strategy against the traffic of enslaved Africans into Cuba.

A Matter of "National Dignity": Anti–Slave Trade Policies from Within

In a recent publication, Josep Fradera wondered "what was the real significance of the Spanish abolitionism of the 1850s and 1860s after some decades of silence and conformity?"[69] Fradera argued that, for Granville Sharp and James Stephen in Britain, abolitionism represented "Christian purification"; in France, for Alexis de Tocqueville, it was "a possibility for simultaneous moral and political reform"; and for the Utilitarian School, it constituted "a formula for progress, . . . waged labour and free trade."[70] Abolitionism was for Juan de la Pezuela (1853), José Gutierrez de la Concha (1854–1859), and Francisco Serrano y Domínguez (1859–1862), as captains general of Cuba, an opportunity to vindicate "national dignity" and Spaniards' "honor." They all shaped an anti–slave trade discourse that went beyond the traditional "necessary evil" stance and presented abolitionism as the right thing to do.[71] The translation into political action of these discourses varied significantly: Pezuela implemented an abolitionist agenda in Cuba, while Concha and Serrano continued protecting and promoting the slave trade on the island. However, their position was a novelty, a divergence from the mainstream construction of abolitionist ideas in Spain's empire. These discourses share important similarities with anti–slave trade expressions in Portugal and Brazil, where the alleged need "to salvage national honor" contributed to the development of a successful anti–slave trade narrative in the 1840s and 1850s.[72]

The appointment of Pezuela as captain general of Cuba in 1853 responded, fundamentally, to the Spanish government's decision to promote alternative forms of labor force that would gradually reduce the need for new enslaved Africans in a "slow and safe way," as the Spanish government later put it.[73] As captain general of Puerto Rico between 1848 and 1851, Pezuela had been successful in dealing with slave owners' and planters' demands and avoiding the introduction of new enslaved Africans after the slave trade had been virtually eradicated in this colony from 1842.[74] Certainly, Cuba represented a much more challenging context, considering the structural importance that slavery and the slave trade had on the island. However, during his time as captain general of Cuba, Pezuela issued orders liberating all slaves illegally imported since 1835, allowed marriage between Black women and white men, authorized freedmen to serve in the colonial militia, and threatened anyone suspected of being involved in the slave trade with expulsion from the island.[75]

By the time Pezuela was appointed captain general, the Spanish government, headed by Luis José Sartorius (1820–1871), Count of San Luis, was particularly concerned about the part that Joseph Crawford, the British consul in Havana, was playing in the colony. The Spanish cabinet believed that he had established himself as "an alternative authority to the Captain General with a navy at his service not smaller than ours."[76] The appointment of Pezuela, and the fear among Cuban slave owners that he would implement an anti–slave trade agenda, had the effect of temporarily stimulating the slave trade and provoked the British consul to complain, once again and with much reason, that "the slave trade [in Cuba] flourishes."[77]

The Spanish cabinet perceived that this kind of statement, although perfectly accurate, was damaging the country's international image and believed that the Spanish authorities should be "ready to defend our rights and our dignity. If Spain is afraid it will achieve nothing and will lose her honor."[78] The government ordered more officials and troops to be deployed on the island to suppress any possible slave insurrection and to have all military forces in Cuba ready for all contingencies.[79] The government also suggested the possibility of buying some space in a "respectable French newspaper" to influence the international public opinion and make the case for the Spanish interest.[80]

When Pezuela arrived in Havana, he was received with great skepticism by Cuban planters, slave owners, and bureaucrats.[81] He was an outsider to Cuban society, and, as Cayuela has argued, "he was opposed not only to the slave trade, but also to the institution of slavery."[82] Pezuela considered the eradication of the slave trade to be essential, as, "even if the insolent English try to confuse us all with their violent and exaggerated accusations, they are essentially right in their complaint."[83] Similarly to Valdés in 1841, by acknowledging Spain's responsibility, Pezuela admitted that anti–slave trade policies had been fundamentally insufficient until then. The captain general described a complex network of interests in which everyone on the island was integrated, and he concluded that Spain should take a final decision once and for all: to break the international agreements with Britain and face the consequences or to authorize the inspection of the slave plantations, to effectively fight against—and eradicate—the Spanish slave trade. Pezuela believed that this second option "was hard, but right" and requested that the Spanish government legislate to this end.[84]

On March 22, 1854, the Spanish government passed three decrees with two alleged goals: to stop the slave trade and to promote the introduction of free workers to the island.[85] This new legislation instructed the colonial authorities to create a register of all slaves on the island, so all new slaves found in Cuba "will not be considered as such."[86] The Spanish government clarified to the captain general that these new orders did not repeal the Penal Law of 1845, and that article 9 of this law was still in place, and therefore, "by no means shall you proceed . . . to make inquiries within the plantations to ascertain the origin of the slaves in them."[87] This impossible balance between effectively fighting against the slave trade, as Madrid was demanding, on the one hand, and the impossibility of the authorities entering the plantations, on the other, was broken by the captain general's decree of May 3, 1854. On that date Pezuela partially authorized the colonial authorities to enter and inspect plantations. To do so, the captain general of Cuba adopted a very lax interpretation of the Penal Law of 1845 and pointed out that these visits would not "disturb . . . the owners."[88] Pezuela's decree established that in the period of one month from any known arrival of a slave vessel to Cuba, the authorities would be able to inspect the plantations and if any Black person who had not been previously included in the slave register was to be found, they would be declared free.[89]

The reaction of the Cuban planters to Pezuela's decree of May 1854 was immediate and overwhelming, and only three months after publication, the Spanish government ordered its repeal.[90] As Luis Martínez-Fernández has argued, "Pezuela managed to alienate virtually all the powerful elements of Cuban society and his actions helped spark a new wave of Cuban annexationism and United States filibusterism."[91] A few days after the publication of Pezuela's decree authorizing the searching of the plantations, the US consul in Havana reported to Washington that Cuba was "on the eve of a fearful revolution."[92] In August 1854 the government of one day's duration headed by Fernando Fernández de Córdova (1809–1883) determined that the decree was in clear violation of the Penal Law of 1845 and that a "local authority" had no right to interpret or overwrite a law that had been passed by the Cortes.[93] One month later, in September 1854, Pezuela was dismissed, and José Gutiérrez de la Concha was appointed as his successor. For Pezuela, the fulfillment of Spain's international agreements was the right thing to do, and the inspection of the plantations the only way to effectively enforce the law. He overestimated Madrid's willingness to adopt new measures to this end, and, less than one year after his arrival in Cuba, the opposition of planters and slave owners was enough to have him removed from his post.

The appointment of Gutiérrez de la Concha responded to the decision of the new Spanish government, led by Baldomero Espartero, to give reassurance to the Cuban slave owners and de-escalate the tension between the colonial elites and the metropolis. The support that the Cuban colonial elite gave to the military uprising and revolution of 1854, which put an end to the so-called Decada Moderada and brought the Progressive Party into power, crucially explains the "planned laxity" that Concha adopted against the slave trade.[94] On paper, however, the Spanish government continued to order the new captain general to enforce the law and to stop the slave trade.[95] The risk of losing British support in case of an American attempt to conquer Cuba inclined the Spanish government to publicly stress the need to stop the slave trade into the island, reaffirm its commitment to protect the institution of slavery, and find alternative forms of workforce. During his first mandate in Cuba (1850–1852), Concha captured and executed Narciso López in 1851 and adopted a permissive attitude toward the slave trade: during this time the number of slaves introduced each year rose from 3,098, in 1850, to 8,098, in 1852.[96]

Concha saw the slave trade as a "political problem" that directly affected the international standing and diplomatic stance of Spain.[97] During his second mandate in Cuba, he effectively developed Spain's "balancing-act strategy" by publicly supporting anti–slave trade rhetoric, in line with Pezuela's stance, while protecting the slave trade and providing reassurance to the slave owners.[98] Concha repealed his predecessor's most controversial decrees and opposed the inspection of plantations by officials.[99] In 1855 the slave trader Captain James Smith commented in an interview with the American magazine *De Bow's Review* that since Concha was back in Havana, the slave trade was "flourishing as ever." He described Concha as an abolitionist only "in words" and compared his attitude with his predecessor's: "He talks a great deal, but Pezuela acted. From time immemorial, the planter's estate has been sacred. But Pezuela respected nothing. He seized the negroes wherever he could find them, even on the plantations. By this he incurred the enmity of the planters; and he would probably have been assassinated if he had not been recalled."[100]

Nevertheless, Concha did develop an anti–slave trade position that fed into the formation of a new stage in the construction of abolitionist discourses in Spain, even if it did not yield direct political interventions in support of abolition. His rhetoric constituted a new position that went beyond the traditional humanitarian critique and the "necessary evil" discourse. In one of his first instructions to his subordinates, Concha defined the slave trade as "immoral and damaging" and praised the efforts made by Pezuela, promising to stop the slave trade "and make it disappear."[101] The reasons he gave focused on the preservation of Spain's "honor": "The frank, sincere, and absolute repression of this infamous traffic is a duty for the government in compliance with the Treaties. It is not less for the authorities of this Island; and it is a matter of honor for all of them. The trade in Negroes, then, must disappear completely, and it will disappear."[102] Concha later justified his inaction against the slave trade on the basis of the "deeply contradictory" orders that he had received from the Spanish government, which aimed to eradicate a practice, deeply rooted in Cuban society, without altering or disturbing anyone on the island.[103]

At the end of his mandate, the captain general ruled that, under some extraordinary circumstances, the authorities would have the right to inspect the plantations; but these instructions were strongly rejected and withdrawn by the Spanish government.[104] Concha responded that denying the right of the colonial authorities to visit the plantations virtually nullified any attempt to stop the slave trade, and he pointed out that it should be not just the government's "right" but also its duty to enforce the law.[105] Concha concluded that without the capacity to inspect the plantations, the slave trade and the "violent and well-founded complaints of the British government" would continue no matter what else he did.[106] After five years as captain general, Concha believed that the position of the Spanish government was unsustainable, and in December 1859 he resigned. During his mandate the number of slaves introduced into Cuba had drastically increased year after year, and by 1859 it was the highest ever: at least 26,290.[107]

The British authorities and anti–slave trade activists were astonished. In November 1859 Crawford reported that the Cuban slave trade had reached "gigantic proportions."[108] When Francisco Serrano y Domínguez arrived in Havana as the newly appointed captain general in 1859, his orders were almost identical to those that Pezuela and Concha had received: to stop the slave trade, and to comply with the international agreements to this effect, but also not to conduct any search in any plantation, as this could damage "the moral strength that the owners so much need [and which could] stir in the minds of the negroes a desire for insubordination."[109]

In terms of Serrano's political action against the slave trade, he proposed the creation of a new war fleet of steam vessels to patrol Cuba's coast and fight against the traffic before the slaves were landed. This proposal was accepted by the Spanish government but not implemented until 1865.[110] Cayuela has pointed out that Serrano "developed the same behavior" as Concha, adopting a public rhetoric contrary to the slave trade but, at the same time, providing patronage and protection to slave owners and traders.[111] This is generally true, as Serrano continued to develop an anti–slave trade discourse that focused on "national honor" and "dignity," but there was also an important novelty: Serrano argued in favor of declaring the slave trade to be piracy.

In his instruction to his subordinates of July 1861, Serrano defined slave traders as "speculators" who "congratulate themselves in avoiding the law and increasingly compromise the dignity of the country."[112] For Serrano, Spain's dignity was in danger, as the slave trade "demoralizes and disturbs the administration of the country . . . and provides reasonable pretexts for the noble character of the Spanish nation to be denigrated."[113] Preserving slavery in Cuba would be a much more difficult task if Spain did not fulfill its international obligations and eventually tackle "the depressive and constant control of a foreign agent."[114] For all these reasons, Serrano ordered all Spanish authorities in Cuba to fight against the slave trade and requested the Spanish government "to declare piracy . . . the slave trade," adding his voice to a traditional demand of the British government.[115]

Successive Spanish governments had been extremely reluctant to declare the slave trade to be piracy, and the British Foreign Office had relinquished this demand that had formerly been a top priority in its negotiations with Spain after 1855.[116] Captain General Concha had been consulted at that time about the possible consequences of adopting this measure, and in his reply he predicted catastrophic consequences if such punishment were to be meted out: "If, under the Criminal Code, this offense [the slave trade] is punishable with death; one of two things may happen: either the enormity of the punishment would make it illusory in most cases, or that if it were to become effective a lake of blood would open between Cuba and Spain that would not be possible to cover . . . it would compromise the security of the Island."[117]

The position of the Spanish governments had not changed much since 1855, and Serrano's request was rejected.[118] They believed that punishing an activity, one that was not even openly condemned by the Cuban public, with the death penalty would weaken the authority of Spanish officialdom on the island. Madrid suggested that the only sensible way to put an end to the slave trade was to provide an alternative workforce for Cuba that would make the slave trade unnecessary. This "slow and safe way," as the Spanish government defined it, was in their opinion the only reasonable option left.[119]

Although very different in their commitment to ending the slave trade, Pezuela's, Concha's, and Serrano's perspectives converged in emphasizing the damage to Spain's "national dignity" that the systematic violation of the law was causing. These discourses, although innovative in the Cuban context, bore strong similarities to anti–slave trade ideas put forward by the Portuguese and Brazilian authorities from the 1830s up to the 1850s. In these cases the protection of national honor against Britain's "warlike acts" found a successful common ground that eventually mobilized public opinion toward anti–slave trade positions.[120]

As João Pedro Marques has argued for the Portuguese case, in the second half of the 1830s, Sá da Bandeira (1795–1876), prime minister of Portugal, responded to British diplomatic pressure by adopting a "short and unsentimental" anti–slave trade discourse that stressed national honor and Anglophobic nationalism. This "risky strategy," as Marques put it, aimed to "involve the nation in a subject it viewed as foreign or with a certain amount of indifference."[121] Gradually, this "unsentimental" rhetoric gained ground in Portuguese society, and before 1840, deputies and journalists added to the British-imported humanitarian reasons other ideas, like "political expediency or to salvage national honour."[122]

From 1840 onward Portuguese public opinion steadily shifted to the idea that the slave trade had to cease because Portugal's international prestige was in danger. Politicians, both in government and in the Portuguese parliament, who had traditionally advocated resisting British interference using nationalist rhetoric, came to see abolition, as Marques put it, "as an unavoidable necessity, not only for humanitarian reasons or future economic interests, but mainly because Portugal's respectability was at stake."[123] Marques concluded that, twenty years after Palmerston's Act, which put Portugal's sovereignty on the ropes, the "Portuguese ruling classes changed sides, not so much because the country had been taken up in a wave of anti-slavery, but because the defense of sovereignty and national honor had forced them to match the pace set by Britain."[124]

A similar phenomenon can be identified in the Brazilian case. Britain's unilateral and hostile approach to the Brazilian slave trade became law in 1845. The implementation of the Aberdeen Act and its later interpretation of 1850, which authorized the British navy to capture any slave trade vessels, even in Brazilian waters and ports, was seen as an "act of vandalism" and "warlike" by large sectors of Brazilian society. This strategy was soon defined as "an insult to our dignity as an independent people," even by antislavery activists like Joaquim Nabuco.[125] As in the Portuguese case, national dignity was seen to be jeopardized by British pressure, and in 1850 Paulino Soares de Sousa, Brazilian minister of foreign affairs, declared that the British strategy "wounds deeply every feeling of dignity and national spirit in the country."[126] In a further similarity to the Portuguese case, a true commitment to fighting against the slave trade by all means was seen as the only plausible solution to the crisis. In 1849 Brazilian priest and politician Venâncio Henriques de Resende concluded, "If we are weak, we have still a force . . . capable of making England lower her flag, . . . sincerity and good faith, reason and justice. Let the government take the lead and be the first to repress the traffic."[127]

This approach was embraced by the vast majority of the Brazilian political class, who could not tolerate "the number of insults which we shall have daily to suffer," as Soares de Sousa put it in his speech to the country's Chamber of Deputies in July 1852.[128] By this time, the slave trade had virtually ended in Brazil, and "both sides claimed the credit." For the Brazilian authorities, the eradication of the slave trade was the consequence of their true commitment to persuading the Brazilian people. Eusebio de Quiroz (1812–1868), minister of justice between 1848 and 1852, defined it as "a revolution in public opinion," which, by embracing "the ideas of the age in which we live," reclaimed sovereignty and national independence from Britain.[129]

Therefore, in Brazil and Portugal anti–slave trade discourses that appealed to a sense of "national honor" or "dignity" contributed to successfully transforming anti-British nationalism into anti–slave trade policies that were approved by large sections of the public. For the Spanish case, David Murray has suggested that "under relentless pressure from Britain to modify or replace the law, Spanish politicians took to defending it in patriotic terms against what they termed unwarranted foreign interference," but these "patriotic terms" also operated to justify the adoption of anti–slave trade policies.[130]

In Britain, Palmerston's government and abolitionist activists alike appealed to this rhetoric to highlight Spain's "bad faith to those treaties contracted with England."[131] Palmerston, who had become prime minister in June 1859, accused the Spanish authorities of lacking "the slightest feeling of national honour and good faith," and the abolitionist conference gathered in London in June 1861 emphasized that "remonstrances have been tried to the utmost extent compatible with the national honour and dignity."[132]

Anti–slave trade discourses based on patriotic rhetoric were echoed in the Spanish context by central figures of Spain's colonial government, such as Pezuela, Concha, and Serrano, but unlike in Portugal and Brazil, they failed to persuade the Spanish government to alter its strategy. The "safe and slow way" defended in Madrid was presented as the only viable solution, short of the kinds of drastic measures that would risk Spain's dominion over Cuba. Although they did not produce any tangible outcome, anti–slave trade discourses that appealed to "national honor" are important to understanding the complex picture of abolitionist ideas in the second half of the nineteenth century in Spain and to defining a more comprehensive description of the circulation of anti–slave trade discourses in the Atlantic World. Contrary to what has traditionally been stressed in the historiography, not only external demands impacted and altered Spain's policies on the slave trade.[133] Internal dissension and alternative discourses from within the Spanish administration also informed and tested the strength of Spain's dexterous "balancing-act strategy."

"THE OPINION HAS CHANGED HERE": THE END OF THE SLAVE TRADE

The second half of the 1860s saw the end of the slave trade in the Atlantic World, as the arrival of enslaved Africans to Cuba finally ceased after four centuries.[134] As Harris has rightly argued, "the greatest challenge to the integrity of the slave trade was not the inequality of their financial arrangements but political action."[135] A combination of international and domestic factors contributed to this outcome: the outbreak of the American Civil War in 1861, the signing of the Anglo-American Lyons-Seward Treaty of 1862, the abolition of slavery in the United States in 1865, the radicalization of important sectors of British abolitionism, and the institutionalization of the Spanish abolitionist movement—the weight of these combined factors decisively tipped the scales to abolition, and the trade ebbed away.

At the beginning of the 1860s, the prospect of eradicating the slave trade in Cuba was remote, to say the least.[136] In 1860 the slave trade into Cuba was at a record level.[137] The demand for new slaves was high, and the price paid for them showed no signs of reduction.[138] The expansion of the rail network and the mechanization of the sugar factories stimulated Cuba's agriculture production, which strongly relied on enslaved workers. Far from reducing the dependency on slavery, the industrialization and mechanization of Cuba's economy accelerated the need for more labor, which at first translated into a need for more slaves.[139]

Joseph Crawford, British consul in Havana, who by this time had been in his post for seventeen years (and who was now also judge of the Mixed Commission Court), looked over the situation in Cuba with great pessimism, and recommended that the British "abandon our efforts of persuasion with Spain . . . and proceed to the immediate adoption of the most energetic measures to compel its observance."[140] More-aggressive postures gradually started to gain ground in Britain, and belligerent rhetoric was openly used by Prime Minister Palmerston in Parliament. In February 1861, at the House of Commons, he defined Spain's attitude as "shameless" and "disgraceful," to conclude, in an unprecedented statement, that "Spain has given us good cause for war."[141] After decades of consistent diplomatic and military struggle against the slave trade, Spain represented for Britain the epitome of political frustration.

The outbreak of the American Civil War in 1861 "buried American annexationism for the time being" and facilitated much more aggressive and confrontational rhetoric against Spain's "balancing-act strategy."[142] The unilateral actions against Portugal and Brazil were again presented as successful templates by British officials and abolitionist activists. The notion that "a certain amount of coercion" was required to stop the slave trade became commonplace in Britain's political debate, with the support, for the first time, of traditional pacifist antislavery leaders.[143] By the beginning of 1860, important sectors within the British and Foreign Anti-Slavery Society had abandoned their pacifist stance and driven the abolitionist conference held in London in July 1861 to "demand a more energetic course" from the British government against Spain's impassive attitude.[144]

On the other side of the Atlantic, the Union government of Abraham Lincoln aimed to reaffirm its antislavery commitment and signed an international agreement with Britain authorizing a mutual right of search of suspected slave vessels. In 1862 the Lyons-Seward Treaty contemplated, as a war measure, this new policy, which had crucial consequences in isolating Spain's position and hindered, even further, the capacity of slave traders to successfully transport enslaved people from the African coasts to Cuba.[145] The impact of the agreement was immediate and overwhelming. In 1862 more than 10,382 enslaved Africans arrived in Cuba, while in 1863 the number declined to 5,649. This trend continued until 1866, when only 722 enslaved Africans arrived in the island. As Murray and, more recently, Harris have pointed out, the sudden effect of the Lyons-Seward Treaty responded to the central role that New York played in financing, supporting, and organizing slave expeditions from the African coasts to Havana.[146] As Robert Shufeldt, US consul in Havana, wrote in 1861, "however humiliating may be the confession, the fact nevertheless is beyond question that nine tenths of vessels engaged in the Slave Trade are American."[147] The Lyons-Seward Treaty stopped this forever.

As Matthew Mason concluded in a recent article, "the Lyons-Seward Treaty . . . effectively ended the slave trade to Cuba," and this was also the perception of contemporary politicians, both in Britain and the United States, who considered the agreement decisive in stopping the Atlantic slave trade.[148] William Seward, US secretary of state, wrote, "If I have done nothing else worthy of self-congratulation, I deem this treaty sufficient to have lived for," and Sen. Charles Sumner, chair of the Senate Foreign Relations Committee, informed the British ambassador Richard Lyons about its ratification "with tears of joy in his eyes."[149] In Britain a similar analysis was shared by politicians and newspapers, Conservative and Liberal alike. Henry Brougham, a historical leader of the British antislavery movement, argued in the House of Lords that this international agreement was "in many respects the most important event that had occurred during the period of his sixty years warfare against the African Slave Trade."[150] Taylor Milne pointed out that the gradual reduction of slaves introduced to Cuba after 1862 "was not solely attributable to the disappearance of the American flag from the traffic" but, as Murray later put it, was the coup de grâce to the transatlantic slave trade.[151]

Between 1861 and the end of the decade, as New York's importance faded, the Spanish ports of Cadiz, Barcelona, and Bilbao experienced "growing importance" in the context of the final years of the slave trade in the Atlantic World.[152] The cause for the final decline should be located in the new "potency of suppression policies within the Spanish empire."[153]

In Spain the beginning of the 1860s saw the institutionalization of the Spanish antislavery movement around the Sociedad Abolicionista Española, founded in Madrid in 1865. The role of the Puerto Rican Julio Vizcarrondo (1829–1889), a Protestant priest and journalist, was essential in the creation of the society and in defining its political strategy.[154] Vizcarrondo was linked to progressive and reformist movements on both sides of the Atlantic and got in touch with the American abolitionist movement through his wife, Harriet Brewster, a Quaker from Philadelphia. In 1850 Vizcarrondo was pushed into exile from Puerto Rico, where he had started a career as a journalist. He moved to the United States, where he married and started to build up a network of contacts linked to political reformism. In 1854 they moved to Puerto Rico and, in 1863, after manumitting their slaves, went to Spain. In Madrid, Vizcarrondo, together with the intellectuals Antonio Angulo and Félix Bona, founded the *Revista hispano-americana*, which became a hub for antislavery and progressive ideas in Spain. Vizcarrondo and Brewster attended several international meetings of the antislavery movement, and Vizcarrondo later became correspondent member of the BFASS and secretary of the committee of the Anti-Slavery Conference held in Paris in August 1867.[155]

In December 1864 Vizcarrondo organized a meeting at his house to discuss coordinated political initiatives against slavery in the Spanish Antilles with abolitionist politicians and intellectuals.[156] On April 2, 1865, on the occasion of the fifty-fourth anniversary of Agustín de Argüelles's speech at the Cortes of Cadiz, the Sociedad Abolicionista Española was established. In July of the same year, the first issue of *El abolicionista español*, the newspaper of the society, was published and widely distributed among its members.

In its first years of operation, the society acquired more than seven hundred members and organized two main public events: in December 1865 and June 1866.[157] The first one took place at the Teatro de Variedades in Madrid, where the stage was decorated with "the names of Lincoln, Wilberforce, . . . Enriqueta [Harriet Beecher] Stowe, Orense, and other supporters of the abolitionist cause."[158] The second event was a poetry contest at the Madrid theater Jovellanos, and the first prize was won by the Spanish poet and social reformer Concepción Arenal.[159]

The combination of these international and domestic factors contributed to making the continuation of the slave trade impossible, forcing Spain's political actors to adapt to the new reality, reassess their position, and build a new narrative that could sustain it. The idea that the end of the slave trade had become inevitable established a new political consensus after 1862, and the Spanish authorities urgently tried to claim some agency over the process.

Six months after the Lyons-Seward Treaty was signed into law by Abraham Lincoln in June 1862, General Domingo Dulce y Garay was appointed captain general of Cuba. Like his predecessors, Dulce received clear instructions to eradicate the slave trade in Cuba, but this time the Spanish government was compelled to adopt an ambitious anti–slave trade agenda.[160] In July 1863 Madrid gave Dulce extraordinary powers to prosecute and expel any officials involved in the slave trade, thus consolidating and extending the authoritarian model of his predecessors in the post. Using these arbitrary powers, Dulce expelled Francisco Duramoña and Antonio Tuero in February 1863, on suspicion of being involved in at least two slave trade expeditions.[161] He prosecuted Julián Zulueta, "the Island's most powerful slave trader" and an éminence grise within the Office of the Captain General throughout the nineteenth century. This was followed in June 1863 by the suspension of Pedro Navascues, governor of Havana, when he was accused of corruption related to the slave trade.[162] These decisions were "a vivid public signal" of the new policy against the slave trade.[163]

Dulce established a strong and efficient collaboration with the British authorities in Cuba, with whom he coordinated a strategy to fight against the slave trade on the island and put pressure on the Spanish government to extend his military and judicial powers. Britain recognized the effective work undertaken by Dulce following his appointment, and as Lord John Russell conceded in the summer of 1863, "the good intentions of the Captain General" were beyond question.[164] For its part, the United States diplomatic mission in Madrid also urged the Spanish government to adopt legislative changes that would replace the inefficient Penal Law of 1845. In March 1864 the Ministry of State produced a report in response to the American ambassador, endorsing his suggestions and stressing the need for political reforms:[165] "It seems that the time has come for H.M.'s Government to devote its full attention to this matter, and in anticipation of any demands, it should seek to adopt a procedure that, without attacking the legitimate rights acquired in accordance with the law, shows that the Spanish government, which is not in favour of emancipation, does not want to feed, however, slavery with the import of captive Negroes from the African coasts."[166]

Dulce's reformist agenda was more ambitious than what the Spanish government was prepared to accept. Dulce "clearly advocated an English-like solution: immediate emancipation with compensation to the slave owners and apprenticeship contracts for the former slaves."[167] The Spanish cabinet, however, was committed to the protection of the institution of slavery.

In June 1865 the public outcry after the violent military repression of student protests in Madrid forced the conservative government of General Narváez to step down and led to the subsequent return to power, for the third time, of General Leopoldo O'Donnell. The second government of the Unión Liberal party lasted less than a year, persevering until June 1866, but its actions had significant consequences with regard to the slave trade.[168] In November 1865 the Spanish authorities acknowledged that "the Law of 1845 cannot fulfill the aspirations of the government" and announced their intention to put a new bill to the Cortes as soon as possible.[169] The Spanish overseas minister, Antonio Cánovas del Castillo (1828–1897), presented at the Cortes in April 1866 the Law for the Repression and Punishment of the Slave Trade with the support of the former captains general Concha and Pezuela. In July 1866 the senate voted in favor of the law, which was eventually introduced as a Royal Decree, or executive order, in September. In May of 1867, the newly elected Cortes that followed the resignation of O'Donnell in July 1866 passed the law, which was finally proclaimed in Cuba in September 1867.[170]

The law established the death penalty for masters, pilots, pursers, and petty officers if they attempted to resist arrest, either at sea or ashore. This decision finally complied with the long-held request of the British authorities to declare the slave trade to be piracy, as this law, without using the word, provided the same punishment.[171] The 1866 law contemplated life imprisonment for all the other members of the crew if an officer were killed during the arrest and seizure of the slave trade vessel. It also authorized, in some cases, the colonial authorities to inspect the plantations and ordered the creation of a new slave register to discourage planters from purchasing new slaves.[172] In practical terms the new legislation was successful, as no new landings were recorded by the Spanish or British authorities in Cuba, although they almost certainly continued, on a small scale, into the late 1860s. The Mixed Commission Court in Havana did not operate after 1867, and in 1871 the court in Sierra Leone was closed down too.

In February 1865, during the discussion of the bill in the Spanish Cortes, Deputy Benito Posada Herrera called the government's attention to "what will happen the day that in the Americas and all over the world there will not be more slaves than the Spanish ones on the Island of Cuba" and affirmed that stopping the slave trade was a matter of great urgency to prevent "a revolution in that land."[173] In January 1866 the government emphasized its commitment to eradicating the slave trade as the best way of preserving and protecting slavery in Cuba. They argued that "public opinion in our overseas provinces has started to understand that slavery can be preserved without the traffic," but for many deputies it was obvious that stopping the slave trade would necessarily weaken slavery itself.[174] The parliamentary commission that was responsible for analyzing the bill concluded, in June 1866, that slavery "should be conceptualized . . . as a crisis, whose future must be prepared adequately and gradually" and that "it should and can . . . last for a longer time, but limited to its current conditions and proportions."[175] In a similar vein, Cánovas del Castillo argued that the best way to protect slavery in Cuba was to stop the slave trade: "It is possible that the world will still tolerate for some time the existence of slavery within Cuba, as a domestic issue; this will be possible, as long as it is an isolated issue that concerns only the internal organization of Spanish society; but if we allow it to become an international question; if we allow it to acquire a European character, I assure you one thing that you already know: that the world will not tolerate it."[176]

Even a slave-owning deputy, José Luis Riquelme y Gómez, participated in this new rhetoric and publicly condemned the slave trade.[177] He believed, however, that the law would be inefficient in stopping it and would only cause "great terror to the owners."[178] On the other side of the political spectrum, the Sociedad Abolicionista Española also believed that without abolishing slavery the eradication of the slave trade was impossible, and it called for "such an odious institution to be abolished once and for all."[179] Similarly, Senator Luís María Pastor Copo concluded that the complex network of corruption and profit behind the slave trade would cause the law to fail, and for this reason he went as far as to argue in favor of the abolition of slavery.[180]

Apart from these critical voices, the bill found broad support. All the political actors that had traditionally supported the "necessity of the slave trade" and had presented it as a "necessary evil" now celebrated a new era in which, as Cánovas argued, "the opinion had changed": "Today, gentlemen, the conditions are different, the opinion has changed here, as it has changed on the Island of Cuba, due to the outcome of the civil war in the United States. Since then there is not a person who fails to understand the absolute necessity of ending completely and absolutely the trade; this way, we will have on our side reason and justice and we will be able to sustain the great interests that in Cuba are linked to the question of slavery. . . . We have at this moment . . . the almost unanimous opinion . . . that the time has come for the slave trade to disappear."[181]

For the first time, British diplomatic influence in the drafting and approval of anti–slave trade legislation in Spain was very limited. As David Murray has pointed out, "Britain was not inclined to push for any more concessions," ignoring the request of the BFASS and other abolitionist activists, to demand Spain's abolition of slavery too.[182] After all, the law generally responded to all the demands for which Britain had been fighting since 1807. The law was presented by the Spanish authorities as a symbol of Spain's final, united, and determined commitment to ending the slave trade. Fifty-five years after Argüelles's speech at the Cortes of Cadiz, Spain approved a comprehensive and effective law against the slave trade, which, crucially, it had no other option but to enforce.

Conclusions

Murray was right in arguing that "no historian can say with any certainty when the last slave landing occurred in Cuba," but it is certain that during the first half of the 1860s, the end of the slave trade was perceived by everyone on both sides of the Atlantic as inevitable. During the 1850s, however, there was no sign of such decline, and the Spanish governments successfully protected and promoted the illicit traffic, in an increasingly complex political environment. It was thanks to this complex alignment of international actors and the upsurge of imperial rivalries that the Spanish authorities could successfully perform their "balancing act" to rebuff the persistent demands of the British government for more effective measures and contain the threat of "warlike acts" following the examples of Portugal and Brazil. On both counts Spain had its way, and the slave trade in its empire had grown to "gigantic" proportions by 1859.[183]

However, it was also during the 1850s that a new abolitionist rhetoric, with clear similarities to Portuguese and Brazilian anti–slave trade discourses, was shaped in Cuba by three successive captains general: Pezuela, Concha, and Serrano. An abolitionist discourse emphasized the need to "salvage national honor" and characterized the abolitionist cause as the correct course of action. This discourse added a new layer of intricacy to the development of abolitionist ideas in Spain during the "lengthy hiatus," as Fradera put it, between the early abolitionist discourses of the 1810s and the ending of the slave trade.[184]

A progression of developments—the American Civil War, the Lyons-Seward Treaty, emancipation in the States, the radicalization of British abolitionism, and the institutional turn of the Spanish abolitionists—quickly sank the Atlantic slave trade. The Spanish state risked sinking with it if it could not adapt to the new reality represented by these profound changes. Spanish political actors were left scrabbling to assert some degree of agency over the process, in vain; when Cánovas proclaimed in 1866 "that the time has come for the slave trade to disappear," it already had.[185] The end of the slave trade in Spanish Cuba, the last redoubt of the transatlantic trade, brought to a close four hundred years of brutal mass traffic of Africans to the Americas.

Epilogue

This book has set out to understand how abolitionist ideas were received, shaped, and transformed in Spain's Atlantic empire, and the central role that British activists, diplomats, and successive governments played in advancing the abolitionist cause. In so doing it has brought to attention the complex and uneven development of abolitionist and antiabolitionist discourses in Spain's public life, from the beginning of the nineteenth century to the end of the transatlantic trade.

Starting from the premise that the Spanish abolitionist movement was never likely to develop along the same lines as the British, the French, or the American versions, this study has rejected previously dominant teleological narratives that have framed antislavery ideas as a natural development of pre-existing anti–slave trade discourses. This explanation, in which the British case is taken to be paradigmatic, fails to explain the process comprehensively, in all of its irregularity. Moreover, the chronological analysis adopted in this book has allowed us to emphasize the disruptions, absences, and contradictions in the development of abolitionist ideas in Spain's empire. This work demonstrates that anti–slave trade and antislavery ideas coexisted, in both contradictory and complementary ways, and were advanced by a multiplicity of institutions and political actors: Liberal and absolutist, progressive and conservative, egalitarian and racist.

The early history of Spanish abolitionism is a story of political failure, in which anti–slave trade and antislavery ideas remained marginal and limited to the endeavors of a few activists. The forerunners—Isidoro de Antillón, José María Blanco White, José Guridi, and Agustín de Argüelles—challenged the moral legitimacy of the slave trade for the first time and defined the *odious commerce* as "horrendous, atrocious and inhumane."[1] For their part, antiabolitionists rose to meet this challenge through the successful reconfiguration of their claims to legitimacy, founded upon an arsenal of appeals to and for racism, imperialism, and prosperity. When "the empire was coming apart" and "the idea of a general reform" had been abandoned, abolitionism was seen by some as a dangerous tendency and by others as unattainable.[2]

British ideological, political, military, and diplomatic influence was central after 1807 to the shaping of abolitionist ideas and policies in Spain. The secret negotiations between Argüelles and the British ambassador in Cadiz, weeks before the former presented his proposal to the Cortes, and the correspondence between Toreno and William Wilberforce in 1821 corroborate this. However, British pressure also worked in the opposite direction. The establishment and operation of Havana's Mixed Commission Court and the British Foreign Office's "abrasive approach" fueled Anglophobic sentiment among the Cuban and Spanish populations, consolidating antiabolitionist discourses and the depiction of anti–slave trade ideas as a foreign threat to Cuba's political and economic stability. Antiabolitionist actors found in the "necessary evil" argument a popular and strong refrain with which to confront anti–slave trade policies.

After the death of Fernando VII and the reopening of the Spanish Cortes in 1836, the idea that opposing British abolitionism was "a matter of self-preservation" permeated wide sectors of Spanish and Cuban public opinion. In a context in which Britain's power was perceived as overwhelming and Spanish officials were forced to negotiate new anti–slave trade legislation, a discourse of victimhood further reinforced the protection of slavery and the slave trade as a matter of national sovereignty and independence. The notion of "self-preservation" operated in both a racist and an imperialist way. As Vicente Sancho put it in the Cortes of 1836, freedom and equality for the slaves would mean "extermination and death" for the white people of Cuba. Furthermore, the protection of slavery and the slave trade was presented as essential for the preservation of Spain's sovereignty over the island. To protect the last of its overseas dominions from independence or annexation was the paramount priority for Spanish politicians on both sides of the chamber.

Throughout the first half of the nineteenth century, antiabolitionist discourses remained as strong as the slave trade itself. As this study shows, even in the aftermath of the Conspiracy of La Escalera (1844), José Antonio Saco's racist anti–slave trade discourse remained marginal. In the 1850s the slave trade was more profitable and dynamic than ever before and, after decades of diplomatic and military struggle, Spain's "balancing-act strategy" represented a source of deep political frustration for Britain. The Spanish authorities managed to consistently ignore London's demands for more effective anti–slave trade legislation and, simultaneously, stopped the British cabinet from resorting to unilateral action. Annexationist tensions were running high, and a US-controlled Cuba was, for Britain, too high a price for abolition.

The signature of the Lyons-Seward Treaty in 1862 and the abolition of slavery in the United States put an end to the transatlantic slave trade. By then the sense that the traffic was in its death throes had given rise to a new political consensus, and the Spanish authorities urgently tried to claim some agency over the process. New laws were passed, and the Spanish deputies congratulated themselves for having done the right thing as well as having achieved a strategic goal. The ultimate abolition of the slave trade in Spain was thus presented as the best way to preserve slavery and to protect the country's sovereignty over Cuba.

However, this narrative did not go unchallenged. From 1865 the Sociedad Abolicionista Española sought to gradually shift the traditional premises of the debate, maturing into a truly counterhegemonic movement.[3] After 1868 the concurrent and deeply intertwined Glorious Revolution in Spain and Ten Years' War in Cuba further transformed the political landscape and led to the emergence of new political actors on both sides of the Atlantic. Headed by Spanish and Puerto Rican activists, the Society mobilized against slavery "because of its centrality to the imperial order" that had been founded in the 1830s, altering the very essence of abolitionist politics and challenging the gradualist laws put in place by subsequent Spanish governments until 1886, when slavery was ultimately abolished in Cuba, thirteen years after it had been banned in Puerto Rico.[4]

Throughout the nineteenth century, very few people in Spain campaigned to stop the slave trade, still less to abolish slavery. Even when that was the case, the reasons that moved them were not always humanitarian, liberal, or egalitarian. This book has revealed a much more complex picture, in which abolitionist ideas intertwined with other—often appalling and often materialistic—interests and aspirations. But not always: when Domingo Vila confessed at the 1837 Revolutionary Cortes that he could not find "any repugnance" in himself "at the thought that a man of color might sit" next to him in the parliament, he was showing the way to a better society, one he thought was worth fighting for.[5]

Notes

INTRODUCTION

1. *Hansard*, Lords sitting, 5 Feb. 1807, vol. 8, 662.

2. Throughout this book, the term "discourse" is recurrently used as a concept to describe sources produced by politicians, authorities, intellectuals, and activists. It is essential to be actively aware of the limits of intellectual history, and how discourses, ideas, and concepts must be considered in relation to wider interpretative contexts. As suggested by John Pocock, the role of historians is to understand and inhabit the gap between "thinking" and "experience" by analyzing both the historical context in which the ideas or discourses take place and what he calls the "languages, rhetoric, idioms, paradigms or modes of utterance." Both Pocock and Quentin Skinner argue for a methodology based on context, intention, and aims to understand the distance between historical facts and language. On this point, the Foucauldian idea of "discourse" becomes the center of the paradigm represented by Pocock. He persuasively defines "discourse" as "a sequence of speech acts performed by agents within a context finished ultimately by social practices and historical situations, but also . . . by the political languages by means of which the acts are to be performed." Dominick LaCapra, *Rethinking Intellectual History* (Ithaca: Cornell University Press, 1990), 31–36; John G. A. Pocock, *Political Thought and History* (Cambridge: Cambridge University Press, 2009), 17, 67, 101; Quentin Skinner, "Meaning and Understanding in the History of Ideas," *History and Theory* 8, no. 1 (1969), 3–53; Quentin Skinner and J. Schneewind, *La filosofía de la historia* (Barcelona: Paidós, 1990), 237.

3. In this book, the terms "Spanish," "Spanish abolitionism" and "Spanish liberalism" generally refer to *Spain/European Spanish* and not to the fullness of the *Spanish-speaking* Atlantic. Similarly, "Spaniard" is used to refer to *European Spanish* and does not include Spaniards from Cuba that are referred to as "Cubans." The term "Cuban colonial elite" widely refers to Cuban and Spanish-born subjects that formed a political and economic elite in the island.

4. *Diario de las Sesiones de Cortes*, April 2, 1811, p. 812.

5. Bernard Bailyn, *Atlantic History: Concept and Contours* (Cambridge: Harvard University Press, 2005), 101.

6. Emily Berquist, "Early Anti-Slavery Sentiment in the Spanish Atlantic World, 1765–1817," *Slavery & Abolition* 31, no. 2 (2010): 181–82, https://doi.org/10.1080/01440391003711073.

7. Arthur F. Corwin, *Spain and the Abolition of Slavery in Cuba, 1817–1886* (Austin: University of Texas Press, 1967); David R. Murray, *Odious Commerce: Britain, Spain and the Abolition of the Cuban Slave Trade* (Cambridge: Cambridge University Press, 2002). Originally published 1980.

8. Josep M. Fradera, "La participació catalana en el tràfic d'esclaus (1789–1845)," *Recerques*, no. 16 (1984): 119–40; Josep M. Fradera, "Why Were Spain's Overseas Laws Never Enacted?," in *Spain, Europe and the Atlantic World: Essays in Honour of John H. Elliott*, ed. Richard L. Kagan and Geoffrey Parker (Cambridge: Cambridge University Press, 1995); Josep M. Fradera, "Raza y ciudadanía: El factor racial en la delimitación de los derechos de los Americanos," in *Gobernar colonias*, ed. Josep M. Fradera (Barcelona: Peninsula, 1999); Josep M. Fradera, "Moments in a Postponed Abolition," in *Slavery and Antislavery in Spain's Atlantic Empire*, ed. Josep M. Fradera and Christopher Schmidt-Nowara (New York: Berghahn, 2013); Christopher Schmidt-Nowara, *Empire and Antislavery: Spain, Cuba and Puerto Rico, 1833–1874* (Pittsburgh: University of Pittsburgh Press, 1999); Schmidt-Nowara, "Wilberforce Spanished: Joseph Blanco White and Spanish Antislavery, 1808–1814," in *Slavery and Antislavery in Spain's Atlantic Empire*, ed. Josep M. Fradera and Christopher Schmidt-Nowara (New York: Berghahn, 2013); José A. Piqueras, "La política de los intereses en Cuba y la revolución (1810–1814)," in *Las guerras de independencia en la América española*, ed. Marta Terán and José Antonio Serrano Ortega (Zamora: El Colegio de Michoacán, 2002); José A. Piqueras, "Leales en época de insurrección: La élite criolla cubana entre 1810 y 1814," in *Visiones y revisiones de la independencia americana*, ed. Izaskun Álvarez and Julio Sánchez (Salamanca: Universidad de Salamanca, 2014); Manuel Barcia, *The Great African Slave Revolt of 1825* (Baton Rouge: Louisiana State University Press, 2012); Manuel Barcia, *Seeds of Insurrection. Domination and Resistance on Western Cuban Plantations, 1808–1848* (Baton Rouge: Louisiana State University Press, 2008); Kate Ferris, "Modelos de abolición: Estados Unidos y la política cultural española y la abolición de la esclavitud en Cuba, 1868–1874," in *Visiones del liberalismo: Política, identidad y cultura en la España del siglo XIX*, ed. Alda Blanco and Guy Thomson (Valencia: Universitat de València, 2008); Berquist, "Early Anti-slavery Sentiment in the Spanish Atlantic World, 1765–1817"; Albert García Balañà, "Antislavery before Abolitionism: Networks and Motives in Early Liberal Barcelona, 1833–1844," in *Slavery and Antislavery in Spain's Atlantic Empire*, ed. Josep M. Fradera and Christopher Schmidt-Nowara (New York: Berghahn, 2013).

9. Fradera, "Moments in a Postponed Abolition," 264.

10. Rafael María de Labra, *La abolición de la esclavitud en las Antillas Españolas* (Madrid: Imprenta de J. E. Morete, 1869), 111.

11. Javier Fernández Sebastián, *La aurora de la libertad: Los primeros liberalismos en el mundo iberoamericano* (Madrid: Marcial Pons Historia, 2012), 14.

12. Gabriel Paquette, "Introduction: Liberalism in the Early Nineteenth-Century Iberian World," *History of European Ideas* 41, no. 42 (2015): 9.

13. Fradera, "Moments in a Postponed Abolition," 264.

14. Fradera, "Moments in a Postponed Abolition," 277.

15. Duncan Bell, "What Is Liberalism?," *Political Theory* 42, no. 6 (2014).

16. Bell, "What Is Liberalism?," 686–87.

17. Bell, "What Is Liberalism?," 688–89.

18. Jorge Cañizares-Esguerra, "Some Caveats about the 'Atlantic' Paradigm," *History Compass* 1 (2003): 1; Jorge Cañizares-Esguerra, *How to Write History of the New World: Histories, Epistemologies, and Identities in the Eighteenth Century Atlantic World* (Stanford: Stanford University Press, 2001); see also Daniel T. Rodgers, *Atlantic Crossings: Social Politics in a Progressive Era* (Cambridge: Harvard University Press, 2000); Bailyn, *Atlantic History*.

19. Juan Luis Simal Durán, "La esclavitud como concepto político en el primer liberalismo hispano," in *Ayeres en discusión: Temas clave de historia contemporánea hoy*, ed. María Encarna Nicolás Marín and Carmen González Martínez (Murcia: Universidad de Murcia, 2008), 2; Paquette, "Introduction: Liberalism in the Early Nineteenth-Century Iberian World."

Chapter 1

1. Gabriel Paquette, "The Dissolution of the Spanish Atlantic Monarchy," *Historical Journal* 52, no. 1 (2009): 177; Sherry Johnson, *The Social Transformation of Eighteenth-Century Cuba* (Gainesville: University Press of Florida, 2001); José Luis Belmonte Postigo, "A Caribbean Affair: The Liberalisation of the Slave Trade in the Spanish Caribbean, 1784–1791," *Culture & History Digital Journal* 8, no. 1 (June 2019): 14.

2. Josep M. Fradera, *Colonias para después de un imperio* (Barcelona: Edicions Bellaterra, 2005), 34–35; Josep M. Fradera and Christopher Schmidt-Nowara, *Slavery and Antislavery in Spain's Atlantic Empire* (New York: Berghahn, 2013), 259; Christopher Schmidt-Nowara, "Wilberforce Spanished: Joseph Blanco White and Spanish Antislavery, 1808–1814," in *Slavery and Antislavery in Spain's Atlantic Empire*, ed. Josep M. Fradera and Christopher Schmidt-Nowara (New York: Berghahn, 2013), 158.

3. Manuel Moreno Fraginals, *The Sugarmill: The Socioeconomic Complex of Sugar in Cuba, 1760–1860* (New York: Monthly Review Press, 2008), originally published 1976; Javier Alvarado, "El régimen de legislación especial para ultramar y la cuestión abolicionista en España durante el siglo XIX," in *La supervivencia del derecho español en Hispanoamérica durante la época independiente*, ed. Instituto de Investigaciones Jurídicas, Universidad Nacional Autónoma de México, 1–30 (Mexico City: UNAM, 1998).

4. Moreno Fraginals, *Sugarmill*, 16.

5. Alfonso W. Quiroz, "Implicit Costs of Empire: Bureaucratic Corruption in Nineteenth-Century Cuba," *Journal of Latin American Studies* 35, no. 3 (2003): 474.

6. Quiroz, "Implicit Costs of Empire: Bureaucratic Corruption in Nineteenth-Century Cuba," 474.

7. Moreno Fraginals, *Sugarmill*, 166n52.

8. Moreno Fraginals, *Sugarmill*, 60.

9. Candelaria Saiz Pastor, "Liberales y esclavistas: El dominio colonial español en Cuba (1833–1868)," doctoral thesis, History and Economics, Universidad de Alicante, 1990, 227–30.

10. Moreno Fraginals, *Sugarmill*, 61.

11. Moreno Fraginals, *Sugarmill*, 61.

12. Domenico Losurdo, *Liberalism: A Counter-History* (New York: Verso Books, 2011), 35–65.

13. Losurdo, *Liberalism*, 35–37.

14. Losurdo, *Liberalism*, 58–61.

15. Alvarado, "Régimen de legislación especial," 3–4.

16. Jeremy Adelman, *Sovereignty and Revolution in the Iberian Atlantic* (Princeton: Princeton University Press, 2006), 88; Schmidt-Nowara, "Wilberforce Spanished," 158.

17. Christopher Schmidt-Nowara, "National Economy and Atlantic Slavery: Protectionism and Resistance to Abolitionism in Spain and the Antilles, 1854–1874," *Hispanic American Historical Review* 78, no. 4 (1998): 628.

18. Schmidt-Nowara, "National Economy and Atlantic Slavery," 609.

19. Fradera, "Moments in a Postponed Abolition," 268.

20. He had published in 1794 the work *Descripción orográfica, política y física de Albarracin,* which allowed him to become a member of the Academia de Ciencias. During the Napoleonic invasion of Spain in 1808, he participated in the defense of the city of Zaragoza. In 1809 he moved to Seville and started to contribute to the newspaper *Semario patriótico,* a radical Liberal publication directed by Manuel José Quintana. He became a deputy in the Cortes of Cadiz in 1812. After the dissolution of the Cortes, he was the victim of a murder attempt by a group of Absolutists and died as result of the injuries in 1814, while being driven to Zaragoza, where he was going to be executed after being sentenced to death. "Los diputados fracasan en las Cortes de Cádiz que promulgaron la Constitución de 1812," Conmemoración del 120 Aniversario del a Abolición de la Esclavitud en España, Centre d'Estudis, Debats i Tertúlies, accessed November 14, 2020, http://www.cedt.org/perabol1.htm.

21. Fradera, "Moments in a Postponed Abolition," 266.

22. Isidoro de Antillón, *Disertación sobre el origen de la esclavitud de los negros* (Madrid, 1811), 83.

23. Antillón, *Disertación sobre el origen de la esclavitud de los negros,* 83.

24. Schmidt-Nowara, "Wilberforce Spanished," 168.

25. Schmidt-Nowara, "Wilberforce Spanished," 168.

26. Antillón, *Disertación sobre el origen de la esclavitud de los negros,* 65.

27. Antillón, *Disertación sobre el origen de la esclavitud de los negros,* 66.

28. Antillón, *Disertación sobre el origen de la esclavitud de los negros,* 84.

29. Schmidt-Nowara, "Wilberforce Spanished," 168.

30. Fradera, "Moments in a Postponed Abolition," 266. Antillón, and others, had more leeway to publish under the Cádiz regime when the Inquisition and its *previa censura* (censorship) were abolished, and freedom to publish decreed. The Peninsular War (1807–1814) was a military conflict fought by Bourbon Spain and Portugal, assisted by Great Britain, against the invading and occupying forces of the First French Empire for control of the Iberian Peninsula during the Napoleonic Wars.

31. Antillón, *Disertación sobre el origen de la esclavitud de los negros,* 4.

32. Antillón, *Disertación sobre el origen de la esclavitud de los negros,* 104.

33. Antillón, *Disertación sobre el origen de la esclavitud de los negros,* 104.

34. Martin Murphy, *Blanco White: Self-Banished Spaniard* (London: Yale University Press, 1989); Roberto Breña, "José María Blanco White y la independencia de América: ¿Una postura proamericana?," *Historia constitucional* 3 (2002); Fernando Durán, *José María Blanco White, o, La conciencia errante* (Sevilla: Fundación José Manuel Lara, 2005); Schmidt-Nowara, "Wilberforce Spanished."

35. Manuel Moreno Alonso, *La forja del liberalismo en España: Los amigos españoles de Lord Holland, 1793–1840* (Madrid: Congreso de los Diputados, 1997); Schmidt-Nowara, "Wilberforce Spanished," 159.

36. Durán, *José María Blanco White, o, La conciencia errante*, 159–60.

37. Durán, *José María Blanco White, o, La conciencia errante*, 159–60.

38. Durán, *José María Blanco White, o, La conciencia errante*, 168.

39. The Cortes of Cadiz was a constituent assembly that first gathered in San Fernando on September 24, 1810, later transferred to Cadiz in 1811, during the Peninsular War. The Cortes debated, drafted, and proclaimed the Spanish Constitution of 1812.

40. Schmidt-Nowara, "Wilberforce Spanished," 161.

41. *El Español* (1811), vol. 3, p. 149.

42. *El Español* (1811), vol. 3, p. 150.

43. *El Español* (1811), vol. 3, p. 150.

44. *El Español* (1811), vol. 3, p. 150.

45. *El Español* (1811), vol. 3, p. 466–79; *El Español* (1811), vol. 4, pp. 3–25; *El Español* (1811), vol. 4, pp. 109–19.

46. *El Español* (1811), vol. 3, p. 467.

47. Schmidt-Nowara, "Wilberforce Spanished," 161–62.

48. Blanco White to William Wilberforce, December 15, 1813, MS. Wilberforce, c. 51, ff. 84–85, Special Collections, BL.

49. The African Institution was founded in 1807 after British abolitionists succeeded in ending the slave trade based in the United Kingdom. The institution was formed to create a viable, "civilized refuge" for freed slaves in Sierra Leone, Africa.

50. Wayne Ackerson, *The African Institution and the Antislavery Movement in Great Britain* (Lampeter: Edwin Mellen Press, 2005), 97; *Eighth Report of the Directors of the African Institution, Read at the Annual General Meeting, on March 23, 1814* (London: Ellerton and Henderson, 1814).

51. Blanco White was a former Catholic priest who had converted to Anglicanism in 1812. José María Blanco White, *Bosquexo del comercio de esclavos* (Sevilla: Alfar, 1999 [1814]), 184–94; Berquist, "Early Anti-Slavery Sentiment in the Spanish Atlantic World," 193; Schmidt-Nowara, "Wilberforce Spanished," 159.

52. Schmidt-Nowara, "Wilberforce Spanished," 170.

53. Berquist, "Early Anti-Slavery Sentiment in the Spanish Atlantic World, 1765–1817," 189–90.

54. Christine Benavides, "Isidoro de Antillón y la abolición de la esclavitud," in *Las élites y la Revolución de España (1808–1814): Estudios en homenaje al Profesor Gérard Dufour* (Alicante: Biblioteca Virtual Miguel de Cervantes [Publicaciones de la Universidad de Alicante], 2017), 95, originally published 2010.

55. Benavides, "Isidoro de Antillón y la abolición de la esclavitud," 90; Fradera, "Mo-

ments in a Postponed Abolition," 266; Berquist, "Early Anti-Slavery Sentiment in the Spanish Atlantic World," 193.

56. Schmidt-Nowara, "Wilberforce Spanished," 170–71.

57. Paula E. Dumas, *Proslavery Britain: Fighting for Slavery in an Era of Abolition* (New York: Palgrave Macmillan, 2016), 10–11.

58. Leví Marrero, *Cuba: Economía y sociedad*, vol. 12 (Madrid: Editorial Playor, 1984–1987), 146–47; Ada Ferrer, "Cuban Slavery and Atlantic Antislavery," in *Slavery and Antislavery in Spain's Atlantic Empire*, ed. Josep M. Fradera and Christopher Schmidt-Nowara (New York: Berghahn, 2013); David Eltis, *Economic Growth and the Ending of the Transatlantic Slave Trade* (New York and Oxford: Oxford University Press, 1987); "Trans-Atlantic Slave Trade—Database," Slave Voyages, accessed September 9, 2017, https://www.slavevoyages.org.

59. Murray, *Odious Commerce*, 26.

60. Ferrer, "Cuban Slavery and Atlantic Antislavery," 149.

61. Robert Isaac Wilberforce and Samuel Wilberforce, *The Correspondence of William Wilberforce*, vol. 2 (London: John Murray, 1840), 77–79.

62. Wilberforce and Wilberforce, *Correspondence of William Wilberforce*, 2:134–35.

63. Wilberforce and Wilberforce, *The Correspondence of William Wilberforce*, 2:134–35.

64. Murray, *Odious Commerce*, 27; Roger Anstey, *The Atlantic Slave Trade and British Abolition, 1760–1810* (London: Macmillan, 1975); Seymour Drescher, *Capitalism and Antislavery: British Mobilization in a Comparative Perspective* (Oxford: Oxford University Press, 1987).

65. Robert Isaac Wilberforce and Samuel Wilberforce, *The Life of William Wilberforce*, vol. 3 (London: John Murray, 1838), 369.

66. Alicia Laspra Rodríguez, "Andrés Ángel de la Vega Infanzón: Un reformista anglófilo," *Historia constitucional*, no. 14 (2013).

67. Wilberforce and Wilberforce, *Life of William Wilberforce*, 3:371–72.

68. Wilberforce and Wilberforce, *Life of William Wilberforce*, 3:382–84.

69. Canning to the Marquis of Wellesley, draft, no. 13, July 8, 1809. FO 72/75, TNA.

70. Murray, *Odious Commerce*, 51.

71. José María Portillo Valdés, "Cuerpo de nación, pueblo soberano: La representación política en la crisis de la monarquía hispana," *Ayer*, no. 61 (2006): 51.

72. Fradera, "Moments in a Postponed Abolition," 268.

73. C. W. Crawley, "French and English Influences in the Cortes of Cadiz, 1810–1814," *Cambridge Historical Journal* 6, no. 2 (1939).

74. Joaquín Varela Suanzes-Carpegna, "La Constitución de Cádiz y el primer liberalismo español," *Teoría y derecho: Revista de pensamiento jurídico*, no. 10 (2011); Laspra Rodríguez, "Andrés Ángel de la Vega Infanzón."

75. *Diario de las Sesiones de Cortes*, January 9, 1811, p. 327. Domingo García Quintana should not be confused with Manuel José Quintana (1772–1857), radical writer and poet, a central figure in Antillón's circle of liberals, and who also worked on the radical newspaper *Semanario patriotico*. See Fernando Durán, *Crónicas de Cortes del Semanario patriótico* (Cádiz: Fundación Municipal de Cultura, 2003).

76. *Diario de las Sesiones de Cortes*, January 9, 1811, p. 327.

77. *Diario de las Sesiones de Cortes*, April 2, 1811, p. 810.

78. "Notas de los expedientes pasados a las comisiones de las Cortes desde 1811 a 1814," P-01–000001–0062-0001, f. 23, ACD. *Diario de las Sesiones de Cortes*, April 2, 1811, p. 810.

79. Dumas, *Proslavery Britain*, 11.

80. Fradera, "Moments in a Postponed Abolition," 262. On the constitutional debates on the political participation of the Indigenous populations, see Portillo, "Jurisprudencia constitucional en espacios indígenas: Despliegue municipal de Cádiz en Nueva España," *Anuario de historia del derecho español* 81 (2011); and Portillo, "Cuerpo de nación, pueblo soberano," 61.

81. Fradera, "Moments in a Postponed Abolition," 146; Ada Ferrer, *Freedom's Mirror: Cuba and Haiti in the Age of Revolution* (Cambridge: Cambridge University Press, 2014); María Dolores González-Ripoll et al., *El rumor de Haití en Cuba: Temor, raza y rebeldía, 1789–1844* (Madrid: Consejo Superior de Investigaciones Científicas, 2004); Jeremy D. Popkin, *Facing Racial Revolution. Eyewitness Accounts of the Haitian Revolution* (Chicago: University of Chicago Press, 2007).

82. *Diario de las Sesiones de Cortes*, April 2, 1811, pp. 810–12.

83. *Diario de las Sesiones de Cortes*, April 2, 1811, pp. 810–12.

84. *Diario de las Sesiones de Cortes*, April 2, 1811, pp. 810–12.

85. *Diario de las Sesiones de Cortes*, April 2, 1811, p. 812.

86. José Antonio Saco, *Historia de la esclavitud de la raza africana en el Nuevo Mundo y en especial en los paises americo-hispanos*, vol. 4, ed. Fernando Ortiz (Havana: Cultural S.A., 1938), 86, originally published 1879.

87. Corwin, *Spain and the Abolition of Slavery in Cuba, 1817–1886*, 23. William Wilberforce closely followed this negotiation. He was informed directly from the Foreign Office. See Hamilton to Wilberforce, May 2, 1811. FO 72/121, TNA. In the context of the Peninsular War, the *Regencia* refers to the Spanish executive power headed by a president.

88. Henry Wellesley to Richard Wellesley, Marquis of Wellesley, No. 38, April 13, 1811. FO 72/110, TNA.

89. Saco, *Historia de la esclavitud de la raza africana*, 88.

90. Schmidt-Nowara, "Wilberforce Spanished," 165–66.

91. Saco, *Historia de la esclavitud de la raza africana*, 98.

92. Saco, *Historia de la esclavitud de la raza africana*, 99–102.

93. Saco, *Historia de la esclavitud de la raza africana*, 112.

94. Saco, *Historia de la esclavitud de la raza africana*, 101–2.

95. Barcia, *Great African Slave Revolt of 1825*, 26–28; Ferrer, *Freedom's Mirror*; González-Ripoll et al., *El rumor de Haití en Cuba*; David P. Geggus, *The Impact of the Haitian Revolution in the Atlantic World* (Columbia: University of South Carolina Press, 2001).

96. Saco, *Historia de la esclavitud de la raza africana*, 105–10; Piqueras, "La política de los intereses en Cuba y la revolución"; Piqueras, "Leales en época de insurrección."

97. Barcia, *Great African Slave Revolt of 1825*, 26–28. On the influence of the Hai-

tian Revolution in the development of antiabolitionist discourses in Cuba, see Ferrer, *Freedom's Mirror*; González-Ripoll et al., *El rumor de Haití en Cuba*; Geggus, *Impact of the Haitian Revolution in the Atlantic World*.

98. Saco, *Historia de la esclavitud de la raza africana*, 89–90.

99. Barcia, *Great African Slave Revolt of 1825*, 27.

100. Manuel Barcia, "'Un coloso sobre la arena': Definiendo el camino hacia la plantación esclavista en Cuba, 1792–1825," *Revista de Indias* 71, no. 251 (2011): 65–66.

101. Barcia, "Coloso sobre la arena," 65–66.

102. Matt D. Childs, *The 1812 Aponte Rebellion in Cuba and the Struggle against Atlantic Slavery* (Chapel Hill: University of North Carolina Press, 2006); Barcia, "Coloso sobre la arena," 65–66; Ferrer, *Freedom's Mirror*; Stephan Palmié, *Wizards and Scientists: Explorations in Afro-Cuban Modernity* (Durham, NC: Duke University Press, 2002); José Luciano Franco, "La conspiración de Aponte, 1812," in *Ensayos históricos*, ed. José Luciano Franco, 127–90.

103. Muñoz Torrero was also chair of the Constitution Committee at the Cortes. Fradera, "Moments in a Postponed Abolition," 269.

104. José A. Piqueras, *Azúcar y esclavitud en el final del trabajo forzado* (Madrid: FCE de España, 2002), 474.

105. *Diario de las Sesiones de Cortes*, November 23, 1813, p. 279.

106. John Lynch, *The Spanish American Revolutions, 1808–1826* (New York: W. W. Norton, 1973); Jorge I. Domínguez, *Insurrection or Loyalty: The Breakdown of the Spanish American Empire* (Cambridge: Harvard University Press, 1980); Michael P. Costeloe, *Response to Revolution: Imperial Spain and the Spanish American Revolutions, 1810–1840* (New York: Cambridge University Press, 1986); Jaime E. Rodríguez, *The Independence of Spanish America* (New York: Cambridge University Press, 1998); John Charles Chasteen, *Americanos: Latin America's Struggle for Independence* (New York: Oxford University Press, 2008). In the new independent republics, abolitionist ideas will develop faster and more successfully than in Spain. Venezuela, New Granada, Mexico, and the United Provinces of the Río de la Plata developed anti–slave trade and antislavery legislation during the period 1811–1823. See Marcela Echeverri, *Indian and Slave Royalists in the Age of Revolution: Reform, Revolution and Royalism in the Northern Andes, 1780–1825* (New York: Cambridge University Press, 2016); Muriel Laurent, *Contrabando, poder y color en los albores de le República: Nueva Granada, 1822–1824* (Bogotá: Universidad de los Andes, 2014); Marixa Lasso, *Myths of Harmony: Race and Republicanism during the Age of Revolution, Colombia, 1795–1831* (Pittsburgh: University of Pittsburgh Press, 2007); Aline Helg, *Slave No More: Self-Liberation before Abolitionism in the Americas* (Chapel Hill: University of North Carolina Press, 2019); Aline Helg, *Liberty and Equality in Caribbean Colombia, 1770–1835* (Chapel Hill: University of North Carolina Press, 2004); Aline Helg, "The Limits of Equality: Free People of Color and Slaves during the First Independence of Cartagena, Colombia (1810–15)," *Slavery & Abolition* 20 (1999): 1–30, Harold A. Bierck Jr., "The Struggle for Abolition in Gran Colombia," *Hispanic American Historical Review* 33, no. 3 (1953): 365–86.

107. Dumas, *Proslavery Britain*, 2–3, 6.

108. Schmidt-Nowara, "Wilberforce Spanished," 165–66.

109. Berquist, "Early Anti-Slavery Sentiment in the Spanish Atlantic World," 194.

110. Berquist, "Early Anti-Slavery Sentiment in the Spanish Atlantic World," 195.

111. *Diario de las Sesiones de Cortes*, April 2, 1811, p. 812.

CHAPTER 2

1. Fradera, "Moments in a Postponed Abolition," in *Slavery and Antislavery in Spain's Atlantic Empire*, ed. Josep M. Fradera and Christopher Schmidt-Nowara (New York: Berghahn, 2013), 270.

2. David R. Murray, *Odious Commerce: Britain, Spain and the Abolition of the Cuban Slave Trade* (Cambridge: Cambridge University Press, 2002), 50, originally published 1980.

3. Manuel Barcia, *The Great African Slave Revolt of 1825* (Baton Rouge: Louisiana State University Press, 2012), 26.

4. Murray, *Odious Commerce*, 50; Paul Michael Kielstra, *The Politics of the Slave Trade in Britain and France, 1814–1848* (New York: Saint Martin's Press, 2000); Seymour Drescher, "Public Opinion and Parliament in the Abolition of the British Slave Trade," in *The British Slave Trade: Abolition, Parliament and People*, ed. Stephen Farrell, Melanie Unwin, and James Walvin (Edinburgh: Edinburgh University Press, 2007); Seymour Drescher, *Capitalism and Antislavery: British Mobilization in a Comparative Perspective* (New York: Oxford University Press, 1987).

5. This was an unprecedented number of signatures, considering that the population of the British Isles in 1814 was 16,456,303 people. Seymour Drescher, "British Abolitionism and Imperialism," in *Abolitionism and Imperialism in Britain, Africa, and the Atlantic*, ed. Derek R. Peterson (Athens: Ohio University Press, 2010), 134–35.

6. This policy was clearly stated by the Foreign Office to the British ambassador in Spain in July 1814. Castlereagh to Wellesley, No. 27, draft, July 30, 1814, FO 72/158, TNA. "In the present temper of the Parliament and of the Nation on the subject of the slave trade, any attempt on the part of Prince Regent's Ministers to prevail on Parliament to raise a Loan for State continuing to carry on a traffic in slaves would be utterly vain and hopeless." Castlereagh to Wellesley, No. 27, draft, July 30, 1814, FO 72/158, TNA; Wellesley to Castlereagh, August 25, 1814, British and Foreign State Papers (1815–1816), 926 (London: James Ridgway and Sons, 1838).

7. The Treaty of Peace, Friendship, and Alliance was signed in Madrid in July 1814 and ratified by the Spanish king in August 1814. It was part of various agreements that Spain subscribed with other European powers at the end of the Peninsular War and the Napoleonic Wars. In the treaty both nations agreed to establish a close diplomatic and political collaboration, to draft as soon as possible a new trade agreement that would grant Britain preferential access to the Spanish American markets, and Spain promised not to establish any future agreements or secret negotiation with France that could be detrimental to the British interests. Alejandro del Cantillo Jovellanos, *Tratados, convenios y declaraciones de paz y de comercio que han hecho con las potencias estranjeras los monarcas españoles de la Casa de Borbón* (Madrid: Imp. de Alegría y Charlain, 1843), 732–34.

8. Guadalupe Jiménez Codinach, *La Gran Bretaña y la independencia de México, 1808–1821* (Mexico: Fondo de Cultura Económica, 1991).

9. "Artículo Adicional III del Tratado entre Gran Bretaña y España del 4 de julio de 1814, firmado en Madrid el 28 de agosto de 1814," in Julia Moreno García, "España y Gran Bretaña durante el siglo XIX: La abolición de la trata y la esclavitud," thesis, History, Universidad Complutense de Madrid, 1984, 78–79.

10. "Additional Article to the Treaty between Great Britain and Spain, of the 5th July, 1814. Signed at Madrid, the 28th August 1814," British and Foreign State Papers (1815–1816), 923.

11. Murray, *Odious Commerce*, 50–51; Manuel Barcia, "'Un coloso sobre la arena': Definiendo el camino hacia la plantación esclavista en Cuba, 1792–1825," *Revista de Indias* 71, no. 251 (2011): 66–67; Fradera, "Moments in a Postponed Abolition," 270.

12. Murray, *Odious Commerce*, 50–51.

13. Murray, *Odious Commerce*, 50–54.

14. Wellesley to Castlereagh, private, August 26, 1814, FO 72/160, TNA. In this regard, Pope Pius VII's decision to start lobbying for the abolition of the slave trade after his return to Rome in 1814 had a significant impact. Murray, *Odious Commerce*, 52.

15. Wellesley to Castlereagh, August 31, 1814, British and Foreign State Papers (1815–1816), 929.

16. Barcia, *Great African Slave Revolt of 1825*, 26–28; Gabriel Paquette, "The Dissolution of the Spanish Atlantic Monarchy," *Revista de Indias* 71, no. 251 (2011): 197.

17. José A. Piqueras, "La política de los intereses en Cuba y la revolución (1810–1814)," in *Las guerras de independencia en la América española*, ed. Marta Terán and José Antonio Serrano Ortega (Zamora: El Colegio de Michoacán, 2002); José A. Piqueras, "Leales en época de insurrección: La élite criolla cubana entre 1810 y 1814," in *Visiones y revisiones de la independencia americana*, ed. Izaskun Álvarez and Julio Sánchez (Salamanca: Universidad de Salamanca, 2014); Luis Alonso Álvarez, "Comercio exterior y formación de capital financiero: El tráfico de negros hispano-cubano, 1821–1868," *Anuario de estudios americanos* 51, no. 2 (1994).

18. Wellesley to Castlereagh, August 31, 1814, British and Foreign State Papers (1815–1816), 929; José A. Piqueras, "La siempre fiel isla de Cuba, o la lealtad interesada," *Historia mexicana* 229 (2008): 427–86.

19. Murray, *Odious Commerce*, 51.

20. This is a very significant amount, considering that the British government's budget in 1814 was £66 million. Richard Cooper, "William Pitt, Taxation, and the Needs of War," 94–103; Murray, *Odious Commerce*, 51, 53.

21. The Duke of San Carlos to Wellesley, October 22, 1814, British and Foreign State Papers (1815–1816), 933.

22. Earl Bathurst to Wellesley, November 11, 1814, British and Foreign State Papers (1815–1816), 934.

23. Wellesley to Castlereagh, No. 60, July 6, 1814. FO 72/160, TNA; Wellesley to Castlereagh, January 26, 1815, British and Foreign State Papers (1815–1816), 934–35; Barcia, *Great African Slave Revolt of 1825*, 27.

24. Paquette, "Introduction: Liberalism in the Early Nineteenth-Century Iberian World," 97.

25. Barcia, *Great African Slave Revolt of 1825*, 27.

26. Robert Paquette, *Sugar Is Made with Blood: The Conspiracy of La Escalera and the Conflict between Empires over Slavery in Cuba* (Middletown, CT: Wesleyan University Press, 1988), 98–99.

27. Barcia, "Coloso sobre la arena," 66–67; Betty Fladeland, "Abolitionist Pressures on the Concert of Europe, 1814–1822," *Journal of Modern History* 38, no. 4 (1966): 355–73; Jerome Reich, "The Slave Trade at the Congress of Vienna—A Study in English Public Opinion," *Journal of Negro History* 53, no. 2 (1968): 129–43; Murray, *Odious Commerce*, 50–56.

28. Murray, *Odious Commerce*, 50; Kielstra, *Politics of the Slave Trade in Britain and France*; Drescher, "Public Opinion and Parliament in the Abolition of the British Slave Trade"; Drescher, *Capitalism and Antislavery*.

29. Arthur F. Corwin, *Spain and the Abolition of Slavery in Cuba, 1817–1886* (Austin: University of Texas Press, 1967), 25.

30. Gabriel Paquette, "The Intellectual Impact of International Rivalry," in *Enlightenment, Governance and Reform in Spain and Its Empire, 1759–1808* (New York: Palgrave Macmillan, 2008): 37–38.

31. Barcia, "Coloso sobre la arena," 67; Claudio Martínez de Pinillos to the Consulate of Havana, No. 66, Madrid, November 1, 1814, Gobierno Superior Civil, leg. 1099, exp. 40587, ANC.

32. Paquette, *Sugar Is Made with Blood*, 98–99.

33. David Todd, *Free Trade and Its Enemies in France, 1814–1851* (Cambridge: Cambridge University Press, 2015), 41; Kielstra, *Politics of the Slave Trade in Britain and France, 1814–1848*, 22–55.

34. British and Foreign State Papers (1815–1816), 944–45; Moreno García, "España y Gran Bretaña durante el siglo XIX," 153.

35. Tratados siglo XIX, No. 35, despacho 419, August 29, 1815, AMAE; Moreno García, "España y Gran Bretaña durante el siglo XIX," 154.

36. Vaughan to Cevallos, August 29, 1815, enclosed in Vaughan to Castlereagh, No. 10, August 30, 1815, FO 71/176, TNA.

37. Vaughan to Cevallos, August 23, 1815, enclosed in Vaughan to Castlereagh, No. 10, August 30, 1815, FO 71/176, TNA.

38. *Acuerdo de la Junta Consular, en virtud de lo acordado en el Congreso de Viena acerca del comercio de negros*, July 27, 1815, Colección Vidal Morales y Morales, tomo 78, No. 52, BNC.

39. Tratados siglo XIX, No. 35, despacho 419, August 29, 1815, AMAE; Moreno García, "España y Gran Bretaña durante el siglo XIX," 155–56.

40. Murray, *Odious Commerce*, 57.

41. The Council of the Indies (*Real y Supremo Consejo de Indias*) was founded in 1524, abolished by the Cortes of Cadiz in 1812, and reestablished by Fernando VII in 1814. Its main role was to give advice to the king on political, judicial, or spiritual issues related to the American colonies, but, as a council, it did not have a legislative role. At this time the Council of the Indies and the State Council (*Consejo de Estado*) were the most important advisory institutions in Spain.

42. "Proceedings of the Council of the Indies of Spain, Relative to the Expediency

of the Abolition, by His Catholic Majesty, of the Slave Trade Carried on by Spanish Subjects. Madrid, February 1816," *British and Foreign State Papers (1816–1817)*, 516–36 (London: James Ridgway and Sons, 1838). And also, F.O. 72/185, TNA.

43. "Proceedings of the Council of the Indies of Spain, Relative to the Expediency of the Abolition," 516–36.

44. "Proceedings of the Council of the Indies of Spain, Relative to the Expediency of the Abolition," 516–36.

45. This sentence embodies a very strong and significant message considering the Wars for Independence in the Spanish American territories. "Proceedings of the Council of the Indies of Spain, Relative to the Expediency of the Abolition," 516–36.

46. *Diario de las Sesiones de Cortes*, April 2, 1811, vol. 185, p. 812.

47. "Proceedings of the Council of the Indies of Spain, Relative to the Expediency of the Abolition," 516–36.

48. "Proceedings of the Council of the Indies of Spain, Relative to the Expediency of the Abolition," 516–36.

49. Corwin, *Spain and the Abolition of Slavery in Cuba, 1817–1886*, 27.

50. Murray, *Odious Commerce*, 58; Moreno García, "España y Gran Bretaña durante el siglo XIX," 152–56.

51. Fernando Armario Sanchez, "Esclavitud y abolicionismo durante la regencia de Espartero," in *Esclavitud y derechos humanos: La lucha por la libertad del negro en el siglo XIX*, ed. Francisco de Solano and Agustín Guimerá (Madrid: CSIC, 1990), 379.

52. The report is signed by Francisco Requena, Francisco Ybañez Leyba, Francisco Arango y Parreño, Francisco Xavier Caro de Torquemada, José Navia y Bolaños, Bruno Vallarino, and Mariano González de Merchante. "Opinion of the Dissentient Members of the Council of the Indies, against the Immediate Abolition of the Slave Trade. Madrid, February 1816," *British and Foreign State Papers (1816–1817)*, 536–43.

53. "Opinion of the Dissentient Members of the Council of the Indies, against the Immediate Abolition of the Slave Trade. Madrid, February 1816," 536–43.

54. "Opinion of the Dissentient Members of the Council of the Indies, against the Immediate Abolition of the Slave Trade. Madrid, February 1816," 536–43.

55. "Opinion of the Dissentient Members of the Council of the Indies, against the Immediate Abolition of the Slave Trade. Madrid, February 1816," 536–43.

56. "Opinion of the Dissentient Members of the Council of the Indies, against the Immediate Abolition of the Slave Trade. Madrid, February 1816," 536–43.

57. "Opinion of the Dissentient Members of the Council of the Indies, against the Immediate Abolition of the Slave Trade. Madrid, February 1816," 536–43.

58. "Opinion of the Dissentient Members of the Council of the Indies, against the Immediate Abolition of the Slave Trade. Madrid, February 1816," 536–43.

59. "Reply of the Majority of the Council, to the Opinion of the Members who Oppose the Immediate Abolition of the Slave Trade," *British and Foreign State Papers (1816–1817)*, 543–49.

60. José Antonio Saco, *Historia de la esclavitud de la raza africana en el Nuevo Mundo y en especial en los paises americo-hispanos*, vol. 4, ed. Fernando Ortiz (Havana: Cultural S.A., 1938, originally published 1879), 101–2.

61. Murray, *Odious Commerce*, 58. The Council of State (Consejo de Estado), is the supreme consultative council of the Spanish government. The institution of the Council of State has existed intermittently in Spain since 1812, and it was dedicated to advising the king, primarily about foreign policy.

62. Vaughan to Castlereagh, No. 16, March 14, 1816, FO 72/185, TNA.

63. Wayne Ackerson, *The African Institution and the Antislavery Movement in Great Britain* (Lampeter: Edwin Mellen Press, 2005), 97; *Eighth Report of the Directors of the African Institution, Read at the Annual General Meeting, on March 23, 1814* (London: Ellerton and Henderson, 1814).

64. Murray, *Odious Commerce*, 60.

65. Vaughan to Castlereagh, No. 26, April 9, 1816, FO 72/186, TNA; Murray, *Odious Commerce*, 60. See note 147.

66. Vaughan to Castlereagh, No. 61, July 23, 1816, FO 72/186, TNA; Murray, *Odious Commerce*, 61.

67. Murray, *Odious Commerce*, 61.

68. Harrison to Hamilton, October 26, 1816, FO 72/195, TNA; Murray, *Odious Commerce*, 61.

69. Murray, *Odious Commerce*; Corwin, *Spain and the Abolition of Slavery in Cuba, 1817–1886*; Jenny S. Martinez, *The Slave Trade and the Origins of International Human Rights Law* (Oxford: Oxford University Press, 2012); Berquist, "Early Anti-Slavery Sentiment in the Spanish Atlantic World, 1765–1817," *Slavery & Abolition* 31, no. 2 (2010): 181–82, https://doi.org/10.1080/01440391003711073.

70. Murray, *Odious Commerce*, 69.

71. Tratados siglo XIX, No. 35, despacho 11, December 3–15, 1816, AMAE; Moreno García, "España y Gran Bretaña durante el siglo XIX," 173.

72. Tratados siglo XIX, No. 35, despacho 11, December 3–15, 1816, AMAE; Moreno García, "España y Gran Bretaña durante el siglo XIX," 173.

73. Corwin, *Spain and the Abolition of Slavery in Cuba, 1817–1886*, 25.

74. Murray, *Odious Commerce*, 69.

75. Estado, Esclavitud (Negros), leg. 8029 and 8030, AHN; *British and Foreign State Papers (1816–1817)*, 33–74.

76. Estado, Esclavitud (Negros), leg. 8029, AHN; Corwin, *Spain and the Abolition of Slavery in Cuba, 1817–1886*, 28–29. See note 147.

77. Murray, *Odious Commerce*, 69.

78. Murray defended that this second element was the crucial factor that motivated the agreement. Murray, *Odious Commerce*, 69.

79. Vaughan to Castlereagh, No. 128, November 30, 1816, FO 72/188, TNA.

80. The correspondence between the Spanish king and the Russian emperor during the negotiation of the treaty was published in December 1823 by the *Morning Chronicle*, and months later by the Spanish newspaper published in London *El español constitucional*.

81. Wellesley to Castlereagh, No. 107, August 13, 1817, FO 72/199, TNA.

82. Murray, *Odious Commerce*, 69.

83. Murray, *Odious Commerce*, 69.

84. "Commons Sitting of June 10, 1819," HCPP, accessed November 14, 2020, https://api.parliament.uk/historic-hansard/sittings/1819/jun/10.

85. Moreno García, "España y Gran Bretaña durante el siglo XIX," 872. Also, Jennifer L. Nelson, "Liberated Africans in the Atlantic World: The Courts of Mixed Commission in Havana and Rio de Janeiro, 1819–1871," PhD thesis, University of Leeds, 2015, 39.

86. Paquette, "Intellectual Impact of International Rivalry," 37–38.

87. Barcia, *Great African Slave Revolt of 1825*, 26–27.

88. Alvarado, "Régimen de legislación especial," 6.

89. Don Luis de Onis to Mr. Adams, Translation, Washington, May 4, 1818, *British and Foreign State Papers (1819–1820)*, 374–75 (London: James Ridgway, 1834).

90. Martinez, *The Slave Trade and the Origins of International Human Rights Law*, 37. See also Nelson, "Liberated Africans in the Atlantic World," 36.

91. "Trans-Atlantic Slave Trade—Database," Slave Voyages, accessed December 7, 2015, https://www.slavevoyages.org.

92. "Trans-Atlantic Slave Trade—Database," Slave Voyages, accessed December 7, 2015, https://www.slavevoyages.org.

93. The *doceañistas* were a moderate faction of Liberals who advocated for the restoration and implementation of the Constitution of 1812. The *exaltados* were a progressive faction of Liberals. In comparison to the *doceañistas*, they advocated for more radical policies and criticized the limitations of the Constitution of 1812.

94. William Wilberforce to Lord Holland, Kensington Gore, Monday, April 3, 1820, Wilberforce and Wilberforce, *Correspondence of William Wilberforce*, 324–26.

95. William Wilberforce to Agustín de Argüelles, March 28, 1820, Wilberforce and Wilberforce, *Correspondence of William Wilberforce*, 430.

96. William Wilberforce to Agustín de Argüelles, March 28, 1820, Wilberforce and Wilberforce, *Correspondence of William Wilberforce*, 430–31.

97. William Wilberforce to Agustín de Argüelles, March 28, 1820, Wilberforce and Wilberforce, *Correspondence of William Wilberforce*, 431.

98. William Wilberforce to Agustín de Argüelles, March 28, 1820, Wilberforce and Wilberforce, *Correspondence of William Wilberforce*, 431–32.

99. Agustín de Argüelles to William Wilberforce, Madrid, October 28, 1820, MS Wilberforce c. 44 f. 10, BL.

100. Agustín de Argüelles to William Wilberforce, Madrid, October 28, 1820, MS Wilberforce c. 44 f. 10, BL.

101. Agustín de Argüelles to William Wilberforce, Madrid, October 28, 1820, MS Wilberforce c. 44 f. 10, BL.

102. Agustín de Argüelles to William Wilberforce, Madrid, October 28, 1820, MS Wilberforce c. 44 f. 10, BL. Jesús Sanjurjo, "Negros o esclavos: La retórica de la esclavitud en la prensa española del exilio londinense (1818–1825)," *Anuario de estudios atlánticos*, no. 62 (2016): 1–14.

103. Fradera, "Moments in a Postponed Abolition," 270.

104. The Mixed Commission Courts were a series of joint courts set up by the British government with Dutch, Spanish, or Portuguese representation following treaties

agreed to in 1817 and 1818. By 1820 there were six courts in Rio de Janeiro, Havana, and Suriname, and three in Freetown.

105. Don Santiago Usoz to Viscount Castlereagh, Translation, London, May 20, 1820, *British and Foreign State Papers (1820–1821)*, 208–10 (London: James Ridgway and Son, 1830). See also *Documentos acerca de las representaciones de la Junta Consular al gobierno de España solicitando una prórroga para el tráfico de negros*, Havana, March 4 and 7, 1820, Colección Vidal Morales y Morales, tomo 78, No. 120, BNC.

106. Evaristo Perez de Castro to Henry Wellesley, Translation, July 27, 1820, *British and Foreign State Papers (1820–1821)*, 224–25.

107. *British and Foreign State Papers (1820–1821)*, 246–48; Nelson, "Liberated Africans in the Atlantic World," 46.

108. Nelson, "Liberated Africans in the Atlantic World," 46–47; 230.

109. Evaristo Perez de Castro to Henry Wellesley, Translation, February 27, 1821, FO 72/244, TNA.

110. Joaquín Varela Suanzes-Carpegna, *Historia del levantamiento, guerra y revolución de España por el Conde de Toreno* (Madrid: Centro de Estudios Políticos y Constitucionales, 2008), vii–viii.

111. José María Queipo de Llano y Ruiz de Saravia, Conde de Toreno to William Wilberforce, Paris, January 27, 1821, MS Wilberforce c. 50 f. 1, BL.

112. José María Queipo de Llano y Ruiz de Saravia, Conde de Toreno to William Wilberforce, Paris, January 27, 1821, MS Wilberforce c. 50 f. 1, BL.

113. Wellesley to Castlereagh, No. 40, March 7, 1821, FO 72/244, TNA; Murray, *Odious Commerce*, 82–83. See also Corwin, *Spain and the Abolition of Slavery in Cuba, 1817–1886*, 36; Rafael Marquese, Márcia Berbel, and Tâmis Parron, *Slavery and Politics: Brazil and Cuba, 1790–1850* (Albuquerque: University of New Mexico Press, 2016), 96–97.

114. Wellesley to Castlereagh, No. 40, March 7, 1821, FO 72/244, TNA.

115. Wellesley to Castlereagh, No. 50, March 26, 1821, FO 72/244, TNA.

116. "That a special commission be formed so that, in accordance with Article 6 of the Treaty signed on the 23rd of September of 1817, between England and Spain, it may, as soon as possible, adopt the necessary measures in order to suppress the traffic of slaves from Africa, conveniently adapting the laws in order to end this shameful and inhumane traffic." *Diario de las Sesiones de Cortes*, March 23, 1821, vol. 26, p. 640.

117. *Diario de las Sesiones de Cortes*, March 23, 1821, vol. 26, p. 640.

118. Wellesley to Castlereagh, No. 50, March 26, 1821, FO 72/244, TNA.

119. *Diario de las Sesiones de Cortes*, April 2, 1821, vol. 36, p. 831.

120. Barcia, *Great African Slave Revolt of 1825*, 36–38; Barcia, *Seeds of Insurrection*, 80–85.

121. Barcia, *Great African Slave Revolt of 1825*, 36–38; Barcia, *Seeds of Insurrection*, 80–85.

122. Saco, *Historia de la esclavitud de la raza africana*, 140–41.

123. Saco, *Historia de la esclavitud de la raza africana*, 142.

124. Barcia, *Seeds of Insurrection*, 80.

125. Barcia, *Seeds of Insurrection*, 80.

126. Barcia, *Seeds of Insurrection*, 80.

127. González-Ripoll et al., *El rumor de Haití en Cuba*, 158.

128. Juan Bernardo O'Gavan, *Observaciones sobre la suerte de los negros del África, considerados en su propia patria y trasladados a las Antillas españolas: Y reclamación contra el tratado firmado con los ingleses en el año 1817* (Madrid: Imprenta del Universal, 1821), 11, in *Colección facticia de Vidal Morales*, 082, Morales, tomo 92, No. 13, BNC.

129. Barcia, *Great African Slave Revolt of 1825*, 37–38.

130. O'Gavan, *Observaciones sobre la suerte de los negros del África*, 12.

131. Fradera, "Moments in a Postponed Abolition," 270.

132. John Bowring, *Autobiographical Recollections of Sir John Bowring* (London: Henry S. King, 1877), 99–100.

133. Gregorio Alonso, "'A Great People Struggling for Their Liberties': Spain and the Mediterranean in the Eyes of the Benthamites," *History of European Ideas* (2014): 3–4.

134. Alonso, "Great People Struggling for Their Liberties," 3–4.

135. Hervey to Castlereagh, No. 103, October 3, 1821, FO 72/248, TNA.

136. Hervey to Castlereagh, No. 103, October 3, 1821, FO 72/248, TNA.

137. John Bowring, *Contestación a las observaciones de D. Juan Bernardo O'Gavan, sobre la suerte de los negros de África y reclamación contra el tratado celebrado con los ingleses en 1817* (Madrid: Imprenta de D. León Amarita, 1821).

138. Bowring, *Contestación a las observaciones de D. Juan Bernardo O'Gavan*, 3–4.

139. Bowring, *Contestación a las observaciones de D. Juan Bernardo O'Gavan*, 18–19.

140. Bowring, *Contestación a las observaciones de D. Juan Bernardo O'Gavan*, 20–21.

141. José A. Piqueras, *Felix Varela y la prosperidad de la patria criolla* (Madrid: Fundación Mapfre and Doce Calles, 2007); Moreno Alonso, *La forja del liberalismo en España: Los amigos españoles de Lord Holland, 1793–1840*; Alberto Gil Novales, *Las sociedades patrióticas (1820–1823)*, vol. 1 (Madrid: Tecnos, 1975); Jesús Raúl Navarro García, *Entre esclavos y constituciones (el colonialismo liberal de 1837 en Cuba)* (Sevilla: CSIC—Escuela de Estudios Hispano-Americanos (EEHA), 1991); Enriqueta Vila and Lucia Vila, *Los abolicionistas españoles: Siglo XIX* (Madrid: Ediciones de Cultura Hispánica, 1996). The *Trienio Liberal*, or Liberal Triennium, was a period of three years, between 1820 and 1823, when a Liberal government ruled Spain after a military uprising in January 1820 by the lieutenant-colonel Rafael de Riego against the absolutist rule of Ferdinand VII.

142. Alonso, "Great People Struggling for Their Liberties," 10–11.

143. *Consideraciones dirigidas a los habitantes de la Europa sobre la iniquidad del comercio de los negros* (London: George Smallfield, 1822); *Clamores de los africanos contra los europeos sus opresores, ó Exámen del detestable comercio llamado de negros* (London: J. G. Barnard, 1823).

144. Juan B. Vilar, *Intolerancia y libertad en la España contemporánea: Los orígenes del protestantismo español actual* (Madrid: Istmo, 1994), 72.

145. Julia Moreno García, "La cuestión de la trata en el Trienio Liberal (1820–1823)," *Cuadernos de historia contemporánea* extra 1 (2003). On the Penal Code of 1822, see Manuel Torres Aguilar, *Génesis parlamentaria del Código penal de 1822* (Messina:

SICANIA University Press. Università degli Studi di Messina, 2008); Juan B. Cañizares Navarro, "El Código penal de 1822: Sus fuentes inspiradoras: Balance historiográfico (desde el s. XX)," *Glossae: European Journal of Legal History*, no. 10 (2013).

146. *Código penal español decretado por las Cortes en 8 de junio y sancionado por el Rey y mandado promulgar el nueve de julio de 1822* (Madrid: Imprenta Nacional, 1822), 55, accessed November 14, 2020, https://books.google.co.uk/books?id=UqDLuuX4oUUC.

147. *British and Foreign State Papers (1820–1821)*, 177–79; Viscount Castlereagh to the Earl of Clancarty, Foreign Office, November 11, 1819 (Enclosure 2) Commodore Sir G. Collier to the Lords of the Admiralty. (Extract.)

148. Fradera, "Moments in a Postponed Abolition," 270.

149. Lionel Hervey to Castlereagh, No. 78, June 30, 1822, FO 72/256, TNA.

150. Eloy Martín Corrales, "La esclavitud negra en la Cataluña entre los siglos XVI y XIX," in *Negros y esclavos: Barcelona y la esclavitud atlántica (siglos XVI–XIX)*, ed. Martín Rodrigo y Alharilla and Lizbeth Chaviano Pérez (Barcelona: Icaria, 2017), 29–32; Eduardo Galván, *La abolición de la esclavitud en España: Debates parlamentarios, 1810–1886* (Madrid: Dickinson, 2014), 52–56.

151. Martín Corrales, "Esclavitud negra en la Cataluña," 29–32.

152. Martín Corrales, "Esclavitud negra en la Cataluña," 29–32.

153. Galván, *Abolición de la esclavitud en España*, 65–66.

154. Barcia, *Great African Slave Revolt of 1825*, 37–38. For a biographical study of Felix Varela, see Piqueras, *Felix Varela y la prosperidad de la patria criolla*; Manuel Maza, *Por la vida y el honor: El presbítero Félix Varela en las Cortes de España, 1882–1823* (Madrid: Editorial Nacional, 1987); Eduardo Torres-Cuevas, *Félix Varela: Ética y anticipación del pensamiento de la emancipación cubana* (Havana: Imagen Contemporánea, 1991).

155. Olga Portuondo, *Cuba: Constitución y liberalismo* (Santiago de Cuba: Editorial Oriente, 2008), 143.

156. Saco, *Historia de la esclavitud de la raza africana*, 5–17.

157. Saco, *Historia de la esclavitud de la raza africana*, 15.

158. Saco, *Historia de la esclavitud de la raza africana*, 15.

159. Saco, *Historia de la esclavitud de la raza africana*, 16.

160. Barcia, *Great African Slave Revolt of 1825*, 37–38.

161. Saco, *Historia de la esclavitud de la raza africana*, 17; Jorge Castellanos and Isabel Castellanos, *Cultura afrocubana*, vol. 1 (Miami: Editorial Universal, 1988), 228.

162. Saco, *Historia de la esclavitud de la raza africana*, 9.

163. Piqueras, *Felix Varela y la prosperidad de la patria criolla*; Maza, *Por la vida y el honor*; Torres-Cuevas, *Félix Varela*.

164. Fradera, "Moments in a Postponed Abolition," 264.

165. Fradera, "Moments in a Postponed Abolition," 270.

166. September 20, 1858, Ultramar, Cuba, leg. 2923, No. 279, AHN; Moreno García, "España y Gran Bretaña durante el siglo XIX," 770–71.

Chapter 3

1. Vicente Llorens, *Liberales y románticos* (Madrid: Castalia, 1979, originally published 1954).

2. Daniel Muñoz and Gregorio Alonso, *Londres y el liberalismo hispánico* (Madrid and Frankfurt am Main: Iberoamericana-Vervuert, 2011); Juan Luis Simal, *Emigrados: España y el exilio internacional, 1814–1834* (Madrid: Centro de Estudios Políticos y Constitucionales, 2013); Juan Francisco Fuentes Aragonés, "'Cherchez la femme': Exiliadas y liberales en la Década Ominosa (1823–1833)," *Historia constitucional* 13 (2012): 383–405.

3. Jesús Sanjurjo, "Negros o esclavos: La retórica de la esclavitud en la prensa española del exilio londinense (1818–1825)," *Anuario de estudios atlánticos* 62, no. 62 (2016): 1–14.

4. Fradera, "Moments in a Postponed Abolition," in *Slavery and Antislavery in Spain's Atlantic Empire*, ed. Josep M. Fradera and Christopher Schmidt-Nowara (New York: Berghahn, 2013), 283.

5. Llorens, *Liberales y románticos*, 23.

6. Llorens, *Liberales y románticos*, 288.

7. Catherine Davies, "The Contemporary Response of the British Press to the 1812 Constitution," in *1812 Echoes: The Cadiz Constitution in Hispanic History, Culture and Politics*, ed. Stephen G. H. Roberts and Adam Sharman (Newcastle upon Tyne: Cambridge Scholars, 2013), 106; Llorens, *Liberales y románticos*, 51.

8. Davies, "Contemporary Response of the British Press to the 1812 Constitution," 110.

9. Davies, "Contemporary Response of the British Press to the 1812 Constitution," 110.

10. Davies, "Contemporary Response of the British Press to the 1812 Constitution," 105.

11. *El español constitucional, El Telescopio, Los ocios de los españoles emigrados, Museo Universal de Ciencias y Artes, Correo y político de Londres, El emigrado observador*, and *Semanario de agricultura*. Llorens, *Liberales y románticos*, 287.

12. Llorens, *Liberales y románticos*, 300; Davies, "Contemporary Response of the British Press to the 1812 Constitution," 110.

13. *El español constitucional*, March 1824, p. 17.

14. *El español constitucional*, March 1824, pp. 16–20.

15. *El español constitucional*, March 1824, p. 16.

16. Llorens, *Liberales y románticos*, 302.

17. Llorens, *Liberales y románticos*, 323–24.

18. Neptalí Zúñiga, *Rocafuerte y el periodismo en Inglaterra* (Quito: Imprenta del Ministerio del Tesoro, 1947), iii.

19. Agustín Argüelles, *Apéndice a la sentencia pronunciada en 11 de mayo de 1825 por la Audiencia de Sevilla contra los 63 diputados de las Cortes de 1822 y 1823* (London: Imprenta de Carlos Wood e hijo, 1834); Agustín Argüelles, *Examen histórico de la reforma constitucional que hicieron las Cortes Generales y Estraordinarias . . .* (London: Imprenta de Carlos Wood e hijo, 1835).

20. Manuel Moreno Alonso, "Confesiones políticas de Don Agustín de Argüelles," *Revista de estudios políticos* 54 (1986): 226–61.

21. *Diario de las Sesiones de Cortes*, March 10, 1837, p. 2039.

22. Fradera, "Moments in a Postponed Abolition," 274–75; Fradera, *Colonias para después de un imperio*, 183–326.

23. Paquette, "The Intellectual Impact of International Rivalry," in *Enlightenment, Governance and Reform in Spain and Its Empire, 1759–1808* (New York: Palgrave Macmillan, 2008), 29–55; "Introduction: Liberalism in the Early Nineteenth-Century Iberian World," *History of European Ideas* 41, no. 2 (2015): 1–13.

24. Jennifer L. Nelson, "Liberated Africans in the Atlantic World: The Courts of Mixed Commission in Havana and Rio de Janeiro, 1819–1871," PhD thesis, University of Leeds, 2015, 206.

25. Kilbee to Hamilton, March 4, 1822, FO 84/18; David R. Murray, *Odious Commerce: Britain, Spain and the Abolition of the Cuban Slave Trade* (Cambridge: Cambridge University Press, 2002, originally published 1980), 76–77.

26. Murray, *Odious Commerce*, 76–77.

27. As Kilbee reported in 1825, "I have good reasons for saying that with very few exceptions, all the employees under the Government are directly or indirectly engaged in the Traffic." Murray, *Odious Commerce*, 76–77.

28. Jameson to Clanwillian, September 1, 1821, FO 84/13; Murray, *Odious Commerce*, 76–77.

29. Murray, *Odious Commerce*, 108.

30. Nelson, "Liberated Africans in the Atlantic World," 46.

31. Kilbee to Planta, January 22 and October 8, 1825, FO 84/39; Kilbee to Planta, February 2, 1825, FO 72/304; Murray, *Odious Commerce*, 78.

32. Nelson, "Liberated Africans in the Atlantic World," 230–31.

33. Francisco Vives to Francisco Cea Bermúdez, January 6, 1825, included in Ezpeleta to Francisco Cea Bermúdez, Estado, leg. 8036, AHN.

34. Nelson, "Liberated Africans in the Atlantic World," 50.

35. Kilbee to Canning, no. 2, January 1, 1825, FO 84/39; Murray, *Odious Commerce*, 84–85.

36. Council of State Report, May 15, 1822, Estado, leg. 8031, AHN.

37. Nelson, "Liberated Africans in the Atlantic World," 47.

38. *British and Foreign State Papers (1829–1830)*, 608 (London: James Ridgway, 1834).

39. *British and Foreign State Papers (1829–1830)*, 608.

40. Hervey to Castlereagh (Marquess of Londonderry), Private 2, June 7, 1822, FO 72/255, TNA.

41. "Comunicación del encargado de negocios de S.M. en los Estados Unidos, al intendente, fecha Filadelfia 31 de marzo de 1823, solicitando auxilio [por su situación económica] y acompañando el periódico titulado 'Aurora General Advertiser' correspondiente al viernes 28 de marzo de 1823, con una proclama dirigida a españoles y cubanos sobre los rumores de cesión de la Isla a Inglaterra," Asuntos Políticos, leg. 113, exp. 67, AHC, and Asuntos Políticos, leg. 50, exp. 30.

42. "Comunicación del encargado de negocios de S.M. en los Estados Unidos, al intendente, fecha Filadelfia 31 de marzo de 1823, solicitando auxilio [por su situación económica] y acompañando el periódico titulado 'Aurora General Advertiser' corre-

spondiente al viernes 28 de marzo de 1823, con una proclama dirigida a españoles y cubanos sobre los rumores de cesión de la Isla a Inglaterra," Asuntos Políticos, leg. 113, exp. 67, AHC, and Asuntos Políticos, leg. 50, exp. 30.

43. "Real Orden de 12 de Julio de 1827. Da cuenta de las tramas que se urgen en Londres para estimular a los habitantes de esta Isla a que se subleven contra el Gobierno de SM," Asuntos Políticos, leg. 32, exp. 26, ANC.

44. "Real Orden de 12 de Julio de 1827. Da cuenta de las tramas que se urgen en Londres para estimular a los habitantes de esta Isla a que se subleven contra el Gobierno de SM," Asuntos Políticos, leg. 32, exp. 26, ANC.

45. Lars Schoultz, *The Infernal Little Cuban Republic: The United States and the Cuban Revolution* (Chapel Hill: University of North Carolina Press, 2009), 19; Murray, *Odious Commerce*, 86; Robin Blackburn, *The Overthrow of Colonial Slavery, 1776–1848* (London: Verso, [1988] 2011), 396.

46. Murray, *Odious Commerce*, 86; Blackburn, *Overthrow of Colonial Slavery, 1776–1848*, 396.

47. On the development of Anglophobic discourses and "conspiratorial views" with regard to British abolitionist efforts in the United States in the 1840s, see Leonardo Marques, *The United States and the Transatlantic Slave Trade to the Americas, 1776–1867* (New Haven: Yale University Press, 2016), 158–60.

48. A. Findlay and W. M. Smith to Viscount Palmerston, Sierra Leone, December 28, 1831, *British and Foreign State Papers (1832–1833)*, vol. 20 (London: James Ridgway and Sons, 1836), 147–48.

49. Tratados siglo XIX, No. 64, Madrid, May 21, 1823, AMAE; Moreno García, "España y Gran Bretaña durante el siglo XIX: La abolición de la trata y la esclavitud," thesis, History, Universidad Complutense de Madrid, 1984, 267–69.

50. Tratados siglo XIX, No. 64, Madrid, May 21, 1823, AMAE; Moreno García, "España y Gran Bretaña durante el siglo XIX," 272.

51. Tratados siglo XIX, No. 64, Madrid, May 21, 1823, AMAE; Moreno García, "España y Gran Bretaña durante el siglo XIX," 272–73.

52. O'Gavan, *Observaciones sobre la suerte de los negros del África, considerados en su propia patria y trasladados a las Antillas españolas: Y reclamación contra el tratado firmado con los ingleses en el año 1817*, 11. In *Colección facticia de Vidal Morales*, 082, Morales, tomo 92, No. 13, BNC.

53. W. S. Macleay to Viscount Palmerston, Havana, January 2, 1832, *British and Foreign State Papers (1832–1833)*, 147–48.

54. Tratados siglo XIX, No. 64, Madrid, April 19, 1828, AMAE; Moreno García, "España y Gran Bretaña durante el siglo XIX," 277–78.

55. Council of State Report, January 19, 1829, Estado, leg. 8022, AHN; Moreno García, "España y Gran Bretaña durante el siglo XIX," 279–81; Murray, *Odious Commerce*, 94–95.

56. Fradera, "Moments in a Postponed Abolition," 273–74; Candelaria Saiz Pastor, "Las finanzas públicas en Cuba: La etapa de las desviaciones de fondos a la península, 1823–1866," in *Las Haciendas públicas en el Caribe hispano durante el siglo XIX*, ed. Inés Roldán de Montaud (Madrid: CSIC, 2008).

57. Council of State Report, January 19, 1829, Estado, leg. 8022, AHN; Moreno García, "España y Gran Bretaña durante el siglo XIX," 279–81; Murray, *Odious Commerce*, 94–95.

58. David F. Ericson, *The Debate over Slavery: Antislavery and Proslavery Liberalism in Antebellum America* (New York: New York University Press, 2000), 22–23. See also Harold D. Tallant, *Evil Necessity: Slavery and Political Culture in Antebellum Kentucky* (Lexington: University Press of Kentucky, 2003); John P. Kaminski, *Necessary Evil? Slavery and the Debate over the Constitution* (Madison: Madison House, 1995); Drew Gilpin Faust, *The Ideology of Slavery: Proslavery Thought in the Antebellum South, 1830–1860* (Baton Rouge: Louisiana State University Press, 1981); Domenico Losurdo, *Liberalism: A Counter-History* (New York: Verso Books, 2011), 35–65.

59. Ericson, *Debate over Slavery*, 23. The Missouri Compromise refers to the legislation passed by the 16th United States Congress on May 8, 1820. The measures provided for the admission of Maine as a free state along with Missouri as a slave state, thus maintaining the balance of power between North and South. As part of the compromise, slavery was prohibited north of the 36°30' parallel, excluding Missouri. On the Missouri crisis, see Robert Pierce Forbes, *The Missouri Compromise and Its Aftermath: Slavery and the Meaning of America* (Chapel Hill: Univerity of North Carolina Press, 2007).

60. Murray, *Odious Commerce*, 94–95.

61. Council of State Report, January 19, 1829, Estado, leg. 8022, AHN; Moreno García, "España y Gran Bretaña durante el siglo XIX," 280, 282.

62. Council of State Report, January 19,1829, Estado, leg. 8022, AHN; Moreno García, "España y Gran Bretaña durante el siglo XIX," 280–81.

63. Council of State Report, January 19, 1829, Estado, leg. 8022, AHN; Moreno García, "España y Gran Bretaña durante el siglo XIX," 282.

64. Council of State Report, January 19, 1829, Estado, leg. 8022, AHN; Moreno García, "España y Gran Bretaña durante el siglo XIX," 281; Murray, *Odious Commerce*, 94–95.

65. Tratados siglo XIX, No. 64, Madrid, January 8, 1830, AMAE; Moreno García, "España y Gran Bretaña durante el siglo XIX," 283–84.

66. Moreno García, "España y Gran Bretaña durante el siglo XIX," 285.

67. Murray, *Odious Commerce*, 93.

68. Henry U. Addington to Viscount Palmerston, Madrid, February 9, 1832, *British and Foreign State Papers (1832–1833)*, 187–88.

69. Henry U. Addington to Chevalier de Salmon, Madrid, February 5, 1831, *British and Foreign State Papers (1831–1832)*, vol. 19 (London: James Ridgway, 1834), 472–73.

70. Henry U. Addington to Chevalier de Salmon, Madrid, February 13, 1831, *British and Foreign State Papers (1831–1832)*, 478–79; Moreno García, "España y Gran Bretaña durante el siglo XIX," 289–90.

71. Viscount Palmerston to Henry U. Addington, Foreign Office, March 26, 1831, *British and Foreign State Papers (1831–1832)*, 479–80.

72. Viscount Palmerston to Henry U. Addington, Foreign Office, March 26, 1831, *British and Foreign State Papers (1831–1832)*, 479–80.

73. Viscount Palmerston to Henry U. Addington, Foreign Office, March 26, 1831, *British and Foreign State Papers (1831–1832)*, 479–80.

74. Tratados siglo XIX, No. 64, Madrid, February 1831, AMAE; Moreno García, "España y Gran Bretaña durante el siglo XIX," 293–94.

75. Moreno García, "España y Gran Bretaña durante el siglo XIX," 294.

76. Henry U. Addington, Esq., to the Count de la Alcudia, Aranjuez, May 24, 1832, *British and Foreign State Papers (1832–1833)*, 192–93.

77. Schmidt-Nowara, "Wilberforce Spanished: Joseph Blanco White and Spanish Antislavery, 1808–1814," in *Slavery and Antislavery in Spain's Atlantic Empire*, ed. Josep M. Fradera and Christopher Schmidt-Nowara (New York: Berghahn, 2013), 168.

78. Saco, *Historia de la esclavitud de la raza africana*, 16.

79. Villiers to Palmerston, March 8 and July 14, 1834, Clarendon Mss., c. 451, cited in Murray, *Odious Commerce*, 99.

80. Report of the Commission, October 26, 1833, Estado, leg. 8015, AHN; Murray, *Odious Commerce*, 98.

81. Royal Orders of November 28, 1824; January 2, 1826; June 30, 1828; March 4, 1830; and August 2, 1830.

82. Murray, *Odious Commerce*, 100–101.

83. Moreno García, "España y Gran Bretaña durante el siglo XIX," 318. Jenny S. Martinez, *The Slave Trade and the Origins of International Human Rights Law* (Oxford: Oxford University Press, 2012), 37, 168. The impact of French abolitionism in Spain is also significant during this period. French abolitionists were translated into Spanish too, and even some direct collaborations were established (Mariano Torrente and Abbé Henri Grégoire, for example). See Rossignol, "Jacques-Pierre Brissot and the Fate of Atlantic Antislavery during the Age of Revolutionary Wars," in *War, Empire and Slavery, 1770–1830*, ed. Richard Bessel, Nicholas Guyatt, and Jane Rendall (London: Palgrave Macmillan, 2010), 139–56; Jeremy D. Popkin and Richard H. Popkin, eds., *The Abbé Grégoire and His World* (Dordrecht: Springer Netherlands, 2000).

84. With the exceptions "of the Territories in the Possession of the East India Company," the "Island of Ceylon" and "the Island of Saint Helena" (these exceptions were eliminated in 1843).

85. Seymour Drescher, *Capitalism and Antislavery: British Mobilization in a Comparative Perspective* (Oxford: Oxford University Press, 1987); Christopher L. Brown, *Moral Capital: Foundations of British Abolitionism* (Chapel Hill: University of North Carolina Press, 2006); David Brion Davis, *The Problem of Slavery in Western Culture* (New York: Oxford University Press, 1966); *Economic Growth and the Ending of the Transatlantic Slave Trade* (New York: Oxford University Press, 1987); Robin Blackburn, *The American Crucible : Slavery, Emancipation and Human Rights* (New York: Verso, 2011).

86. Richard Huzzey, *Freedom Burning: Anti-slavery and Empire in Victorian Britain* (Ithaca: Cornell University Press, 2012), 70.

87. Huzzey, *Freedom Burning*, 65.

88. Ana Guerrero Latorre, Sisinio Pérez Garzón, and Germán Rueda Hernanz, *Historia política* (Madrid: Istmo, 2013), 185–91.

89. Mark Lawrence, *Spain's First Carlist War, 1833–40* (London: Palgrave Macmillan, 2014).

90. Murray, *Odious Commerce*, 100–101.

91. Kiple suggested that around twenty-two thousand enslaved Africans died from cholera during the period 1833–1836. In a more recent work, Adrián López Denis has reinterpreted Kiple's data and clarified that, although the figure provided by Ricafort was undoubtedly exaggerated, the number of deaths was closer to twenty-five thousand enslaved Africans. Kenneth F. Kiple, "Cholera and Race in the Caribbean," *Journal of Latin American Studies* 17, no. 1 (1985): 159–61; Franklin W. Knight, *Slave Society in Cuba during the Nineteenth Century* (Madison: University of Wisconsin Press, 1970), 34–35, 54–55; Adrián López Denis, "Disease and Society in Colonial Cuba, 1790–1840," PhD diss., University of California, Los Angeles, 2007. On the political and ideological response in Cuba to the cholera epidemic of 1833, see also J. Selene Zander, "Contagious Invasions: The 1833 Cholera Epidemic in Havana," *Revista de estudios hispánicos* 49, no. 1 (2005): 3–23.

92. Kiple, "Cholera and Race in the Caribbean," 159–61; Knight, *Slave Society in Cuba during the Nineteenth Century*, 34–35, 54–55.

93. Murray, *Odious Commerce*, 99.

94. Murray, *Odious Commerce*, 96–99.

95. Villiers to Zea Bermudez, December 31, 1833, *British and Foreign State Papers (1834–1835)*, vol. 23 (London: James Ridgway and Sons, 1852), 56.

96. Villiers to Palmerston, July 18, 1834, cited in Murray, *Odious Commerce*, 99.

97. Villiers to Martínez de la Rosa, April 14, 1835, Tratados del siglo XIX, No. 64, AMAE; Moreno García, "España y Gran Bretaña durante el siglo XIX," 379.

98. Proyecto de Tratado, April 1825, Tratados del siglo XIX, No. 64, AMAE; Moreno García, "España y Gran Bretaña durante el siglo XIX," 386.

99. Treaty between His Majesty and the Queen Regent of Spain, during the Minority of her Daughter, Donna Isabella the Second of Spain, for the Abolition of the Slave Trade, June 28, 1835, *British and Foreign State Papers (1834–1835)*, 344.

100. Treaty between His Majesty and the Queen Regent of Spain, during the Minority of her Daughter, Donna Isabella the Second of Spain, for the Abolition of the Slave Trade, June 28, 1835, *British and Foreign State Papers (1834–1835)*, 351–53; Murray, *Odious Commerce*, 100.

101. Treaty between His Majesty and the Queen Regent of Spain, during the Minority of her Daughter, Donna Isabella the Second of Spain, for the Abolition of the Slave Trade, June 28, 1835, *British and Foreign State Papers (1834–1835)*, 344, 45–47; Murray, *Odious Commerce*, 100. The Penal Law was only passed after ten years, in 1845.

102. Treaty between His Majesty and the Queen Regent of Spain, during the Minority of her Daughter, Donna Isabella the Second of Spain, for the Abolition of the Slave Trade, June 28, 1835, *British and Foreign State Papers (1834–1835)*, 355.

103. Murray, *Odious Commerce*, 106–7; Alfonso W. Quiroz, "Implicit Costs of Empire: Bureaucratic Corruption in Nineteenth-Century Cuba," *Journal of Latin American Studies* 35, no. 3 (2003), 484; Juan Pérez de la Riva, "Introducción: El general don

Miguel Tacón y su época," in *Correspondencia reservada del Capitan General don Miguel Tacon con el gobierno de Madrid, 1834–1836* (Havana: Biblioteca Nacional José Martí, 1964), 44.

104. Murray, *Odious Commerce*, 102; Martinez, *Slave Trade and the Origins of International Human Rights Law*, 83–84.

105. Murray, *Odious Commerce*, 100–102; "Trans-Atlantic Slave Trade—Database," Slave Voyages, accessed August 15, 2015, https://www.slavevoyages.org.

106. Murray, *Odious Commerce*, 107.

107. Murray, *Odious Commerce*, 106–7; Quiroz, "Implicit Costs of Empire," 484; Riva, "Introducción: El general don Miguel Tacón y su época," 44.

108. Quiroz, "Implicit Costs of Empire," 481.

109. Miguel Tacón to [unknown], Barcelona, June 27, 1844, Estado, leg. 8035, AHN. Reference and original transcription provided by Prof. Manuel Barcia.

110. This practice continued until 1839, when the British parliament passed the legislation known as Palmerston's Act, which authorized British war vessels to capture all Portuguese ships suspected of being slavers and to try them at the British Vice-Admiralty courts. The use of the American flag to avoid the Treaty of 1835 ceased in 1842 with the signing of a bilateral agreement between Britain and the United States that ruled that a US naval squadron would be based at the west coast of Africa to seize suspected slavers flying the American flag. Leslie Bethell, *The Abolition of the Brazilian Slave Trade* (Cambridge: Cambridge University Press, 1970); João Pedro Marques, *The Sounds of Silence: Nineteenth-Century Portugal and the Abolition of the Slave Trade* (New York: Berghahn Books, 2006); Don Fehrenbacher, *The Slaveholding Republic: An Account of the United States Government's Relations to Slavery* (New York: Oxford University Press, 2001), 135–204; John A. E. Harris, "Circuits of Wealth, Circuits of Sorrow: Financing the Illegal Transatlantic Slave Trade in the Age of Suppression, 1850–66," *Journal of Global History* 11, no. 3 (2016): 410.

111. Murray, *Odious Commerce*, 104.

112. Palmerston to Walden, May 6, 1837, Britain, Parliamentary Papers, Accounts and Papers 1837–38, vol. 50, p. 39.

113. Nicholas Trist accused the British authorities of blatant hypocrisy and argued that "British struggle against Cuban slave trade was aimed at favouring Brazilian cotton production (which has British capital) to the detriment of its U.S. counterparts"; as Leonardo Marqués has shown, Trist's accusation "that the British were as immersed in the slave trade as the Americans definitely had some truth to it." Marques, *United States and the Transatlantic Slave Trade to the Americas, 1776–1867*, 132–36; Murray, *Odious Commerce*, 106.

114. David Turnbull, *Travels in the West, Cuba: With Notices of Porto Rico and the Slave Trade* (London: Longman, Orme, Brown, Green and Longmans, 1840), 442–43.

115. Martinez, *Slave Trade and the Origins of International Human Rights Law*, 106; Eltis, *Economic Growth and the Ending of the Transatlantic Slave Trade*, 83.

116. Eltis, *Economic Growth and the Ending of the Transatlantic Slave Trade*, 83.

117. Manuel Barcia and Effie Kesidou, "Innovation and Entrepreneurship as Strategies for Success among Cuban-Based Firms in the Late Years of the Transatlantic Slave

Trade," *Business History* 60, no. 4 (2017); 546; Harris, "Circuits of Wealth, Circuits of Sorrow."

118. Murray, *Odious Commerce*, 103; Eltis, *Economic Growth and the Ending of the Transatlantic Slave Trade*, 142–43. Soon after, in October 1836, the British consul in Havana, Charles Tolmé, already predicted the new strategies that the slave traders would use to avoid the new legislation. Tolmé to Palmerston, October 15, 1836, FO 84/201, TNA.

119. Barcia and Kesidou, "Innovation and Entrepreneurship as Strategies for Success among Cuban-Based Firms in the Late Years of the Transatlantic Slave Trade," 554–55.

120. Murray, *Odious Commerce*, 112.

121. Eltis, *Economic Growth and the Ending of the Transatlantic Slave Trade*, 84–85.

122. Eltis, *Economic Growth and the Ending of the Transatlantic Slave Trade*, 84–85.

123. Murray, *Odious Commerce*, 112; Huzzey, *Freedom Burning*, 64.

124. Murray, *Odious Commerce*, 99.

125. Commodore Hayes to Admiralty, January 20, 1831, cited in Eltis, *Economic Growth and the Ending of the Transatlantic Slave Trade*, 84–85. On slave ships seized as prizes during the Royal Navy's anti–slave trade patrols, see Robert Burroughs, "Eyes on the Prize: Journeys in Slave Ships Taken as Prizes by the Royal Navy," *Slavery & Abolition* 31, no.1 (2010): 99–115.

126. [Edward Villiers], "Correspondence Relating to the Slave Trade; New Treaty with Spain," *Edinburgh Review* 128 (July 1836): 393. Cited in Murray, *Odious Commerce*, 99.

Chapter 4

1. The Estatuto Real of 1834 (or Royal Statute) was a *charte octroyée* of Spain under the rule of Maria Christina, wife of the deceased King Ferdinand VII of Spain, who ruled as queen regent during the infancy of her daughter Queen Isabella II of Spain. It came into effect on April 10, 1834. The Motín de La Granja de San Ildefonso was a military uprising that took place in Spain in August 1836 during the regency of María Cristina de Borbón in which a group of garrison sergeants and the royal guard of the palace of La Granja de San Ildefonso (Segovia) forced the queen regent to reenact the Constitution of 1812 and to appoint a progressive Liberal government chaired by José María Calatrava.

2. Josep M. Fradera, "Raza y ciudadanía: El factor racial en la delimitación de los derechos de los Americanos," in *Gobernar colonias*, ed. Josep M. Fradera (Barcelona: Peninsula, 1999); Fradera, *Colonias para después de un imperio* (Barcelona: Edicions Bellaterra, 2005), 163; Josep M. Fradera, "Moments in a Postponed Abolition," in *Slavery and Antislavery in Spain's Atlantic Empire*, ed. Josep M. Fradera and Christopher Schmidt-Nowara (New York: Berghahn, 2013); Josep M. Fradera, *La nación imperial (1750–1918): Derechos, representación y ciudadanía en los imperios de Gran Bretaña, Francia, España y Estados Unidos* (Barcelona: Edhasa, 2015); Javier Alvarado, "El régimen de legislación especial para ultramar y la cuestión abolicionista en España durante el siglo XIX," in *La supervivencia del derecho español en Hispanoamérica durante la época independiente*, ed. Instituto de Investigaciones Jurídicas, Universidad Nacional Autónoma de

México, 1–30 (Mexico City: UNAM, 1998); José Antonio Piqueras, "El gobierno de la población heterogénea en la segunda esclavitud," in *Orden político y gobierno de esclavos*, ed. José Antonio Piqueras (Valencia: Centro Francisco Tomás y Valiente UNED Alzira-Valencia and Fundación Instituto de Historia Social, 2016).

3. Fradera, *Colonias para después de un imperio*.

4. "Dictamen de las comisiones reunidas de Ultramar y Constitución, proponiendo que las provincias ultramarinas de América y Asía sean regidas y administradas por leyes especiales," *Diario de las Sesiones de Cortes*, February 12, 1837, pp. 1491–93. Piqueras, "Gobierno de la población heterogénea en la segunda esclavitud," 19–20, 23–24.

5. Piqueras, "Gobierno de la población heterogénea en la segunda esclavitud," 32.

6. Piqueras, "Gobierno de la población heterogénea en la segunda esclavitud," 32.

7. Fradera, *Colonias para después de un imperio*, 157.

8. *Diario de las Sesiones de Cortes*, March 10, 1837, p. 2039.

9. *Diario de las Sesiones de Cortes*, March 10, 1837, pp. 2039–2042.

10. *Diario de las Sesiones de Cortes*, March 10, 1837, p. 2042.

11. José Antonio Saco, *Historia de la esclavitud de la raza africana en el Nuevo Mundo y en especial en los paises americo-hispanos*, vol. 4, ed. Fernando Ortiz (Havana: Cultural S.A., 1938), 85–98, originally published 1879.

12. Fradera, *Colonias para después de un imperio*, 160.

13. *Diario de las Sesiones de Cortes*, April 5, 1837, p. 2508.

14. *Diario de las Sesiones de Cortes*, April 5, 1837, p. 2508.

15. *Diario de las Sesiones de Cortes*, April 5, 1837, p. 2508; and March 25, 1837, p. 2317; Piqueras, "Gobierno de la población heterogénea en la segunda esclavitud," 33–34. On the Haitian Revolution's impact in Cuba, see Fradera, "Moments in a Postponed Abolition," 146; Ferrer, *Freedom's Mirror: Cuba and Haiti in the Age of Revolution* (Cambridge: Cambridge University Press, 2014); María Dolores González-Ripoll et al., *El rumor de Haití en Cuba: Temor, raza y rebeldía, 1789–1844* (Madrid: Consejo Superior de Investigaciones Científicas, 2004); Jeremy D. Popkin, *Facing Racial Revolution: Eyewitness Accounts of the Haitian Revolution* (Chicago: University of Chicago Press, 2007).

16. *Diario de las Sesiones de Cortes*, April 2, 1811, p. 812.

17. Piqueras, "Gobierno de la población heterogénea en la segunda esclavitud," 35–36.

18. Albert García Balañà, "Antislavery before Abolitionism: Networks and Motives in Early Liberal Barcelona, 1833–1844," in *Slavery and Antislavery in Spain's Atlantic Empire*, ed. Josep M. Fradera and Christopher Schmidt-Nowara (New York: Berghahn, 2013), 234.

19. García Balañà, "Antislavery before Abolitionism," 236.

20. *Criollo* refers to a person from Spanish America, especially one of supposedly "pure" Spanish descent.

21. *Diario de las Sesiones de Cortes*, March 10, 1837, pp. 2036–38.

22. *Diario de las Sesiones de Cortes*, March 9, 1837, p. 2037.

23. García Balañà, "Antislavery before Abolitionism," 235.

24. In the context of Spanish America, *pardos* generally refers to mixed-race people, descendants of Europeans, Indigenous Americans, and West Africans.

25. *Diario de las Sesiones de Cortes*, March 9, 1837, p. 2022.

26. Piqueras, "Gobierno de la población heterogénea en la segunda esclavitud," 38.

27. On Saco's position in 1837, see Fradera, *Colonias para después de un imperio*, 165–70; Piqueras, "Gobierno de la población heterogénea en la segunda esclavitud," 39–45; Jesús Raúl Navarro García, *Entre esclavos y constituciones* (Sevilla: CSIC—Escuela de Estudios Hispano-Americanos [EEHA], 1991), 28–33.

28. José Antonio Saco, *Examen analítico del informe de la comisión especial nombrada por las Cortes* (Madrid: Oficina de Don Tomás Jordan, 1837), 25.

29. José Antonio Saco, *Obras*, vol. 2, ed. Eduardo Torres-Cuevas (Havana: Imagen Contemporánea, 2001), 196.

30. On race and national identity in Saco's work, see Josef Opantrny, *José Antonio Saco y la búsqueda de la identidad cubana* (Prague: Univerzita Karlova, 2010).

31. Saco, *Obras*, 2:73–74; Eduardo Torres Cuevas and Arturo Soregui, *José Antonio Saco, acerca de la esclavitud y su historia* (Havana: Editorial de Ciencias Sociales, 1982), 202–5.

32. Saco, *Examen analítico del informe de la comisión especial nombrada por las Cortes*, 125–26.

33. Saco, *Obras*, 1:296.

34. Saco, *Obras*, 4:102.

35. José Antonio Saco, *Paralelo entre la Isla de Cuba y algunas colonias inglesas* (Madrid: Oficina de Don Tomás Jordán, impresor de Cámara de S. M., 1837).

36. Saco, *Obras*, 3:145–46.

37. José Antonio Saco, *Mi primera pregunta ¿La abolición del comercio de esclavos africanos arruinará o atrasará la agricultura cubana?* (Madrid: Imprenta de don Marcilino Calero, 1837).

38. Saco, *Obras*, 2:82–83.

39. Saco, *Obras*, 2:82–83.

40. Saco, *Obras*, 2:117.

41. Saco, *Obras*, 2:125.

42. Domingo del Monte, *La Isla de Cuba tal cual está* (New York: Whittaker, 1836).

43. Alfonso W. Quiroz, "Implicit Costs of Empire: Bureaucratic Corruption in Nineteenth-Century Cuba," *Journal of Latin American Studies* 35, no. 3 (2003): 473–511.

44. Domingo del Monte, "La Isla de Cuba tal cual está," in *Historia de la esclavitud de la raza africana en el Nuevo Mundo y en especial en los paises americo-hispanos*, ed. José Antonio Saco (Havana: Cultural S. A., 1938), 281.

45. Domingo del Monte, *Escritos de Domingo del Monte*, vol. 1 (Havana: Cultural, 1929), 231.

46. Del Monte, *Escritos de Domingo del Monte*, 231.

47. He is the author of the popular aphorism "En la cuestión de los negros, lo menos negro es el negro." José de la Luz y Caballero, *Aforismos* (Havana: Editorial Lex, 1960).

48. José Antonio Fernández de Castro, *Medio siglo de historia colonial de Cuba* (Havana: Ricardo Veloso, 1923), 52–56; Castellanos and Castellanos, *Cultura afrocubana*, vol. 1 (Miami: Editorial Universal, 1988), 273–74.

49. Castellanos and Castellanos, *Cultura afrocubana*, 280.

50. Castellanos and Castellanos, *Cultura afrocubana*, 280.

51. Castellanos and Castellanos, *Cultura afrocubana*, 281.

52. Castellanos and Castellanos, *Cultura afrocubana*, 281.

53. Murray, *Odious Commerce*, 129.

54. Murray, *Odious Commerce*, 129.

55. Castellanos and Castellanos, *Cultura afrocubana*, 246.

56. In fact, during his campaign to be elected as representative for the Cuban city of Santiago, Saco was accused by slave owners of being an abolitionist with links to the British authorities: "sold out to the interests of the British government with regard to [the abolition of] slavery." His friend and supporter, Juan Bautista Segarra, aiming to tackle these allegations and to attract the votes of the planters, asked rhetorically: "When has he [Saco] ever said anything of giving freedom to the Negroes?" Castellanos and Castellanos, *Cultura afrocubana*, 274.

57. Murray, *Odious Commerce*, 129.

58. María del Carmen Barcia, "La abolición de la trata negrera en Cuba," in *IV encuentro de historiadores latinoamericanos y del Caribe* (Havana: Universidad de la Havana, 1983), 11.

59. Murray, *Odious Commerce*, 131.

60. Barcia, "Abolición de la trata negrera en Cuba," 11. Even Wenceslao de Villaurrutia, Saco's close collaborator, considered that Turnbull's words were hard to believe and a generalization. Barcia, "Abolición de la trata negrera en Cuba," 22; Murray, *Odious Commerce*, 129.

61. Romy Sánchez, "Quitter la Très Fidèle: Exilés et bannis au temps du séparatisme cubain, 1834–1879," PhD thesis, Université Paris 1 Panthéon Sorbonne, 2017; Robin Blackburn, *The Overthrow of Colonial Slavery, 1776–1848* (London: Verso, [1988] 2011); Luis Martínez-Fernández, *Fighting Slavery in the Caribbean: Life and Times of a British Family in Nineteenth Century Havana* (London: Routledge, 1998); Charles Henry Brown, *Agents of Manifest Destiny: The Lives and Times of the Filibusters* (Chapel Hill: University of North Carolina Press, 1980).

62. Manuel Barcia, *West African Warfare in Bahia and Cuba: Soldier Slaves in the Atlantic World, 1807–1844* (Oxford: Oxford University Press, 2014), 161–65.

63. Moreno García, "España y Gran Bretaña durante el siglo XIX," 426.

64. Ezpeleta to the Secretary of State, February 1830, Estado, leg. 8023, AHN.

65. Ferrer, *Freedom's Mirror*; González-Ripoll et al., *Rumor de Haití en Cuba*.

66. In 1830 Captain General Vives referred to the "ideas of freedom" that illegally introduced enslaved Africans from Jamaica could bring into Cuba. Similarly, in August 1833, Cuban intendant Claudio Martinez de Pinillos, Count of Villanueva (1782–1853), wrote about the risk of infection of "pernicious ideas" in reference to abolitionist discourses. Vives to the Secretary of State, August 1833, Estado, leg. 8034, AHN.

67. "Diligencias que se han de practicar en averiguación del poseedor de un papel encontrado en el camino real que atraviesa el pueblo de Alquizar, el cual contiene una estampa de una negro aprisionado de una rodilla en tierra, y en el pie de la figura unos versos subversivos escritos en inglés," November 15, 1835, Comisión Militar, leg. 130, exp. 2, ANC.

68. Tacón to the Secretary of State, May 22, 1836, Estado, leg. 8035, AHN.

69. Antonio Brosa to Tacón, May 22, 1837, Estado, leg. 8037, AHN.

70. Antonio Brosa to Tacón, February 20, 1838, Estado, leg. 8037, AHN.

71. De la Barca to the Secretary of State, December 8, 1836, Estado, leg. 8036, AHN.

72. *Comunicación dirigida por Miguel Tacón al Gobernador de la provincia de Cuba tras-cribiéndole otra del Ministro de España en EEUU referente a las actividades de las Asociaciones para la abolición de la esclavitud de los negros,* July 14, 1837, leg. 39, exp. 18, Asuntos Políticos, ANC.

73. Among the seized documents were "The War in Texas, Investigated by Slave-holders, Land Speculators of Philadelphia," published in 1836; "The Speech delivered at the Soiree in honour of George Thompson, Esq." of 1837; "Memoir of Phillips Wheasley," published in Boston in 1834; "The Tale of a New Yorker by a Known Author" published in New York in 1835; and different issues of the periodicals *New York Mirror, Plain Dealer, New Yorker, Albion, Daily Herald, Sun, Morning Courier, New York Weekly Messenger, Norfolk & Portsmouth Herald, Alexandria Gazette, American & Commercial, Transcript,* and *Examiner.* Comisión Militar, leg. 17, exp. 1, ANC.

74. Asuntos Políticos, leg. 40, exp. 1, ANC.

75. Asuntos Políticos, leg. 40, exp. 7, ANC.

76. Murray, *Odious Commerce,* 120.

77. Murray, *Odious Commerce,* 132; Christine Bolt, *The Anti-slavery Movement and Reconstruction: A Study in Anglo-American Co-Operation, 1833–77* (London: Oxford University Press, 1969); James Heartfield, *The British and Foreign Anti-slavery Society, 1838–1956: A History* (Oxford: Oxford University Press, 2016); Richard Huzzey, *Freedom Burning: Anti-slavery and Empire in Victorian Britain* (Ithaca: Cornell University Press, 2012).

78. Murray, *Odious Commerce,* 121.

79. Murray, *Odious Commerce,* 122; Tacón to the Secretary of State, August 31, 1837, Estado, leg. 8022, AHN.

80. Murray, *Odious Commerce,* 120.

81. Murray, *Odious Commerce,* 120. On the relation between national sovereignty, honor, and the slave trade in Portugal, see João Pedro Marques, *The Sounds of Silence: Nineteenth-Century Portugal and the Abolition of the Slave Trade* (New York: Berghahn Books, 2006). For the Spanish case, this aspect is discussed further in the following chapter.

82. Murray, *Odious Commerce,* 123.

83. Nelson, "Liberated Africans in the Atlantic World," 106; Jennifer L. Nelson, "Slavery, Race, and Conspiracy: The HMS *Romney* in Nineteenth-Century Cuba," *Atlantic Studies* 14, no. 2 (2017): 174–95.

84. Murray, *Odious Commerce,* 125.

85. Murray, *Odious Commerce,* 127.

86. Murray, *Odious Commerce,* 126–27.

87. Manuel Llorca-Jaña, "Turnbull, David (1793?–1851)," in *Oxford Dictionary of National Biography* (Oxford: Oxford University Press, 2009).

88. James Kennedy had also accused Tolmé of collaborating with slave traders in the

past. Turnbull, *Travels in the West: Cuba, with Notices of Porto Rico and the Slave Trade*, 43.

89. Huzzey, *Freedom Burning*, 14.

90. Murray, *Odious Commerce*, 132; Bolt, *Anti-slavery Movement and Reconstruction*; Heartfield, *British and Foreign Anti-Slavery Society*; Huzzey, *Freedom Burning*.

91. According to Albert García Balañà, in January 1842 the BFASS suggested to the French Société pour l'Abolition de l'Esclavage, to invite the Spanish subjects José Antonio Saco, Santiago Usoz y Río, and Antonio Bergnes de las Casas to a forthcoming antislavery convention. Bergnes, a Catalan publisher, also appears in the proceedings of the General Anti-Slavery Convention of June 1843 in London. García Balañà, "Antislavery before Abolitionism," 227.

92. Turnbull, *Travels in the West, Cuba*, 342–43.

93. Turnbull, *Travels in the West, Cuba*, 348.

94. Turnbull, *Travels in the West, Cuba*, 349–59, 43.

95. Turnbull, *Travels in the West, Cuba*, viii.

96. Memorandum by Bandiel, April 3, 1840, FO 84/318; *Westminster Review* 34 (June 1840), 151; Murray, *Odious Commerce*, 137–38; Huzzey, *Freedom Burning*, 136–41.

97. Murray, *Odious Commerce*, 139–40.

98. Huzzey, *Freedom Burning*, 70.

99. Girón to the Secretary of State, November 1, 1840, Estado, leg. 8498, AHN.

100. Junta de Fomento de Agricultura y Comercio to the Secretary of State Estado, leg. 8053, November 30, 1840, AHN.

101. Junta de Fomento de Agricultura y Comercio to the Secretary of State Estado, leg. 8053, November 30, 1840, AHN.

102. Murray, *Odious Commerce*, 145. On Antonio Bergnes, see also García Balañà, "Antislavery before Abolitionism."

103. Benjamin Wiffen and Santiago Usoz continued a correspondent relationship after this meeting. Mar Vilar, "La lengua y civilización inglesas en sus relaciones con España a mediados del siglo XIX," *Boletín de la Real Academia de la Historia*, no. 193–1 (1996); Juan B. Vilar and Mar Vilar, *El primer hispanismo británico en la formación y contenidos de la más importante biblioteca española de libros prohibidos: Correspondencia inédita de Luis de Usoz con Benjamin B. Wiffen (1840–1850)* (Sevilla: Editorial MAD, 2010).

104. John Flude Johnson, *Proceedings of the General Anti-Slavery Convention Called by the Committee of the British and Foreign Anti-Slavery Society* (London: John Snow, 1843), 186–87.

105. Armario Sanchez, "Esclavitud y abolicionismo durante la regencia de Espartero," in *Esclavitud y derechos humanos: La lucha por la libertad del negro en el siglo XIX*, ed. Francisco de Solano and Agustín Guimerá (Madrid: CSIC, 1990); Mark Lawrence, *Spain's First Carlist War, 1833–40* (London: Palgrave Macmillan, 2014); Raúl Martín Arranz, "Espartero: Figuras de legitimidad," in *Populismo, caudillaje y discurso demagógico*, ed. José Alvarez Junco (Madrid: CIS/Siglo XXI, 1987); María Cruz Romeo Mateo, "Lenguaje y política del nuevo liberalismo: Moderados y progresistas, 1834–1845," *Ayer*, no. 29 (1998); Adrian Shubert, *Espartero, el Pacificador* (Barcelona: Galaxia Gutenberg, 2018).

106. Murray, *Odious Commerce*.

107. Armario Sanchez, "Esclavitud y abolicionismo durante la regencia de Esparte-ro," 392.

108. Valdés to the Secretary of State, December 31, 1841, Estado, leg. 8565–1, AHN.

109. "Trans-Atlantic Slave Trade—Database," Slave Voyages, accessed December 7, 2015, https://www.slavevoyages.org.

110. In November 1841 Turnbull was arrested in Matanzas, accused of talking "talk to some black slaves about freedom and other similar issues, which may very well alter the state of servitude of those and therefore the public tranquility." November 12, 1841, Estado, leg. 8566(I), AHN.

111. Kennedy admitted he had hired enslaved Africans but argued that he was opposed to owning them. Murray, *Odious Commerce*, 141. Kennedy to Palmerston, December 17, 1840, FO 84/312, TNA.

112. Murray, *Odious Commerce*, 141.

113. Murray, *Odious Commerce*, 142.

114. Manuel Barcia, "Entre amenazas y quejas: Un acercamiento al papel jugado por los diplomáticos ingleses en Cuba durante la conspiración de La Escalera, 1844," *Colonial Latin American Historical Review* 10, no. 1 (2001): 25.

115. Murray, *Odious Commerce*, 145.

116. Murray, *Odious Commerce*, 144, 55.

117. Secretary of State to the British Ambassador in Madrid, July 31, 1841, Estado, leg. 8566–1, AHN.

118. Valdés to the Secretary of State, Estado, November 30, 1841, Estado, leg. 8037, AHN.

119. The Palmerston Act of 1839 authorized British officers and courts to capture and adjudicate upon Portuguese ships and subjects engaged in the slave trade, and therefore the Portuguese flag could no longer protect vessels involved in the slave trade south of the equator. In 1845 the Aberdeen Act authorized the British navy to search and capture any slave trade vessels under the Brazilian flag or without any nationality. Although these laws did not directly refer to Spain, they had an important impact, as many Spanish slave traders sheltered under the, genuine or fraudulent, Portuguese and Brazilian flags. Bethell, *Abolition of the Brazilian Slave Trade*; Leslie Bethell, "Britain, Portugal and the Suppression of the Brazilian Slave Trade: The Origins of Lord Palmerston's Act of 1839," *English Historical Review* 80, no. 8317 (1965): 761–84; Jenny S. Martinez, *Slave Trade and the Origins of International Human Rights Law* (Oxford: Oxford University Press, 2012).

120. Murray, *Odious Commerce*, 156–58.

121. Murray, *Odious Commerce*, 151.

122. Ultramar, Cuba, leg. 4614, AHN; Moreno García, "España y Gran Bretaña durante el siglo XIX," 484–86; Armario Sanchez, "Esclavitud y Abolicionismo durante la Regencia de Espartero," 397–98.

123. Valdés to the Secretary of State, September 13, 1842, Estado, leg. 8038, AHN.

124. Valdés to the Secretary of State, September 13, 1842, Estado, leg. 8038, AHN.

125. Moreno García, "España y Gran Bretaña durante el siglo XIX," 491; September 1842, Ultramar, Cuba, leg. 2910, AHN.

126. September 18, 1842, Ultramar, Cuba, leg. 2810, AHN; Moreno García, "España y Gran Bretaña durante el siglo XIX," 514.

127. Manuel Barcia, *Seeds of Insurrection: Domination and Resistance on Western Cuban Plantations, 1808–1848* (Baton Rouge: Louisiana State University Press, 2008), 91–92.

128. Barcia, *Seeds of Insurrection*, 91–92.

129. The *Código negro* (Black Code) was a compilation of rules, laws, and regulations that affected enslaved Africans in a certain territory.

130. Valdés to the Secretary of State, November 30, 1842, Ultramar, Cuba, leg. 2909, AHN; Moreno García, "España y Gran Bretaña durante el siglo XIX," 509.

131. Barcia, *Seeds of Insurrection*, 92.

132. Nelson, "Liberated Africans in the Atlantic World," 49.

133. Kennedy to Viscount Palmerston, No. 9, Havana, March 6, 1849, HCPP, 1850 (1290) LV.111, p. 17; Nelson, "Liberated Africans in the Atlantic World," 208.

134. "Trans-Atlantic Slave Trade—Database," Slave Voyages, accessed December 7, 2015, https://www.slavevoyages.org; Nelson, "Liberated Africans in the Atlantic World," 184.

135. As Jennifer Nelson has pointed out, Valdés admitted in 1849 that "he knew of more slave ship arrivals than Kennedy was aware of, but that he had too many other priorities to attend to." Kennedy to Viscount Palmerston, No. 9, Havana, March 6, 1849, HCPP, 1850 (1290) LV.111, p. 17.

136. Murray, *Odious Commerce*, 184; Commissioners to Palmerston, No. 60, October 29, 1841, FO 84/395, TNA. The Camino Real de Cuba (Royal Way of Cuba) was a road that ran across (east to west) the island of Cuba from Punta de Maisí, in current Guantanamo Province, to Cabo de San Antonio, in current Pinar del Río.

137. Barcia, "Entre amenazas y quejas," 4. On the Conspiracy of "La Escalera," see José Luciano Franco, *Ensayos históricos* (Havana: Editorial de Ciencias Sociales, 1974); Paquette, *Sugar Is Made with Blood: The Conspiracy of La Escalera and the Conflict between Empires over Slavery in Cuba*; Jonathan Curry-Machado, "How Cuba Burned with the Ghosts of British Slavery: Race, Abolition and the Escalera," *Slavery and Abolition* 25, no. 1 (2004); Manuel Barcia, "Exorcising the Storm: Revisiting the Origins of the Repression of the Conspiracy of La Escalera in Cuba," *Colonial Latin America Historical Review* 15, no. 3 (2006): 311–26; Aisha K. Finch, *Rethinking Slave Rebellion in Cuba: La Escalera and the Insurgencies of 1841–1844* (Chapel Hill: University of North Carolina Press, 2015).

138. Barcia, "Entre amenazas y quejas."

139. Barcia, *Seeds of Insurrection*, 42.

140. On the repression of British subjects and the reaction of the British diplomatic mission in Havana, see Barcia, "Entre amenazas y quejas."

141. Gobierno Superior Civil, leg. 850, exp. 28634, ANC.

142. Barcia, "Entre amenazas y quejas," 17–18.

143. Barcia, "Entre amenazas y quejas," 25.

144. Murray, *Odious Commerce*, 179.

145. Armario Sanchez, "Esclavitud y abolicionismo durante la regencia de Espartero," 402–3.

146. Murray, *Odious Commerce*, 191; Julia Moreno García, "Actitudes de los naciona-listas cubanos ante la Ley Penal de abolición y represión del tráfico de esclavos (1845)," in *Esclavitud y derechos humanos: La lucha por la libertad del negro en el siglo XIX*, ed. Francisco de Solano and Agustín Guimerá (Madrid: CSIC, 1990), 477.

147. Aberdeen to Bulwer, May 9, 1844. Murray, *Odious Commerce*, 196.

148. Aberdeen to Bulwer, May 9, 1844. Murray, *Odious Commerce*, 196.

149. The British government headed by Robert Peel was facing strong opposition regarding its attitude to Cuba and the slave trade, and was accused of a lack of strength against the Spanish government in the British parliament. Murray, *Odious Commerce*, 198–99; Eric Williams, *Capitalism and Slavery* (Chapel Hill: University of North Carolina Press, 1964), 190.

150. Candelaria Saiz Pastor, "La esclavitud como problema político en la España del siglo XIX (1833–1868): Liberalismo y esclavismo," in *Esclavitud y derechos humanos: La lucha por la libertad del negro en el siglo XIX*, ed. Francisco de Solano and Agustín Guimerá (Madrid: CSIC, 1990), 85.

151. Murray, *Odious Commerce*, 199–200.

152. *Diario de las Sesiones de Cortes del Congreso de los Diputados*, January 27, 1845, p. 1390; Saiz Pastor, "Esclavitud como problema político en la España del siglo XIX (1833–1868)," 86.

153. Fradera, "Moments in a Postponed Abolition" 273–74; Saiz Pastor, "Finanzas públicas en Cuba."

154. *Diario de las Sesiones de Cortes del Congreso de los Diputados*, January 27, 1845, p. 1384. In these sentences, Istúriz referred to a quote popularized by Isidoro de Antillón in 1811: "*Si alguno se atreviese todavía, en medio del grito de la naturaleza y de las luces del siglo, a defender este infame sistema, no merecería más contestación, dice un escritor sensible, que el desprecio del filósofo y el puñal del negro.*" Antillón, *Disertación sobre el origen de la esclavitud de los Negros*, 19–20.

155. *Diario de las Sesiones de Cortes del Congreso de los Diputados*, January 27, 1845, p. 1384.

156. *Diario de las Sesiones de Cortes del Congreso de los Diputados*, January 27, 1845, p. 1390; Saiz Pastor, "Esclavitud como problema político en la España del siglo XIX (1833–1868)," 86.

157. *Anti-slavery Reporter* 6, no. 2, January 22, 1845; Murray, *Odious Commerce*, 201.

158. Murray, *Odious Commerce*, 202.

159. "Trans-Atlantic Slave Trade—Database," Slave Voyages, accessed December 7, 2015, https://www.slavevoyages.org.

Chapter 5

1. Cánovas del Castillo, *Diario de las Sesiones de Cortes*, April 18, 1866, 588ff.

2. David R. Murray, *Odious Commerce: Britain, Spain and the Abolition of the Cuban Slave Trade* (Cambridge: Cambridge University Press, 2002, originally published 1980), 202.

3. Leslie Bethell, *The Abolition of the Brazilian Slave Trade* (Cambridge: Cambridge University Press, 1970), 357–59.

4. Arthur F. Corwin, *Spain and the Abolition of Slavery in Cuba, 1817–1886* (Austin: University of Texas Press, 1967), 87–89.

5. Corwin, *Spain and the Abolition of Slavery in Cuba, 1817–1886*, 87–89.

6. Moreno García, "España y Gran Bretaña durante el siglo XIX: La abolición de la trata y la esclavitud," thesis, History, Universidad Complutense de Madrid, 1984, 615.

7. Between 1847 and 1874, there were different initiatives to attract white workers into Cuba as an alternative workforce to the African slaves. Immigration through contract and the indenture of settlers from China, the so-called coolies, reached 120,000 during this time. Moreover, some two thousand Yucatan Indians were also transported under a similar system. Also, between 1854 and 1855, some 1,700 Spanish unfree workers, from the region of Galicia, were introduced to the island. At least five hundred of them died, which caused a public controversy in Spain. Evelyn Hu-Dehart, "Chinese Coolie Labor in Cuba in the Nineteenth Century: Free Labor of Neoslavery," *Contributions in Black Studies* 12 (1994): 38–54; Consuelo Naranjo and Imilcy Balboa Navarro, "Colonos asiáticos para una economía en expansión: Cuba, 1847–1880," *Revista mexicana del Caribe* 8 (1999): 32–65; Benjamin N. Narvaez, "Chinese Coolies in Cuba and Peru: Race, Labor, and Immigration, 1839–1886," PhD diss., University of Texas at Austin, 2010; Izaskun Álvarez Cuartero, "De Tihosuco a La Habana: La venta de indios yucatecos a Cuba durante la Guerra de Castas," *Studia historica: Historia antigua* (2007): 559–76; Candelaria Saiz Pastor, "Liberales y esclavistas: El dominio colonial español en Cuba (1833–1868)," thesis, Universidad de Alicante, 1990, 312–15; Fernando Mendiola, "The Role of Unfree Labour in Capitalist Development: Spain and Its Empire, Nineteenth to the Twenty-First Centuries," *IRSH* 61 (2016): 187–211; Santiago Garrido Buj, "'Los otros esclavos': La sustitución de la mano de obra esclava africana en la Cuba colonial," *Revista de Derecho UNED* 16 (2015): 963–87.

8. Corwin, *Spain and the Abolition of Slavery in Cuba, 1817–1886*, 87–89.

9. Moreno García, "España y Gran Bretaña durante el siglo XIX," 633.

10. Guerrero Latorre, Pérez Garzón, and Rueda Hernanz, *Historia política* (Madrid: Istmo, 2013), 233–36.

11. Leonardo Marques, *The United States and the Transatlantic Slave Trade to the Americas, 1776–1867* (New Haven: Yale University Press, 2016), 176; Bethell, *Abolition of the Brazilian Slave Trade*, 326.

12. Marques, *United States and the Transatlantic Slave Trade to the Americas*, 176.

13. Stanley to Hamilton, April 22, 1850, FO 84/823, TNA.

14. Bethell, *Abolition of the Brazilian Slave Trade*, 326.

15. Marques, *United States and the Transatlantic Slave Trade to the Americas*, 176–77.

16. Marques, *United States and the Transatlantic Slave Trade to the Americas*, 177–80.

17. Bethell, *Abolition of the Brazilian Slave Trade*, 357–59.

18. John A. E. Harris, "Circuits of Wealth, Circuits of Sorrow: Financing the Illegal Transatlantic Slave Trade in the Age of Suppression, 1850–66," *Journal of Global History* 11, no. 3 (2016): 411; Marques, *United States and the Transatlantic Slave Trade to the Americas*, 181–82.

19. Harris, "Circuits of Wealth, Circuits of Sorrow," 427.

20. Bethell, *Abolition of the Brazilian Slave Trade*, 362.

21. Southern, No. 47, August 10, 1852, FO 84/879, TNA; Bethell, *Abolition of the Brazilian Slave Trade*, 360.

22. Bethell, *Abolition of the Brazilian Slave Trade*, 363.

23. Palmerston to Baring, September 3, 1850, quoted in Bethell, *Abolition of the Brazilian Slave Trade*, 344.

24. Moreno García, "España y Gran Bretaña durante el siglo XIX," 639.

25. Moreno García, "España y Gran Bretaña durante el siglo XIX," 639.

26. Moreno García, "España y Gran Bretaña durante el siglo XIX," 639; Corwin, *Spain and the Abolition of Slavery in Cuba, 1817–1886*, 97.

27. Palmerston to Sir George Bonham, September 29, 1850, FO 17/173, TNA.

28. Palmerston to Sir George Bonham, September 29, 1850, FO 17/173, TNA.

29. Richard Huzzey, *Freedom Burning: Anti-slavery and Empire in Victorian Britain* (Ithaca: Cornell University Press, 2012), 64; on imperial rivalries and British imperialism and abolitionism, also see Gabriel Paquette, "The Intellectual Impact of International Rivalry," in *Enlightenment, Governance and Reform in Spain and Its Empire, 1759–1808* (New York: Palgrave Macmillan, 2008); Keith Hamilton and Patrick Salmon, *Slavery, Diplomacy and Empire: Britain and the Suppression of the Slave Trade, 1807–1975* (Brighton: Sussex Academic Press, 2009); Alfred W. McCoy, Josep M. Fradera, and Stephen Jacobson, *Endless Empire: Spain's Retreat, Europe's Eclipse, America's Decline* (Madison: University of Wisconsin Press, 2012); Marcus Wood, *Blind Memory: Visual Representations of Slavery in England and America, 1780–1865* (Manchester: Manchester University Press, 2000).

30. Josef Opatrny, *U.S. Expansionism and Cuban Annexationism in the 1850s* (Prague: Charles University, 1990).

31. Murray, *Odious Commerce*, 239, 381n120.

32. Murray, *Odious Commerce*, 239, 381n120.

33. Murray, *Odious Commerce*, 208; Mark C. Hunter, *Policing the Seas: Anglo-American Relations and the Equatorial Atlantic* (St. John's, NL: International Maritime Economic History Association, 2008).

34. Lars Schoultz, *The Infernal Little Cuban Republic* (Chapel Hill: University of North Carolina Press, 2009), 19; Louis A. Pérez Jr, *Cuba between Empires, 1878–1902* (Pittsburgh: University of Pittsburgh Press, 1983), 178.

35. Thomas Jefferson to James Madison, April 27, 1809, Founders Online, United States National Archives, accessed March 5, 2018, https://founders.archives.gov/.

36. Schoultz, *Infernal Little Cuban Republic*, 19; Murray, *Odious Commerce*, 86; Robin Blackburn, *The Overthrow of Colonial Slavery, 1776–1848* (London: Verso, [1988] 2011), 396.

37. Schoultz, *Infernal Little Cuban Republic*, 19; Louis A. Pérez Jr., *Cuba between Empires* (Pittsburgh: University of Pittsburgh Press, 1983), 178; Robert E. May, *The Southern Dream of a Caribbean Empire, 1854–1861* (Baton Rouge: Louisiana State University Press, 1973).

38. Corwin, *Spain and the Abolition of Slavery in Cuba, 1817–1886*, 99.

39. Tom Chaffin, *Fatal Glory: Narciso Lopez and the First Clandestine U.S. War against Cuba* (Baton Rouge: Louisiana State University Press, 2003), 67–69, 162–65.

40. Rodrigo Lazo, *Writing to Cuba: Filibustering and Cuban Exiles in the United States* (Chapel Hill: University of North Carolina Press, 2005); Chaffin, *Fatal Glory*; Tom Chaffin, "'Sons of Washington': Narciso Lopez, Filibustering, and U.S. Nationalism, 1848–1851," *Journal of the Early Republic* 15, no. 1 (1995): 79–108; Charles Henry Brown, *Agents of Manifest Destiny: The Lives and Times of the Filibusters* (Chapel Hill: University of North Carolina Press, 1980); May, *The Southern Dream of a Caribbean Empire*; Hugh Thomas, *Cuba: The Pursuit of Freedom* (New York: Harper and Row, 1971).

41. Carmen de la Guardia, "Un espacio social propio," in *Mujeres esclavas y abolicionistas en la España de los siglos XVI al XIX*, ed. Aurelia Martín Casares and Rocio Periáñez Gómez (Madrid and Frankfurt am Main: Iberoamericana-Vervuert, 2014), 216–17.

42. Jennifer R. Green and Patricia Kirkwood, "Reframing the Antebellum Democratic Mainstream Transatlantic Diplomacy and the Career of Pierre Soulé," *Civil War History* 61, no. 3 (2015): 212–51; Amos Ettinger, *The Mission to Spain of Pierre Soulé* (New Haven: Yale University Press, 1932). I thank Prof. Adrian Shubert for passing me his notes on Pierre Soulé.

43. May, *Southern Dream of a Caribbean Empire*, 57–59; J. Preston Moore, "Pierre Soule: Southern Expansionist and Promoter," *Journal of Southern History* 21, no. 2 (1955): 203–23; Jay Sexton, "Toward a Synthesis of Foreign Relations in the Civil War Era, 1848–77," *American Nineteenth Century History* 5, no. 3 (2004): 50–73; Sidney Webster, "Mr. Marcy, the Cuban Question and the Ostend Manifesto," *Political Science Quarterly* 8, no. 1 (1893): 1–32; Peter H. Smith, *Talons of the Eagle: Dynamics of U.S.–Latin American Relations* (New York: Oxford University Press, 1996); Ostend Manifesto, October 15, 1854, accessed January 20, 2020, https://en.wikisource.org/wiki/Ostend_Manifesto.

44. Ostend Manifesto, October 15, 1854, accessed January 20, 2020, https://en.wikisource.org/wiki/Ostend_Manifesto.

45. Brown, *Agents of Manifest Destiny*, 141–42, 255–56.

46. David M. Potter, *The Impending Crisis, 1848–1861* (New York: Harper & Row, 1976), 195.

47. Romy Sánchez, "Quitter la Très Fidèle: Exilés et bannis au temps du séparatisme cubain, 1834-1879," doctoral thesis, Université Paris 1 Panthéon Sorbonne, 2017, 73–87, 484–98.

48. Marques, *United States and the Transatlantic Slave Trade to the Americas*, 218; Chaffin, *Fatal Glory*, 11–12. This perception changed in the early 1860s, when James Buchanan's administration saw the annexation of Cuba as "one of the few possible ways to stop the traffic." Marques, *United States and the Transatlantic Slave Trade to the Americas*, 239.

49. Chaffin, *Fatal Glory*, 3–4.

50. December 17, 1847, Ultramar, Sección Cuba, leg. 2913, AHN.

51. Count of Alcoy to the Secretary of State, December 17, 1847, leg. 2913, Ultramar, AHN.

52. Sánchez, "Quitter la Très Fidèle," 79–82.

53. Raúl Cepero Bonilla, *Azúcar y abolición* (Barcelona: Crítica, 1976), 49; Saco, *Obras*, 3:349.

54. Saco, *Obras*, 3:349–50.

55. Sánchez, "Quitter la Très Fidèle," 73–87.

56. *La Verdad* (New York), no. 21, August 10, 1853; Moreno García, "España y Gran Bretaña durante el siglo XIX," 684.

57. José Antonio Saco, *Ideas sobre la incorporación de Cuba a Estados Unidos* (Paris: Imprenta de Panckoucke, 1848), 54–55.

58. Saco, *Ideas sobre la incorporación de Cuba a Estados Unidos*, 54–55.

59. *La Verdad* (New York), no. 83, June 12, 1851; Moreno García, "España y Gran Bretaña durante el siglo XIX," 687–89. In Spanish America, *peninsulares* refers to a Spanish people originally from the Iberian Peninsula.

60. *La Verdad* (New York), no. 83, June 12, 1851; Moreno García, "España y Gran Bretaña durante el siglo XIX," 687–89.

61. Saco, *Obras*, 3:272–73; José A. Matos Arévalo, "José Antonio Saco, pensamiento social: Apuntes sobre el padre Bartolomé de Las Casas," in *El pensamiento lascasiano en la conciencia de América y Europa*, ed. Pablo González Casanova (Mexico City: Universidad Nacional Autónoma de México, 1994), 57–68.

62. Chaffin, *Fatal Glory*, 219.

63. Sánchez, "Quitter la Très Fidèle," 79; Moreno García, "España y Gran Bretaña durante el siglo XIX," 690–91.

64. Brigitte Journeau, *Augusto Conte, memorialista y diplomático* (Alicante: Biblioteca Virtual Miguel de Cervantes, 2016).

65. Conte to Earl of Malmesbury, September 20, 1858, leg. 2923, No. 270, Ultramar, AHN; Moreno García, "España y Gran Bretaña durante el siglo XIX," 769–70.

66. Conte to Earl of Malmesbury, September 20, 1858, leg. 2923, No. 270, Ultramar, AHN; Moreno García, "España y Gran Bretaña durante el siglo XIX," 769–70.

67. On June 18, 1858, the Bishop of Oxford, Samuel Wilberforce (William's son), and Lord Brougham denounced the economic difficulties that the Jamaican sugar producers were facing to compete with the Cuban sugar produced by slaves. The British politicians accused the Spanish authorities of ignoring the international agreements signed with Britain and defended to adopt any possible measure to stop the slave trade into Cuba. June 18, 1858, Ultramar, Cuba, leg. 2922, No. 180, AHN; Moreno García, "España y Gran Bretaña durante el siglo XIX," 751–52.

68. September 20, 1858, Ultramar, Cuba, leg. 2923, No. 279, AHN; Moreno García, "España y Gran Bretaña durante el siglo XIX," 770–71.

69. Fradera, "Moments in a Postponed Abolition," 277.

70. Fradera, "Moments in a Postponed Abolition," 277.

71. Pezuela to the Secretary of State, February 7, 1854, Ultramar, Cuba, leg. 2924, No. 80, AHN.

72. Marques, *Sounds of Silence*, 148–49; Bethell, *Abolition of the Brazilian Slave Trade*, 266, 338.

73. October 25, 1861, Ultramar, Cuba, leg. 2924, AHN; Corwin, *Spain and the Abolition of Slavery in Cuba, 1817–1886*, 115–20, 182.

74. "Trans-Atlantic Slave Trade—Database," Slave Voyages, accessed December 7, 2015, https://www.slavevoyages.org.

75. Corwin, *Spain and the Abolition of Slavery in Cuba, 1817–1886*, 115–20, 182; Luis

Martínez-Fernández, *Fighting Slavery in the Caribbean: Life and Times of a British Family in Nineteenth Century Havana* (London: Routledge, 1998); Robert Steven Levine, *Martin Delany, Frederick Douglass, and the Politics of Representative Identity* (Chapel Hill: University of North Carolina Press, 1997), 294n242; José G. Cayuela Fernández, *Bahía de ultramar: España y Cuba en el siglo XIX: El control de las relaciones coloniales* (Madrid: Siglo XXI, 1993), 228–31, 233–35.

76. "Memoria relativa al estado de nuestras relaciones con Inglaterra," September 23, 1853, Ultramar, Cuba, leg. 2919, AHN; Moreno García, "España y Gran Bretaña durante el siglo XIX," 699–700.

77. Crawford to Clarendon, August 29, 1853, No. 69, FO 84/906, TNA.

78. "Memoria relativa al estado de nuestras relaciones con Inglaterra," September 23, 1853, Ultramar, Cuba, leg. 2919, AHN.

79. "Memoria relativa al estado de nuestras relaciones con Inglaterra," September 23, 1853, Ultramar, Cuba, leg. 2919, AHN.

80. "Memoria relativa al estado de nuestras relaciones con Inglaterra," September 23, 1853, Ultramar, Cuba, leg. 2919, AHN.

81. Corwin, *Spain and the Abolition of Slavery in Cuba, 1817–1886*, 114–15.

82. Cayuela Fernández, *Bahía de ultramar: España y Cuba en el siglo XIX*, 228.

83. Pezuela to the Secretary of State, February 7, 1854, Ultramar, Cuba, leg. 2924, No. 80, AHN.

84. Pezuela to the Secretary of State, February 7, 1854, Ultramar, Cuba, leg. 2924, No. 80, AHN.

85. "Reglamento sobre capitación de esclavos," "Reglamento para la formación de los padrones y un registro civil de esclavos," and "Reglamento para la introducción y régimen de los colonos en Cuba."

86. "Decreto del Consejo de Ministros," March 21, 1854, Ultramar, Cuba, leg. 2912, AHN.

87. "Decreto del Consejo de Ministros," March 21, 1854, Ultramar, Cuba, leg. 2912, AHN.

88. May 10, 1854, No. 35, FO 313/26, TNA.

89. May 10, 1854, No. 35, FO 313/26, TNA.

90. Moreno García, "España y Gran Bretaña durante el siglo XIX," 716–17.

91. Martínez-Fernández, *Fighting Slavery in the Caribbean*, 133.

92. Martínez-Fernández, *Fighting Slavery in the Caribbean*, 133–34.

93. August, 20–21, 1854, Ultramar, Cuba, leg. 2912, AHN.

94. Cayuela Fernández, *Bahía de ultramar: España y Cuba en el siglo XIX*, 230, 236. In the history of Spain, the Decada Moderada was the period from May 1844 to July 1854, during which the Moderate Party continuously held power.

95. Cayuela Fernández, *Bahía de ultramar*, 230–33, 235–36, 238–57.

96. "Trans-Atlantic Slave Trade—Database," Slave Voyages, accessed December 7, 2015, https://www.slavevoyages.org.

97. Cayuela Fernández, *Bahía de ultramar*, 245.

98. Cayuela Fernández, *Bahía de ultramar*, 236.

99. During his mandate in Cuba, Concha established the so-called Sistema de

Cédulas, by which every enslaved person should have an identification certificate. The system soon proved completely ineffective in stopping the slave trade and was used to validate the status of the enslaved who had been illegally introduced into Cuba. Cayuela Fernández, *Bahía de ultramar*, 244–45.

100. *De Bow's Review* 18 (January to July 1855), p. 226, accessed November 14, 2020, https://catalog.hathitrust.org/Record/011984803; Marques, *United States and the Transatlantic Slave Trade to the Americas*, 202–3, 229n.227.

101. May 10, 1854, No. 35, FO 313/26, TNA; Moreno García, "España y Gran Bretaña durante el siglo XIX," 721.

102. May 10, 1854, No. 35, FO 313/26, TNA.

103. June 12, 1857, Ultramar, Cuba, leg. 2921, AHN.

104. Real Orden, January 6, 1856, Ultramar, Cuba, leg. 2921, AHN.

105. Concha to the Secretary of State, February 20, 1856, Ultramar, Cuba, leg. 2921, AHN.

106. Concha to the Secretary of State, February 20, 1856, Ultramar, Cuba, leg. 2921, AHN.

107. "Trans-Atlantic Slave Trade—Database," Slave Voyages, accessed December 7, 2015, https://www.slavevoyages.org.

108. Crawford to Russell, No. 37, November 19, 1859, FO 84/1109, TNA; Murray, *Odious Commerce*, 266.

109. "Instrucciones al Capitán General de Cuba D Fco. Serrano y Dominguez, Conde de S. Antonio," Ministerio de la Guerra y Ultramar, October 20, 1859, Ultramar, Cuba, leg. 2923, AHN; Moreno García, "España y Gran Bretaña durante el siglo XIX," 795–96; Cayuela Fernández, *Bahía de ultramar*, 236.

110. Moreno García, "España y Gran Bretaña durante el siglo XIX," 798.

111. Cayuela Fernández, *Bahía de ultramar*, 236.

112. "Circular del Capitán General Francisco Serrano," July 25, 1861, Ultramar, Cuba, leg. 2924, AHN.

113. "Circular del Capitán General Francisco Serrano," July 25, 1861, Ultramar, Cuba, leg. 2924, AHN.

114. "Circular del Capitán General Francisco Serrano," July 25, 1861, Ultramar, leg. 2924, AHN.

115. "Circular del Capitán General Francisco Serrano," July 25, 1861, Ultramar, Cuba, leg. 2924, AHN.

116. On the slave trade as piracy, see Jenny S. Martinez, *Slave Trade and the Origins of International Human Rights Law* (Oxford: Oxford University Press, 2012), 49–50, 60–61, 64–65, 119–21, 143.

117. May 12, 1855, Ultramar, Cuba, leg. 2925, AHN.

118. Moreno García, "España y Gran Bretaña durante el siglo XIX," 807.

119. "Ordenes al Capitán General de Cuba Francisco Serrano," October 25, 1861, Ultramar, Cuba, leg. 2924, AHN.

120. Marques, *Sounds of Silence*; Bethell, *Abolition of the Brazilian Slave Trade*.

121. Marques, *Sounds of Silence*, 106–8.

122. Marques, *Sounds of Silence*, 148–49.

123. Marques, *Sounds of Silence*, 181.

124. Marques, *Sounds of Silence*, 186.

125. Bethell, *Abolition of the Brazilian Slave Trade*, 266.

126. Paulino to Hudson, February 12, enclosed in Hudson No. 7, February 20, 1850, FO 84/802, TNA; Bethell, *Abolition of the Brazilian Slave Trade*, 317.

127. Paulino to Hudson, No. 7, February 20, 1850, FO 84/802, TNA; Bethell, *Abolition of the Brazilian Slave Trade*, 319.

128. Bethell, *Abolition of the Brazilian Slave Trade*, 338.

129. Bethell, *Abolition of the Brazilian Slave Trade*, 362.

130. Murray, *Odious Commerce*, 270.

131. Murray, *Odious Commerce*, 300.

132. Murray, *Odious Commerce*, 300–301.

133. This historiographical analysis was shared, for example, by Matthew Mason. See Matthew Mason, "Keeping Up Appearances: The International Politics of Slave Trade Abolition in the Nineteenth-Century Atlantic World," *William and Mary Quarterly* 66, no. 4 (2009), 809–32. David Murray and Taylor Milne adopted more-comprehensive approaches but also stressed the prevalence of international and external factors to explain the ending of the slave trade in the Spanish Empire. See Murray, *Odious Commerce*, 299; A. Taylor Milne, "The Lyons-Seward Treaty of 1862," *American Historical Review* 38 (1933): 511–25.

134. The last recorded arrival of a slave trade vessel took place in March 1866, disembarking seven hundred African slaves in Cuba. However, according to Fernando Ortiz, on January 25, 1870, six hundred African slaves arrived to the province of Havana, in what he believed was the last slave vessel to reach the Cuban coast. "Trans-Atlantic Slave Trade—Database," Slave Voyages, accessed May 1, 2018, https://www.slavevoyages .org; Murray, *Odious Commerce*, 324; José Luciano Franco, *Comercio clandestino de esclavos* (Havana: Editorial de Ciencias Sociales, 1980), 389.

135. Harris, "Circuits of Wealth, Circuits of Sorrow," 418.

136. Murray, *Odious Commerce*, 298.

137. "Trans-Atlantic Slave Trade—Database," Slave Voyages, accessed December 7, 2015, https://www.slavevoyages.org.

138. By 1867 more than 40 percent of the world's cane sugar came from Cuba. Alan Dye, *Cuban Sugar in the Age of Mass Production: Technology and the Economics of the Sugar Central, 1899–1929* (Stanford: Stanford University Press, 1998), 27; Manuel Moreno Fraginals, "Plantations in the Caribbean: Cuba, Puerto Rico, and the Dominican Republic in the late Nineteenth Century," in *Between Slavery and Free Labor: The Spanish-Speaking Caribbean in the Nineteenth Century*, ed. Manuel Moreno Fraginals, Frank Moya Pons, and Stanley L. Engerman, 3–21 (Baltimore: Johns Hopkins University Press, 1985).

139. Murray, *Odious Commerce*, 298–99; Laird W. Bergad, "Slave Prices in Cuba, 1840–1875," in *Caribbean Slavery in the Atlantic World: A Student Reader*, ed. Verene A. Shepherd and Hilary McD. Beckles (Oxford: James Currey, 2000), 527–42.

140. Murray, *Odious Commerce*, 299–300.

141. With regard to this debate in the House of Commons, the British satirical

weekly magazine *Punch, or The London Charivari*, reported: "'Profligate, shameless, and disgraceful,' these are not very palatable adjectives to swallow, especially when coupled with the substantive noun 'liar,' which is implied by the expression 'violation of good faith.' The Don can hardly be a man of such proud stomach as he was, if he digests without a qualm the hard words which are here hurled at him, but that we know he owes us far too much to quarrel with us, we might really almost fear that our giving him the lie might be made a *casus belli*." *Punch, or The London Charivari* 40, March 16, 1861, p. 115; Murray, *Odious Commerce*, 300.

142. Murray, *Odious Commerce*, 300; Chaffin, *Fatal Glory*, 222. On the impact of the American Civil War in Spain, see James W. Cortada, *Spain and the American Civil War: Relations at Mid-Century, 1855–1868* (Philadelphia: American Philosophical Society, 1980).

143. Murray, *Odious Commerce*, 303.

144. *Anti-slavery Reporter*, 9–7, July 1, 1861, pp. 152, 158.

145. Milne, "Lyons-Seward Treaty of 1862"; Kinley J. Brauer, "The Slavery Problem in the Diplomacy of the American Civil War," *Pacific Historical Review* 46, no. 3 (1977): 439–69; Edward Keene, "A Case Study of the Construction of International Hierarchy: British Treaty-Making against the Slave Trade in the Early Nineteenth Century," *International Organization* 61, no. 2 (2007): 311–99; Mason, "Keeping Up Appearances"; Harris, "Circuits of Wealth, Circuits of Sorrow," 418–20.

146. Murray, *Odious Commerce*, 306; Harris, "Circuits of Wealth, Circuits of Sorrow," 418–20.

147. Murray, *Odious Commerce*, 306; Frederick C. Drake and R. W. Shufeldt, "Secret History of the Slave Trade to Cuba Written by an American Naval Officer, Robert Wilson Schufeldt, 1861," *Journal of Negro History* 55, no. 3 (1970): 218–35 (229); Franco, *Comercio clandestino de esclavos*, 385–86. On the "post-1850 nexus" dominated by the United States, West Central Africa and Cuba, see Harris, "Circuits of Wealth, Circuits of Sorrow."

148. Mason, "Keeping Up Appearances," 830.

149. Milne, "The Lyons-Seward Treaty of 1862," 514.

150. Milne, "The Lyons-Seward Treaty of 1862," 514.

151. Milne, "Lyons-Seward Treaty of 1862," 516; Murray, *Odious Commerce*, 308; Josep M. Fradera, *Colonias para después de un imperio* (Barcelona: Edicions Bellaterra, 2005), 646–47.

152. Harris, "Circuits of Wealth, Circuits of Sorrow," 419.

153. Harris, "Circuits of Wealth, Circuits of Sorrow," 420; Marques, *United States and the Transatlantic Slave Trade to the Americas*, 252.

154. Paloma Arroyo, "La Sociedad Abolicionista Española, 1864–1886," *Cuadernos de historia moderna y contemporánea*, no. 3 (1982): 127–49; Corwin, *Spain and the Abolition of Slavery in Cuba, 1817–1886*, 154; Luis Martínez-Fernández, *Protestantism and Political Conflict in the Nineteenth-Century Hispanic Caribbean* (New Brunswick, NJ: Rutgers University Press, 1960), 87; Luis A. Figueroa, *Sugar, Slavery and Freedom in Nineteenth-Century Puerto Rico* (Chapel Hill: University of North Carolina Press, 2005), 107–8; Caroline P. Boyd, "A Man for All Seasons: Lincoln in Spain," in *The Glob-*

al Lincoln, ed. Richard Carwardine and Jay Sexton, ch. 11 (New York: Oxford University Press, 2011).

155. *Special Report of the Anti-Slavery Conference: Held in Paris in the Salle Herz, on the Twenty-sixth and Twenty-seventh August, 1867, under the Presidency of Mons. Édouard Laboulaye* (London: Committee of the British and Foreign Anti-slavery Society, 1867); *Anti-slavery Reporter and Aborigines' Friends*, September–October 1889, 234–35; Guardia, "Espacio social propio," 220.

156. Guardia, "Espacio social propio," 213–16.

157. Arroyo, "Sociedad Abolicionista Española, 1864–1886,"129–30.

158. Guardia, "Espacio social propio," 223.

159. Enriqueta Vila Vilar, "Concepción Arenal, feminista y abolicionista," *Minervae Baeticae: Boletín de la Real Academia Sevillana de Buenas Letras* 42 (2014): 311–21 (321). In her work "La esclavitud de los negros," Arenal described the brutality of slavery and demanded, once and for all, its abolition: "*¡Horrible esclavitud! En tu presencia / ¿qué mano generosa, / suscribir quiere la sentencia odiosa / que entrega a la codicia la inocencia? / ¿Quién pone tu dogal, tu marca imprime? / ¿Quién en cólera justa no se inflama? / ¿Quién, angustiado el corazón, no gime / y a Dios y al mundo en su socorro llama? / ¡ESCLAVITUD! ¿Cómo este horrible nombre, / que es opresión, iniquidades, llanto, / fuerza brutal, depravación, espanto, / puede el hombre escuchar? ¡Qué digo el hombre! / Dijérase que aterra, que inspira el horror mismo / en el mar proceloso, en la ancha tierra, / de la región del sol, hasta el abismo.*"

160. Moreno García, "España y Gran Bretaña durante el siglo XIX," 823.

161. Murray, *Odious Commerce*, 311–12; Marques, *United States and the Transatlantic Slave Trade to the Americas*, 254.

162. Harris, "Circuits of Wealth, Circuits of Sorrow," 415; Marques, *United States and the Transatlantic Slave Trade to the Americas*, 254. On Julián Zulueta, see Franco, *Comercio clandestino de esclavos*, 246–49; José G. Cayuela Fernández, "Transferencias de capitales antillanos a Europa: Los patrimonios de Pedro Juan de Zulueta y Ceballos y de Pedro José de Zulueta y Madariaga (1823–1877)," *Estudios de historia social* 44, no. 47 (1988): 191–211; July 11, 1863, Ultramar, Cuba, leg. 2924, AHN; 12 April 1863, Ultramar, Cuba, leg. 3550, AHN; Dulce to Minister of Ultramar, June 28, 1863, exp. 43, leg. 4648, AHN; Moreno García, "España y Gran Bretaña durante el siglo XIX," 321–22; Murray, *Odious Commerce*, 312–13; Corwin, *Spain and the Abolition of Slavery in Cuba, 1817–1886*, 147–48; Quiroz, "Implicit Costs of Empire," 473–511 490–91; Joaquín Buxó de Abaigar, *Domingo Dulce, general isabelino: Vida y época* (Barcelona: Editorial Planeta, 1962), 396–99.

163. Murray, *Odious Commerce*, 311.

164. Russell to Edwardes, No. 8, July 9, 1863, FO 84/1196, TNA; Murray, *Odious Commerce*, 312; Moreno García, "España y Gran Bretaña durante el siglo XIX," 826; Corwin, *Spain and the Abolition of Slavery in Cuba, 1817–1886*, 148.

165. In April 1864 the government of Abraham Lincoln authorized the extradition of José Agustín Argüelles, former lieutenant governor of the district of Colón, who had been accused by Dulce of collaborating in the attempted disembarkation of more

than one thousand African captives aboard a slave steamer owned by Julian Zulueta. Argüelles had escaped to New York, but the US authorities, in an unprecedented decision to collaborate with the Spanish government, arrested him and sent him to Havana.

166. Moreno García, "España y Gran Bretaña durante el siglo XIX," 823.

167. Fradera, *Colonias para después de un imperio*, 647.

168. Fradera, *Colonias para después de un imperio*, 604–5, 649.

169. Ultramar, Cuba, November 6, 1865, leg. 2927, AHN.

170. Murray, *Odious Commerce*, 322; Moreno García, "España y Gran Bretaña durante el siglo XIX," 833.

171. Fradera, *Colonias para después de un imperio*, 647. On slave trade and piracy, see Martinez, *Slave Trade and the Origins of International Human Rights Law*, 49–50, 60–61, 64–65, 119–21, 143.

172. "Disposiciones sobre la represión y castigo del tráfico negrero, mandadas observar por Real decreto de 29 de septiembre de 1866, Cuba, Ultramar, leg. 2928, AHN; "Reglamento para la aplicación de la Ley sobre represión y castigo del tráfico de negros," n.d., Cuba, Ultramar, leg. 2929, AHN; Moreno García, "España y Gran Bretaña durante el siglo XIX," 834–37.

173. *Diario de las Sesiones de Cortes*, February 10 and 17, 1865, p. 410 and p. 548.

174. Eduardo Galván, *La abolición de la esclavitud en España: Debates parlamentarios, 1810–1886* (Madrid: Dickinson, 2014), 108; Marques, *United States and the Transatlantic Slave Trade to the Americas*, 254.

175. *Diario de las Sesiones de Cortes*, June 12, 1866, 2nd appendix; Galván, *Abolición de la esclavitud en España*, 118.

176. *Diario de las Sesiones de Cortes*, July 7, 1866, p. 2499.

177. *Diario de las Sesiones de Cortes*, July 6, 1866, p. 2487.

178. *Diario de las Sesiones de Cortes*, July 6, 1866, p. 2487.

179. The Sociedad Abolicionista Española had an active role during the debates on the Law for the Repression and Punishment of the Slave Trade. In collaboration with Senator Pastor, the society presented to the Cortes a statement in April 1866, denouncing the lack of determination of the Spanish government and demanding the abolition of slavery in Spanish Antillean provinces. The document was signed by prominent politicians and members of the society, including Segismundo Morer, Joaquín María Sanromá, and the Republican leader Emilio Castelar. In July 1866, following the fall of O'Donnell's government, the cabinet headed by General Narváez, as part of his repressive political programme, ordered the dissolution of the society and the closure of *El abolicionista español*, and forced several of its leaders into exile, including Vizcarrondo. It was not until the Revolution of 1868 started that the society was reestablished. By then the slave trade had disappeared, and its efforts would focus on achieving the abolition of slavery in the Spanish Empire. *Diario de las Sesiones de Cortes*, April 20, 1866, p. 617ff. Galván, *Abolición de la esclavitud en España*, 114–15; Arroyo, "Sociedad Abolicionista Española, 1864–1886," 130.

180. *Diario de las Sesiones de Cortes*, 18 April 1866, p. 588ff.

181. *Diario de las Sesiones de Cortes*, 18 April 1866, p. 588ff.

182. Murray, *Odious Commerce*, 323.

183. Crawford to Russell, No. 37, November 19, 1859, FO 84/1109, TNA; Murray, *Odious Commerce*, 266.

184. Fradera, "Moments in a Postponed Abolition," 283.

185. *Diario de las Sesiones de Cortes*, April 18, 1866, p. 588.

Epilogue

1. *Diario de las Sesiones de Cortes*, April 2, 1811, p. 812.

2. Fradera, "Moments in a Postponed Abolition," in *Slavery and Antislavery in Spain's Atlantic Empire*, ed. Josep M. Fradera and Christopher Schmidt-Nowara (New York: Berghahn, 2013), 270.

3. Christopher Schmidt-Nowara, *Empire and Antislavery: Spain, Cuba and Puerto Rico, 1833–1874* (Pittsburgh: University of Pittsburgh Press, 1999), 122–23.

4. Schmidt-Nowara, *Empire and Antislavery*, 125, 174.

5. *Diario de las Sesiones de Cortes*, March 9, 1837, p. 2037.

Bibliography

ARCHIVAL SOURCES

Archivo del Congreso de los Diputados, Madrid

Diario de las Sesiones de Cortes, 1810–1814
Diario de las Sesiones de Cortes, 1820–1823
Diario de las Sesiones de Cortes, 1837
Diario de las Sesiones de Cortes, 1845
Diario de las Sesiones de Cortes, 1865–1866
Notas de los expedientes pasados a las comisiones de las Cortes desde 1811 a 1814

Archivo Histórico Nacional, Madrid

Estado
Ultramar

Archivo del Ministerio de Asuntos Exteriores, Madrid

Tratados Siglo XIX

Archivo Nacional de la República de Cuba, Havana

Asuntos Políticos
Comisión Militar
Gobierno Superior Civil

Biblioteca Nacional de Cuba José Martí, Havana

Colección Vidal Morales y Morales
Colección de Manuscritos Alfonso, Colección Cubana

Bodleian Library, University of Oxford

MS Wilberforce, Special Collections

The National Archives, Kew

FO 17/173
FO 71/176
FO 72/75–256
FO 84/312–1196
FO 313/26

House of Commons Parliamentary Papers
  Accounts and Papers
  Commons Sitting

NEWSPAPERS
  El Español (1811)
  El español constitucional (1814–1820)
  La Verdad (1851)
  *Ocios de los españoles emigrado*s (1824–1827)
  The Anti-slavery Reporter (1861)
  The Anti-slavery Reporter and Aborigines' Friends (1889)

DATABASE
  Trans-Atlantic Slave Trade—Database. 2008. *Slave Voyages,* http://www
    .slavevoyages.org

PUBLICATIONS
  Ackerson, Wayne. *The African Institution and the Antislavery Movement in Great
    Britain.* Lampeter, Wales: Edwin Mellen Press, 2005.
  Adelman, Jeremy. *Sovereignty and Revolution in the Iberian Atlantic.* Princeton:
    Princeton University Press, 2006.
  Alonso, Gregorio. "'A Great People Struggling for Their Liberties': Spain and the
    Mediterranean in the Eyes of the Benthamites." *History of European Ideas* 41,
    no. 2 (2015): 194–204.
  Alonso Álvarez, Luis. "Comercio exterior y formación de capital financiero: El tráf-
    ico de negros hispano-cubano, 1821–1868." *Anuario de estudios americanos* 51,
    no. 2 (1994): 75–92.
  Álvarez Cuartero, Izaskun. "De Tihosuco a La Habana: La venta de indios yu-
    catecos a Cuba durante la Guerra de Castas." *Studia historica: Historia antigua*
    (2007): 559–76.
  Alvarado, Javier. "El régimen de legislación especial para ultramar y la cuestión
    abolicionista en España durante el siglo XIX." In *La supervivencia del derecho
    español en Hispanoamérica durante la época independiente,* edited by Instituto de
    Investigaciones Jurídicas, Universidad Nacional Autónoma de México, 1–30.
    Mexico City: UNAM, 1998.
  Anstey, Roger. *The Atlantic Slave Trade and British Abolition, 1760–1810.* London:
    Macmillan, 1975.
  Antillón, Isidoro de. *Disertación sobre el origen de la esclavitud de los negros.* Madrid,
    1811.
  Argüelles, Agustín. *Apéndice a la sentencia pronunciada en 11 de mayo de 1825 por la
    audiencia de Sevilla contra los 63 diputados de las cortes de 1822 y 1823.* London:
    Imprenta de Carlos Wood e hijo, 1834.
  ———. *Examen histórico de la reforma constitucional que hicieron las cortes generales y
    estraordinarias.* . . . London: Imprenta de Carlos Wood e hijo, 1835.

Armario Sanchez, Fernando. "Esclavitud y abolicionismo durante la regencia de espartero." In *Esclavitud y derechos humanos: La lucha por la libertad del negro en el siglo XIX*, edited by Francisco de Solano and Agustín Guimerá, 377–406. Madrid: CSIC, 1990.

Arroyo, Paloma. "La Sociedad Abolicionista Española, 1864–1886." *Cuadernos de historia moderna y contemporánea*, no. 3 (1982): 127–49.

Bailyn, Bernard. *Atlantic History: Concept and Contours*. Cambridge: Harvard University Press, 2005.

Barcia, Manuel. "Entre amenazas y quejas: Un acercamiento al papel jugado por los diplomáticos ingleses en Cuba durante la conspiración de La Escalera, 1844." *Colonial Latin American Historical Review* 10, no. 1 (2001): 1–25.

———. "Exorcising the Storm: Revisiting the Origins of the Repression of the Conspiracy of La Escalera in Cuba." *Colonial Latin America Historical Review* 15, no. 3 (2006): 311–26.

———. *Seeds of Insurrection. Domination and Resistance on Western Cuban Plantations, 1808–1848*. Baton Rouge: Louisiana State University Press, 2008.

———. *The Great African Slave Revolt of 1825*. Baton Rouge: Louisiana State University Press, 2012.

———. "Un coloso sobre la arena": Definiendo el camino hacia la plantación esclavista en Cuba, 1792–1825." *Revista de Indias* 71, no. 251 (2011): 53–76.

———. *West African Warfare in Bahia and Cuba: Soldier Slaves in the Atlantic World, 1807–1844*. Oxford: Oxford University Press, 2014.

Barcia, Manuel, and Effie Kesidou. "Innovation and Entrepreneurship as Strategies for Success among Cuban-Based Firms in the Late Years of the Transatlantic Slave Trade." *Business History* 60, no. 4 (2017): 542–61.

Barcia, María del Carmen. "La abolición de la trata negrera en Cuba." In *IV encuentro de historiadores latinoamericanos y del Caribe*. Havana: Universidad de la Havana, 1983.

Bell, Duncan. "What Is Liberalism?" *Political Theory* 42, no. 6 (2014): 682–715.

Belmonte Postigo, José Luis "A Caribbean Affair: The Liberalisation of the Slave Trade in the Spanish Caribbean, 1784–1791." *Culture & History Digital Journal* 8, no. 1 (June 2019): 14.

Benavides, Christine. "Isidoro de Antillón y la abolición de la esclavitud." In *Las élites y la revolución de España (1808–1814): Estudios en homenaje al Profesor Gérard Dufour*, 89–103. Alicante: Biblioteca Virtual Miguel de Cervantes [Publicaciones de la Universidad de Alicante], 2017. Originally published 2010.

Bergad, Laird W. "Slave Prices in Cuba, 1840–1875." In *Caribbean Slavery in the Atlantic World: A Student Reader*, edited by Verene A. Shepherd and Hilary McD. Beckles, 527–42 Oxford: Currey, 2000.

Berquist, Emily. "Early Anti-Slavery Sentiment in the Spanish Atlantic World, 1765–1817." *Slavery & Abolition* 31, no. 2 (2010): 181–205. https://doi.org/10.1080/01440391003711073.

Bethell, Leslie. *The Abolition of the Brazilian Slave Trade*. Cambridge: Cambridge University Press, 1970.

———. "Britain, Portugal and the Suppression of the Brazilian Slave Trade: The Origins of Lord Palmerston's Act of 1839." *English Historical Review* 80, no. 317 (1965): 761–84.

Bierck Jr., Harold A. "The Struggle for Abolition in Gran Colombia." *Hispanic American Historical Review* 33, no. 3 (1953): 365–86.

Blackburn, Robin. *The Overthrow of Colonial Slavery, 1776–1848*. London: Verso, 2011. Originally published 1988.

———. *The American Crucible: Slavery, Emancipation and Human Rights*. London: Verso, 2011.

Blanco White, José María. *Bosquexo del comercio de esclavos*. Sevilla: Alfar, 1999 [1814].

Bolt, Christine. *The Anti-slavery Movement and Reconstruction: A Study in Anglo-American Co-Operation, 1833–77*. London: Oxford University Press, 1969.

Bowring, John. *Autobiographical Recollections of Sir John Bowring*. London: Henry S. King, 1877.

———. *Contestación a las observaciones de D. Juan Bernardo O'Gavan, sobre la suerte de los negros de África y reclamación contra el tratado celebrado con los ingleses en 1817*. Madrid: Imprenta de D. León Amarita, 1821.

Boyd, Caroline P. "A Man for All Seasons: Lincoln in Spain." In *The Global Lincoln*, edited by Richard Carwardine and Jay Sexton, ch. 11. New York: Oxford University Press, 2011.

Brauer, Kinley J. "The Slavery Problem in the Diplomacy of the American Civil War." *Pacific Historical Review* 46, no. 3 (1977): 439–69.

Breña, Roberto "José María Blanco White y la independencia de América: ¿Una postura proamericana?" *Historia constitucional* 3 (2002): 1–17.

British and Foreign State Papers (1815–1816). London: James Ridgway and Sons, 1838.

British and Foreign State Papers (1816–1817). London: James Ridgway and Sons, 1838.

British and Foreign State Papers (1819–1820). London: James Ridgway, 1834.

British and Foreign State Papers (1820–1821). London: James Ridgway and Son, 1830.

British and Foreign State Papers (1829–1830). London: James Ridgway, 1834.

British and Foreign State Papers (1831–1832), vol. 19. London: James Ridgway, 1834.

British and Foreign State Papers (1832–1833), vol. 20. London: James Ridgway and Sons, 1836.

British and Foreign State Papers (1834–1835), vol. 23. London: James Ridgway and Sons, 1852.

Brown, Charles Henry. *Agents of Manifest Destiny: The Lives and Times of the Filibusters*. Chapel Hill: University of North Carolina Press, 1980.

Brown, Christopher L. *Moral Capital: Foundations of British Abolitionism*. Chapel Hill: University of North Carolina Press, 2006.

Burroughs, Robert. "Eyes on the Prize: Journeys in Slave Ships Taken as Prizes by the Royal Navy." *Slavery & Abolition* 31, no. 1 (2010): 99–115.

Buxó de Abaigar, Joaquín. *Domingo Dulce, general isabelino: Vida y época*. Barcelona: Editorial Planeta, 1962.

Cantillo Jovellanos, Alejandro del. *Tratados, convenios y declaraciones de paz y de comercio que han hecho con las potencias estranjeras los monarcas españoles de la casa de Borbón*. Madrid: Imp. de Alegría y Charlain, 1843.

Castellanos, Jorge, and Isabel Castellanos. *Cultura afrocubana*. Vol. 1. Miami: Editorial Universal, 1988.

Castells, Irene. *La utopía insurreccional del liberalismo: Torrijos y las conspiraciones liberales de la Década Ominosa*. Barcelona: Crítica, 1989.

Cañizares Navarro, Juan B. "El Código Penal de 1822: Sus fuentes inspiradoras: Balance historiográfico (desde el s. XX)." *Glossae: European Journal of Legal History*, no. 10 (2013): 108–36.

Cañizares-Esguerra, Jorge. *How to Write History of the New World: Histories, Epistemologies, and Identities in the Eighteenth Century Atlantic World*. Stanford: Stanford University Press, 2001.

———. "Some Caveats about the 'Atlantic'" Paradigm. *History Compass* 1 (2003): 1–4.

Cayuela Fernández, José G. *Bahía de ultramar: España y Cuba en el siglo XIX: El control de las relaciones colonials*. Madrid: Siglo XXI, 1993.

———. "Transferencias de capitales antillanos a Europa: Los patrimonios de Pedro Juan de Zulueta y Ceballos y de Pedro José de Zulueta y Madariaga (1823–1877)." *Estudios de historia social* 44, no. 47 (1988): 191–211.

Cepero Bonilla, Raúl. *Azúcar y abolición* (Barcelona: Crítica, 1976).

Chasteen, John Charles. *Americanos: Latin America's Struggle for Independence*. New York: Oxford University Press, 2008.

Chaffin, Tom. *Fatal Glory: Narciso Lopez and the First Clandestine U.S. War against Cuba*. Baton Rouge: Louisiana State University Press, 2003.

———. "'Sons of Washington': Narciso Lopez, Filibustering, and U.S. Nationalism, 1848–1851." *Journal of the Early Republic* 15, no. 1 (1995): 79–108.

Childs, Matt D. *The 1812 Aponte Rebellion in Cuba and the Struggle against Atlantic Slavery*. Chapel Hill: University of North Carolina Press, 2006.

Cooper, Richard. "William Pitt, Taxation, and the Needs of War." *Journal of British Studies* 22, no. 1 (1982): 94–103.

Cortada, James W. *Spain and the American Civil War: Relations at Mid-Century, 1855–1868*. Philadelphia: American Philosophical Society, 1980.

Corwin, Arthur F. *Spain and the Abolition of Slavery in Cuba, 1817–1886*. Austin: University of Texas Press, 1967.

Costeloe, Michael P. *Response to Revolution: Imperial Spain and the Spanish American Revolutions, 1810–1840*. New York: Cambridge University Press, 1986.

Crawley, C. W. "French and English Influences in the Cortes of Cadiz, 1810–1814." *Cambridge Historical Journal* 6, no. 2 (1939): 176–208.

Curry-Machado, Jonathan. "How Cuba Burned with the Ghosts of British Slavery: Race, Abolition and the Escalera." *Slavery and Abolition* 25, no. 1 (2004): 71–93.

Davies, Catherine. "The Contemporary Response of the British Press to the 1812 Constitution." In *1812 Echoes: The Cadiz Constitution in Hispanic History, Culture and Politics*, edited by Stephen G. H. Roberts and Adam Sharman, 103–18. Newcastle upon Tyne: Cambridge Scholars, 2013.

Del Monte, Domingo. *Escritos de Domingo del Monte*. Vol. 1. Havana: Cultural, 1929.

———. *La Isla de Cuba tal cual está*. New York: Whittaker, 1836.

———. "La Isla de Cuba tal cual está." In *Historia de la esclavitud de la raza Africana en el Nuevo Mundo y en especial en los paises americo-hispanos*, edited by José Antonio Saco, 269–96. Havana: Cultural S.A., 1938.

Davis, David Brion. *The Problem of Slavery in Western Culture*. New York: Oxford University Press, 1966.

Domínguez, Jorge I. *Insurrection or Loyalty: The Breakdown of the Spanish American Empire*. Cambridge: Harvard University Press, 1980.

Drake, Frederick C., and R. W. Shufeldt. "Secret History of the Slave Trade to Cuba Written by an American Naval Officer, Robert Wilson Schufeldt, 1861." *Journal of Negro History* 55, no. 3 (1970): 218–35.

Drescher, Seymour. "British Abolitionism and Imperialism." In *Abolitionism and Imperialism in Britain, Africa, and the Atlantic*, edited by Derek R. Peterson, 129–49. Athens: Ohio University Press, 2010.

———. *Capitalism and Antislavery: British Mobilization in a Comparative Perspective*. New York: Oxford University Press, 1987.

———. "Public Opinion and Parliament in the Abolition of the British Slave Trade." In *The British Slave Trade: Abolition, Parliament and People*, edited by Stephen Farrell, Melanie Unwin, and James Walvin, 42–65. Edinburgh: Edinburgh University Press, 2007.

Dumas, Paula E. *Proslavery Britain. Fighting for Slavery in an Era of Abolition*. New York: Palgrave Macmillan, 2016.

Durán, Fernando. *Crónicas de Cortes del "Semanario patriótico."* Cadiz: Fundación Municipal de Cultura, 2003.

———. *José María Blanco White, o, La conciencia errante*. Sevilla: Fundación José Manuel Lara, 2005.

Echeverri, Marcela. *Indian and Slave Royalists in the Age of Revolution: Reform, Revolution and Royalism in the Northern Andes, 1780–1825*. New York: Cambridge University Press, 2016.

Eltis, David. *Economic Growth and the Ending of the Transatlantic Slave Trade*. New York: Oxford University Press, 1987.

Ericson, David F. *The Debate over Slavery: Antislavery and Proslavery Liberalism in Antebellum America*. New York: New York University Press, 2000.

Ettinger, Amos. *The Mission to Spain of Pierre Soulé*. New Haven: Yale University Press, 1932.

Faust, Drew Gilpin. *The Ideology of Slavery: Proslavery Thought in the Antebellum*

South, 1830–1860. Baton Rouge: Louisiana State University Press, 1981.

Fehrenbacher, Don. *The Slaveholding Republic: An Account of the United States Government's Relations to Slavery*. New York: Oxford University Press, 2001.

Fernández de Castro, José Antonio. *Medio siglo de historia colonial de Cuba*. Havana: Ricardo Veloso, 1923.

Fernández Sebastián, Javier. *La aurora de la libertad: Los primeros liberalismos en el mundo iberoamericano*. Madrid: Marcial Pons Historia, 2012.

Ferrer, Ada. "Cuban Slavery and Atlantic Antislavery." In *Slavery and Antislavery in Spain's Atlantic Empire*, edited by Josep M. Fradera and Christopher Schmidt-Nowara, 134–57. New York: Berghahn, 2013.

———. *Freedom's Mirror: Cuba and Haiti in the Age of Revolution*. Cambridge: Cambridge University Press, 2014.

Ferris, Kate. "Modelos de abolición: Estados Unidos y la política cultural española y la abolición de la esclavitud en Cuba, 1868–1874." In *Visiones del liberalismo: Política, identidad y cultura en la España del siglo XIX*, edited by Alda Blanco and Guy Thomson, 195–218. Valencia: Universitat de València, 2008.

Figueroa, Luis A. *Sugar, Slavery and Freedom in Nineteenth-Century Puerto Rico*. Chapel Hill: University of North Carolina Press, 2005.

Finch, Aisha K. *Rethinking Slave Rebellion in Cuba: La Escalera and the Insurgencies of 1841–1844*. Chapel Hill: University of North Carolina Press, 2015.

Fladeland, Betty. "Abolitionist Pressures on the Concert of Europe, 1814–1822." *Journal of Modern History* 38, no. 4 (1966): 355–73.

Forbes, Robert Pierce. *The Missouri Compromise and Its Aftermath: Slavery and the Meaning of America*. Chapel Hill: University of North Carolina Press, 2007.

Fradera, Josep M. *Colonias para después de un imperio*. Barcelona: Edicions Bellaterra, 2005.

———. *La nación imperial (1750–1918): Derechos, representación y ciudadanía en los imperios de Gran Bretaña, Francia, España y Estados Unidos*. Barcelona: Edhasa, 2015.

———. "Moments in a Postponed Abolition." In *Slavery and Antislavery in Spain's Atlantic Empire*, edited by Josep M. Fradera and Christopher Schmidt-Nowara, 256–83. New York: Berghahn, 2013.

———. "La participació catalana en el tràfic d'esclaus (1789–1845)." *Recerques*, no. 16 (1984): 119–40.

———. "Raza y ciudadanía: El factor racial en la delimitación de los derechos de los americanos." In *Gobernar colonias*, edited by Josep M. Fradera, 51–70. Barcelona: Peninsula, 1999.

———. "Why Were Spain's Overseas Laws Never Enacted?" In *Spain, Europe and the Atlantic World: Essays in Honour of John H. Elliott*, edited by Richard L. Kagan and Geoffrey Parker, 333–49. Cambridge: Cambridge University Press, 1995.

Fradera, Josep M., and Christopher Schmidt-Nowara. *Slavery and Antislavery in Spain's Atlantic Empire*. New York: Berghahn, 2013.

Franco, José Luciano. *Comercio clandestino de esclavos*. Havana: Editorial de Ciencias Sociales, 1980.

———. "La conspiración de Aponte, 1812." In *Ensayos históricos*, edited by José Luciano Franco, 127–90. Havana: Editorial de Ciencias Sociales, 1974.

———, ed. *Ensayos históricos*. Havana: Editorial de Ciencias Sociales, 1974.

Fuentes Aragonés, Juan Francisco. "'Cherchez la femme': Exiliadas y liberales en la Década Ominosa (1823–1833)." *Historia constitucional* 13 (2012): 383–405.

Galván, Eduardo. *La abolición de la esclavitud en España: Debates parlamentarios, 1810–1886*. Madrid: Dickinson, 2014.

García Balañà, Albert. "Antislavery before Abolitionism: Networks and Motives in Early Liberal Barcelona, 1833–1844." In *Slavery and Antislavery in Spain's Atlantic Empire*, edited by Josep M. Fradera and Christopher Schmidt-Nowara, 229–55. New York: Berghahn, 2013.

Garrido Buj, Santiago. "'Los otros esclavos': La sustitución de la mano de obra esclava africana en la Cuba colonial." *Revista de derecho UNED* 16 (2015): 963–87.

Geggus, David P. *The Impact of the Haitian Revolution in the Atlantic World*. Columbia: University of South Carolina Press, 2001.

Gil Novales, Alberto. *Las sociedades patrióticas (1820–1823)*. Vol. 1. Madrid: Tecnos, 1975.

González-Ripoll, María Dolores, Consuelo Naranjo, Ada Ferrer, Gloria García, and Josef Opatrny. *El rumor de Haití en Cuba: Temor, raza y rebeldía, 1789–1844*. Madrid: Consejo Superior de Investigaciones Científicas, 2004.

Green, Jennifer R., and Patricia Kirkwood, "Reframing the Antebellum Democratic Mainstream Transatlantic Diplomacy and the Career of Pierre Soulé." *Civil War History* 61, no. 3 (2015): 212–51.

Guardia, Carmen de la. "Un espacio social propio." In *Mujeres esclavas y abolicionistas en la España de los siglos XVI al XIX*, edited by Aurelia Martín Casares and Rocio Periáñez Gómez, 213–34. Madrid and Frankfurt am Main: Iberoamericana-Vervuert (2014).

Guerrero Latorre, Ana, Sisinio Pérez Garzón, and Germán Rueda Hernanz. *Historia política*. Madrid: Istmo, 2013.

Hamilton, Keith, and Patrick Salmon, *Slavery, Diplomacy and Empire: Britain and the Suppression of the Slave Trade, 1807–1975*. Brighton: Sussex Academic Press, 2009.

Harris, John A. E. "Circuits of Wealth, Circuits of Sorrow: Financing the Illegal Transatlantic Slave Trade in the Age of Suppression, 1850–66." *Journal of Global History* 11, no. 3 (2016): 409–29.

Heartfield, James. *The British and Foreign Anti-Slavery Society, 1838–1956: A History*. Oxford: Oxford University Press, 2016.

Helg, Aline. *Liberty and Equality in Caribbean Colombia, 1770–1835*. Chapel Hill: University of North Carolina Press, 2004.

———. "The Limits of Equality: Free People of Color and Slaves during the First Independence of Cartagena, Colombia (1810–15)." *Slavery & Abolition* 20 (1999): 1–30.

———. *Slave No More: Self-Liberation before Abolitionism in the Americas*. Chapel Hill: University of North Carolina Press, 2019.

Huzzey, Richard. *Freedom Burning: Anti-slavery and Empire in Victorian Britain.* Ithaca: Cornell University Press, 2012.

Jiménez Codinach, Guadalupe. *La Gran Bretaña y la independencia de México, 1808–1821.* Mexico: Fondo de Cultura Económica, 1991.

Johnson, John Flude. *Proceedings of the General Anti-Slavery Convention Called by the Committee of the British and Foreign Anti-Slavery Society.* London: John Snow, 1843.

Johnson, Sherry. *The Social Transformation of Eighteenth-Century Cuba.* Gainesville: University Press of Florida, 2001.

Journeau, Brigitte. *Augusto Conte, memorialista y diplomático.* Alicante: Biblioteca Virtual Miguel de Cervantes, 2016.

Kaminski, John P. *Necessary Evil? Slavery and the Debate over the Constitution.* Madison: Madison House, 1995.

Keene, Edward. "A Case Study of the Construction of International Hierarchy: British Treaty-Making against the Slave Trade in the Early Nineteenth Century." *International Organization* 61, no. 2 (2007): 311–99.

Kielstra, Paul Michael. *The Politics of the Slave Trade in Britain and France, 1814–1848.* New York: Saint Martin's Press, 2000.

Kiple, Kenneth F. "Cholera and Race in the Caribbean." *Journal of Latin American Studies* 17, no. 1 (1985): 157–77.

Knight, Franklin W. *Slave Society in Cuba during the Nineteenth Century.* Madison: University of Wisconsin Press, 1970.

Labra, Rafael María de. *La abolición de la esclavitud en las Antillas Españolas.* Madrid: Imprenta de J. E. Morete, 1869.

LaCapra, Dominick. *Rethinking Intellectual History.* Ithaca: Cornell University Press, 1990.

Laspra Rodríguez, Alicia. "Andrés Ángel de la Vega Infanzón: Un reformista anglófilo." *Historia constitucional,* no. 14 (2013): 45–75.

Lasso, Marixa. *Myths of Harmony: Race and Republicanism during the Age of Revolution, Colombia, 1795–1831.* Pittsburgh: University of Pittsburgh Press, 2007.

Laurent, Muriel. *Contrabando, poder y color en los albores de le República: Nueva Granada, 1822–1824.* Bogotá: Universidad de los Andes, 2014.

Lawrence, Mark. *Spain's First Carlist War, 1833–40.* London: Palgrave Macmillan, 2014.

Lazo, Rodrigo. *Writing to Cuba: Filibustering and Cuban Exiles in the United States.* Chapel Hill: University of North Carolina Press, 2005.

Levine, Robert Steven. *Martin Delany, Frederick Douglass, and the Politics of Representative Identity.* Chapel Hill: University of North Carolina Press, 1997.

Llorca-Jaña, Manuel. "Turnbull, David (1793?–1851)." In *Oxford Dictionary of National Biography.* Oxford: Oxford University Press, 2009.

Llorens, Vicente. *Liberales y románticos.* Madrid: Castalia, 1979. Originally published 1954.

López Denis, Adrián. "Disease and Society in Colonial Cuba, 1790–1840." PhD diss., University of California, Los Angeles, 2007.

Losurdo, Domenico. *Liberalism: A Counter-History*. New York: Verso Books, 2011.

Luz y Caballero, José de la. *Aforismos*. Havana: Editorial Lex, 1960.

Lynch, John. *The Spanish American Revolutions, 1808–1826*. New York: W. W. Norton, 1973.

Marques, João Pedro. *The Sounds of Silence: Nineteenth-Century Portugal and the Abolition of the Slave Trade*. New York: Berghahn Books, 2006.

Marques, Leonardo. *The United States and the Transatlantic Slave Trade to the Americas, 1776–1867*. New Haven: Yale University Press, 2016.

Marquese, Rafael, Márcia Berbel, and Tâmis Parron. *Slavery and Politics: Brazil and Cuba, 1790–1850*. Albuquerque: University of New Mexico Press, 2016.

Marrero, Leví. *Cuba: Economía y sociedad*. Vol. 12. Madrid: Editorial Playor, 1984–1987.

Martín Arranz, Raúl. "Espartero: Figuras de Legitimidad." In *Populismo, caudillaje y discurso demagógico*, edited by José Alvarez Junco, 101–28. Madrid: CIS/Siglo XXI, 1987.

Martín Corrales, Eloy. "La esclavitud negra en la Cataluña entre los siglos XVI y XIX." In *Negros y esclavos: Barcelona y la esclavitud atlántica (siglos XVI–XIX)*, edited by Martín Rodrigo y Alharilla and Lizbeth Chaviano Pérez, 17–46. Barcelona: Icaria, 2017.

Martinez, Jenny S. *The Slave Trade and the Origins of International Human Rights Law*. Oxford: Oxford University Press, 2012.

Martínez-Fernández, Luis. *Fighting Slavery in the Caribbean: Life and Times of a British Family in Nineteenth Century Havana*. London: Routledge, 1998.

———. *Protestantism and Political Conflict in the Nineteenth-Century Hispanic Caribbean* New Brunswick, NJ: Rutgers University Press, 1960.

Mason, Matthew. "Keeping Up Appearances: The International Politics of Slave Trade Abolition in the Nineteenth-Century Atlantic World." *William and Mary Quarterly* 66, no. 4 (2009): 809–32.

Matos Arévalo, José A. "José Antonio Saco, pensamiento social: Apuntes sobre el padre Bartolomé de Las Casas." In *El pensamiento lascasiano en la conciencia de América y Europa*, ed. Pablo González Casanova, 57–68. Mexico City: Universidad Nacional Autónoma de México, 1994.

Maza, Manuel. *Por la vida y el honor: El presbítero Félix Varela en las Cortes de España, 1882–1823*. Madrid: Editorial Nacional, 1987.

May, Robert E. *The Southern Dream of a Caribbean Empire, 1854–1861*. Baton Rouge: Louisiana State University Press, 1973.

McCoy, Alfred W., Josep M. Fradera, and Stephen Jacobson, *Endless Empire: Spain's Retreat, Europe's Eclipse, America's Decline*. Madison: University of Wisconsin Press, 2012.

Mendiola, Fernando. "The Role of Unfree Labour in Capitalist Development: Spain and Its Empire, Nineteenth to the Twenty-First Centuries." *IRSH* 61 (2016): 187–211.

Milne, A. Taylor. "The Lyons-Seward Treaty of 1862." *American Historical Review* 38, no. 3 (1933): 511–25.

Moore, J. Preston. "Pierre Soule: Southern Expansionist and Promoter." *Journal of Southern History* 21, no. 2 (1955): 203–23.

Moreno Alonso, Manuel. "Confesiones políticas de Don Agustín de Argüelles." *Revista de estudios políticos* 54 (1986): 226–61.

———. *La forja del liberalismo en España: Los amigos españoles de Lord Holland, 1793–1840.* Madrid: Congreso de los Diputados, 1997.

Moreno Fraginals, Manuel. "Plantations in the Caribbean: Cuba, Puerto Rico, and the Dominican Republic in the late Nineteenth Century," in *Between Slavery and Free Labor: The Spanish-Speaking Caribbean in the Nineteenth Century*, ed. Manuel Moreno Fraginals, Frank Moya Pons, and Stanley L. Engerman, 3–21. Baltimore: Johns Hopkins University Press, 1985.

———. *The Sugarmill. The Socioeconomic Complex of Sugar in Cuba, 1760–1860.* New York: Monthly Review Press, 2008. Originally published 1976.

Moreno García, Julia. "Actitudes de los nacionalistas cubanos ante la ley penal de abolición y represión del tráfico de esclavos (1845)." In *Esclavitud y derechos humanos: La lucha por la libertad del negro en el siglo XIX*, edited by Francisco de Solano and Agustín Guimerá, 478–98. Madrid: CSIC, 1990.

———. "La cuestión de la trata en el Trienio Liberal (1820–1823)." *Cuadernos de historia contemporánea* extra 1 (2003): 157–67.

———. "España y Gran Bretaña durante el siglo XIX: La abolición de la trata y la esclavitud." Doctoral thesis, History, Universidad Complutense de Madrid, 1984.

Murphy, Martin. *Blanco White: Self-Banished Spaniard.* New Haven: Yale University Press, 1989.

Murray, David R. *Odious Commerce: Britain, Spain and the Abolition of the Cuban Slave Trade.* Cambridge: Cambridge University Press, 2002. Originally published 1980.

Muñoz, Daniel, and Gregorio Alonso. *Londres y el liberalismo hispánico.* Madrid: Iberoamericana-Vervuert, 2011.

Naranjo, Consuelo, and Imilcy Balboa Navarro. "Colonos asiáticos para una economía en expansión: Cuba, 1847–1880." *Revista mexicana del Caribe* 8 (1999): 32–65.

Narvaez, Benjamin N. "Chinese Coolies in Cuba and Peru: Race, Labor, and Immigration, 1839–1886," PhD diss., University of Texas at Austin, 2010.

Navarro García, Jesús Raúl. *Entre esclavos y constituciones (el colonialismo liberal de 1837 en Cuba).* Sevilla: CSIC—Escuela de Estudios Hispano-Americanos (EEHA), 1991.

Nelson, Jennifer L. "Liberated Africans in the Atlantic World: The Courts of Mixed Commission in Havana and Rio de Janeiro, 1819–1871." PhD thesis, University of Leeds, 2015.

———. "Slavery, Race, and Conspiracy: The HMS *Romney* in Nineteenth-Century Cuba." *Atlantic Studies* 14, no. 2 (2017): 174–95.

Opatrny, Josef. *José Antonio Saco y la búsqueda de la identidad cubana.* Prague: Univerzita Karlova, 2010.

Ostend Manifesto, October 15, 1854, accessed January 20, 2020, https://en.wiki-source.org/wiki/Ostend_Manifesto.

O'Gavan, Juan Bernardo. *Observaciones sobre la suerte de los negros del África, considerados en su propia patria y trasladados a las Antillas Españolas: Y reclamación contra el tratado firmado con los ingleses en el año 1817.* Madrid: Imprenta del Universal, 1821.

Palmié, Stephan. *Wizards and Scientists: Explorations in Afro-Cuban Modernity.* Durham, NC: Duke University Press, 2002.

Paquette, Gabriel. "The Dissolution of the Spanish Atlantic Monarchy." *Historical Journal* 52, no. 1 (2009): 175–212.

———. "The Intellectual Impact of International Rivalry." In *Enlightenment, Governance and Reform in Spain and Its Empire, 1759–1808.* New York: Palgrave Macmillan, 2008. 29–55.

———. "Introduction: Liberalism in the Early Nineteenth-Century Iberian World." *History of European Ideas* 41, no. 2 (2015): 1–13.

Paquette, Robert. *Sugar Is Made with Blood: The Conspiracy of La Escalera and the Conflict between Empires over Slavery in Cuba.* Middletown: Wesleyan University Press, 1988.

Pérez, Louis A. Jr. *Cuba between Empires, 1878–1902.* Pittsburgh: University of Pittsburgh Press, 1983.

Piqueras, José A. *Azúcar y esclavitud en el final del trabajo forzado.* Madrid: FCE de España, 2002.

———. *Felix Varela y la prosperidad de la patria criolla.* Madrid: Fundación Mapfre and Doce Calles, 2007.

———. "El gobierno de la población heterogénea en la segunda esclavitud." In *Orden político y gobierno de esclavos*, edited by José Antonio Piqueras, 17–52. Valencia: Centro Francisco Tomás y Valiente UNED Alzira-Valencia and Fundación Instituto de Historia Social, 2016.

———. "Leales en época de insurrección: La élite criolla cubana entre 1810 y 1814." In *Visiones y revisiones de la independencia americana*, edited by Izaskun Álvarez and Julio Sánchez, 183–206. Salamanca: Universidad de Salamanca, 2014.

———. "La política de los intereses en Cuba y la revolución (1810–1814)." In *Las guerras de independencia en la América española*, edited by Marta Terán and José Antonio Serrano Ortega, 465–84. Zamora: El Colegio de Michoacán, 2002.

———. "La siempre fiel isla de Cuba, o la lealtad interesada." *Historia mexicana* 229 (2008): 427–86.

Pocock, John G. A. *Political Thought and History.* Cambridge: Cambridge University Press, 2009.

Popkin, Jeremy D. *Facing Racial Revolution: Eyewitness Accounts of the Haitian Revolution.* Chicago: University of Chicago Press, 2007.

Popkin, Jeremy D., and Richard H. Popkin, eds. *The Abbé Grégoire and His World.* Dordrecht: Springer Netherlands, 2000.

Portillo Valdés, José María. "Cuerpo de nación, pueblo soberano: La representación política en la crisis de la monarquía hispana." *Ayer*, no. 61 (2006): 47–76.

———. "Jurisprudencia constitucional en espacios indígenas: Despliegue municipal de Cádiz en Nueva España." *Anuario de historia del derecho español* 81 (2011): 181–206

Portuondo, Olga. *Cuba: Constitución y liberalismo.* Santiago de Cuba: Editorial Oriente, 2008.

Potter, David M. *The Impending Crisis, 1848–1861.* New York: Harper & Row, 1976.

Quiroz, Alfonso W. "Implicit Costs of Empire: Bureaucratic Corruption in Nineteenth-Century Cuba." *Journal of Latin American Studies* 35, no. 3 (2003): 473–511.

Reich, Jerome. "The Slave Trade at the Congress of Vienna—a Study in English Public Opinion." *Journal of Negro History* 53, no. 2 (1968): 129–43.

Riva, Juan Pérez de la. "Introducción: El General Don Miguel Tacón y su época." In *Correspondencia reservada del Capitan General Don Miguel Tacon con el gobierno de Madrid, 1834–1836.* Havana: Biblioteca Nacional José Martí, 1964.

Rodgers, Daniel T. *Atlantic Crossings: Social Politics in a Progressive Era.* Cambridge: Harvard University Press, 2000.

Rodríguez, Jaime E. *The Independence of Spanish America.* New York: Cambridge University Press, 1998.

Romeo Mateo, María Cruz "Lenguaje y política del nuevo liberalismo: Moderados y progresistas, 1834–1845." *Ayer*, no. 29 (1998): 37–62.

Rossignol, Marie-Jeanne. "Jacques-Pierre Brissot and the Fate of Atlantic Anti-slavery during the Age of Revolutionary Wars." In *War, Empire and Slavery, 1770–1830,* edited by Richard Bessel, Nicholas Guyatt, and Jane Rendall, 139–56. London: Palgrave Macmillan, 2010.

Saco, José Antonio. *Examen analítico del informe de la comisión especial nombrada por las cortes.* Madrid: Oficina de Don Tomás Jordan 1837.

———. *Historia de la esclavitud de la raza africana en el Nuevo Mundo y en especial en los paises Americo-Hispanos.* Vol. 4. Edited by Fernando Ortiz. Havana: Cultural S.A., 1938. Originally published 1879.

———. *Ideas sobre la incorporación de Cuba a Estados Unidos.* Paris: Imprenta de Panckoucke, 1848.

———. *Mi primera pregunta ¿La abolición del comercio de esclavos africanos arruinará o atrasará la agricultura cubana?* Madrid: Imprenta de don Marcilino Calero, 1837.

———. *Obras.* Edited by Eduardo Torres-Cuevas. Vols. 1–5. Havana: Imagen Contemporánea, 2001.

———. *Paralelo entre la isla de Cuba y algunas colonias inglesas.* Madrid: Oficina de Don Tomás Jordán, impresor de Cámara de S.M., 1837.

Saiz Pastor, Candelaria. "La esclavitud como problema político en la España del siglo XIX (1833–1868): Liberalismo y esclavismo." In *Esclavitud y derechos humanos: La lucha por la libertad del negro en el siglo XIX*, edited by Francisco de Solano and Agustín Guimerá, 80–98. Madrid: CSIC, 1990.

———. "Las finanzas públicas en Cuba: La etapa de las desviaciones de fondos a la península, 1823–1866." In *Las haciendas públicas en el caribe hispano durante el siglo XIX*, edited by Inés Roldán de Montaud, 68–108. Madrid: CSIC, 2008.

———. "Liberales y esclavistas: El dominio colonial español en Cuba (1833–1868)." PhD thesis, History and Economics, Universidad de Alicante, 1990.

Sánchez, Romy. "Quitter la Très Fidèle: Exilés et bannis au temps du séparatisme cubain, 1834–1879." PhD thesis, Université Paris 1 Panthéon Sorbonne, 2017.

Sanjurjo, Jesús. "Negros o esclavos: La retórica de la esclavitud en la prensa española del exilio londinense (1818–1825)." *Anuario de estudios atlánticos*, no. 62 (2016): 1–14.

Schmidt-Nowara, Christopher. *Empire and Antislavery: Spain, Cuba and Puerto Rico, 1833–1874*. Pittsburgh: University of Pittsburgh Press, 1999.

———. "Wilberforce Spanished: Joseph Blanco White and Spanish Antislavery, 1808–1814." In *Slavery and Antislavery in Spain's Atlantic Empire*, edited by Josep M. Fradera and Christopher Schmidt-Nowara, 158–75. New York: Berghahn, 2013.

Schmidt-Nowara, Christopher. "National Economy and Atlantic Slavery: Protectionism and Resistance to Abolitionism in Spain and the Antilles, 1854–1874." *Hispanic American Historical Review* 78, no. 4 (1998): 603–29.

Schoultz, Lars. *The Infernal Little Cuban Republic: The United States and the Cuban Revolution*. Chapel Hill: University of North Carolina Press, 2009.

Sexton, Jay. "Toward a Synthesis of Foreign Relations in the Civil War Era, 1848–77." *American Nineteenth Century History* 5, no. 3 (2004): 50–73.

Shubert, Adrian. *Espartero, El Pacificador*. Barcelona: Galaxia Gutenberg, 2018.

Simal Durán, Juan Luis. *Emigrados: España y el exilio internacional, 1814–1834*. Madrid: Centro de Estudios Políticos y Constitucionales, 2013.

———. La esclavitud como concepto político en el primer liberalismo hispano." In *Ayeres en discusión: Temas clave de historia contemporánea hoy*, edited by María Encarna Nicolás Marín and Carmen González Martínez, 1–20. Murcia: Universidad de Murcia, 2008.

Skinner, Quentin. "Meaning and Understanding in the History of Ideas." *History and Theory* 8, no. 1 (1969): 3–53.

Skinner, Quentin, and Jerome B. Schneewind. *La filosofía de la historia*. Barcelona: Paidós, 1990.

Smith, Peter H. *Talons of the Eagle: Dynamics of U.S.–Latin American Relations*. New York: Oxford University Press, 1996.

Special Report of the Anti-Slavery Conference: Held in Paris in the Salle Herz, on the Twenty-sixth and Twenty-seventh August, 1867, under the Presidency of Mons. Édouard Laboulaye. London: Committee of the British and Foreign Antislavery Society, 1867.

Tallant, Harold D. *Evil Necessity: Slavery and Political Culture in Antebellum Kentucky*. Lexington: University Press of Kentucky, 2003.

Todd, David. *Free Trade and Its Enemies in France, 1814–1851.* Cambridge: Cambridge University Press, 2015.

Torres Aguilar, Manuel. *Génesis parlamentaria del Código penal de 1822.* Messina: SICANIA University Press, Università degli Studi di Messina, 2008.

Torres-Cuevas, Eduardo. *Félix Varela: Ética y anticipación del pensamiento de la emancipación cubana.* Havana: Imagen Contemporánea, 1991.

Torres-Cuevas, Eduardo, and Arturo Soregui. *José Antonio Saco, acerca de la esclavitud y su historia.* Havana: Editorial de Ciencias Sociales, 1982.

Turnbull, David. *Travels in the West, Cuba: With Notices of Porto Rico and the Slave Trade.* London: Longman, Orme, Brown, Green and Longmans, 1840.

Varela Suanzes-Carpegna, Joaquín. "La Constitución de Cádiz y el primer liberalismo español." *Teoría y derecho: Revista de pensamiento jurídico*, no. 10 (2011): 49–66.

———. *Historia del levantamiento, guerra y revolución de España por el Conde de Toreno.* Madrid: Centro de Estudios Políticos y Constitucionales, 2008.

Vila Vilar, Enriqueta. "Concepción Arenal, feminista y abolicionista." *Minervae Baeticae: Boletín de la Real Academia Sevillana de Buenas Letras* 42 (2014): 311–21.

Vila, Enriqueta, and Lucia Vila. *Los abolicionistas españoles: Siglo XIX.* Madrid: Ediciones de Cultura Hispánica, 1996.

Vilar, Juan B. *Intolerancia y libertad en la España contemporánea: Los orígenes del protestantismo español actual.* Madrid: Istmo, 1994.

Vilar, Juan B., and Mar Vilar. *El primer hispanismo británico en la formación y contenidos de la más importante biblioteca española de libros prohibidos: Correspondencia inédita de Luis de Usoz con Benjamin B. Wiffen (1840–1850).* Sevilla: Editorial MAD, 2010.

Vilar, Mar. "La lengua y civilización inglesas en sus relaciones con España a mediados del siglo XIX." *Boletín de la Real Academia de la Historia* 193, no. 1 (1996): 137–76.

Webster, Sidney. "Mr. Marcy, the Cuban Question and the Ostend Manifesto." *Political Science Quarterly* 8, no. 1 (1893): 1–32.

Wilberforce, Robert Isaac, and Samuel Wilberforce. *The Correspondence of William Wilberforce.* Vol. 2. London: John Murray, 1840.

———. *The Life of William Wilberforce.* Vol. 3. London: John Murray, 1838.

Williams, Eric. *Capitalism and Slavery.* Chapel Hill: University of North Carolina Press, 1964.

Wood, Marcus. *Blind Memory: Visual Representations of Slavery in England and America, 1780–1865.* Manchester: Manchester University Press, 2000.

Zander, J. Selene. "Contagious Invasions: The 1833 Cholera Epidemic in Havana." *Revista de Estudios Hispánicos* 49, no. 1 (2005): 3–23.

Zúñiga, Neptalí. *Rocafuerte y el periodismo en Inglaterra.* Quito: Imprenta del Ministerio del Tesoro, 1947.

Index